Battle for the future

by
Adrian Nastase

BATTLE FOR THE FUTURE

By

Adrian Nastase

English Translation by
Ilinca Anghelescu
Fabiola Hosu
Roxana Petcu

EAST EUROPEAN MONOGRAPHS, BOULDER
DISTRIBUTED BY COLUMBIA UNIVERSITY PRESS, NEW YORK

2001

EAST EUROPEAN MONOGRAPHS, NO. DLXXXV

ISBN 0-88033-483-5

Library of Congress Catalog Control Number 2001-131745

Printed in the United States of America

CONTENTS

Part II

Part III

Part IV

"Whoever masters the past,
master the future: whoever masters
the present masters the past."

George Orwell, 1984

I OFFER THIS BOOK
TO ALL THE PERSONS THAT BUILD ROMANIA
OF THIS MILLENNIUM,
WITH ALL THEIR COURAGE
AND VISION.

I BELIEVE IN THE FUTURE
AND IN ALL OF US.
WE ARE ALL ENGAGED
IN THE BATTLE FOR THE FUTURE.

FINALLY,
A NOTE OF CONSIDERATION
IN MY FATHER'S MEMORY

ADRIAN NĂSTASE

PREFACE
APPEAL TO THE TRUTH

We are being faced with a painful paradox: after an eleven-year quest down the transition "tunnel", the turn of this millennium finally witnesses a decisive encounter – between this period's crashing failure which had massive destructive effects upon the Romanian society and the major stake of the European-NATO integration. Today's Romania seems unable to become tomorrow's future Romania. Nevertheless, it must happen so. Still, the imperative need to join Europe cannot even be put into words unless a wide-ranging political project is undertaken. Yet, who is courageous and strong enough to assume such an undertaking? What is really important for this essential moment? To hold the political power for its own sake, within the limits of a dramatic space, which operates according to the karmic laws of the ancient tragedy or to initiate the risky action of resorting to a rigorous project via the decision making right, already granted after having been awarded the political power? Do we really need politicians overwhelmed with fear that they might lose their privileges, politicians who live in the broken promises Inferno, or responsible politicians who know that, before making any promises, they must persuade people that they are really able to make things happen? However much we may be wishing for this "miracle" to come true, it cannot within a space dominated by actors resorting to political lies or evading responsibility.

The politics of the present can no longer appeal only to hypothetical resources. Confronted with the pressure exercised by the existing reality, all energies are now being channeled toward the idea of pursuing performance. These last few years could be put into a nutshell using just a few phrases: precarious existence; waste of resources and social energies; aimless, targetless resistance, survival... The time has come to develop a long-term philosophy, to project the future, to draft intelligent policies and to responsibly manage the social issues. Time has lost all patience for Romania.

All along its history, mankind has already fallen victim to theories and ideologies based on irresponsibility and demagogy and they all failed into crashing, painful experiments. We can still remember all those conceited, unique solutions which suggested pure demagogy as a way to reach the future state of well-being. Romania was forced to undergo similar experiments, even if they carried the mark of an opposed kind of ideology. Caught between these two ideological extremes, the notions of well-being and national interest got eroded and turned into worthless dust. Romania is now running the risk of entering “an eternity of historic nothingness”, the more so as mankind seems to be developing toward a new stage of its evolution: globalization.

The political momentum of the year 2000 and the transfer of the political power do not bear the sign of a revolution, as it was wrongly claimed in 1996, but that of an **evolution**. A necessary evolution. It was a switch from a utopian, manicheistic concept on political power to a superior stage, where accountability for any decision made and closeness to the citizens have become obligatory constituents of the new governance philosophy. The political power has already been awarded, but we are still to win the political authority which is only conferred by acquiring legitimacy in relation to the citizens as a result of the government’s performance. Even if Romanians no longer expect a miracle, they will not tolerate having their expectations destroyed once more.

All political decisions made today will have to offer solutions for a truly European integration rhythm. They will serve our national interests, in direct keeping with the real possibilities for the Romanian society. Nowadays, the people can no longer be subjected to useless sacrifices, while continuing in the social pauperism process.

The way reality is perceived goes beyond the politicians’ personal destinies. Their personal images and personal fortunes are to be clearly subordinated to concrete, essential political actions. It is imperative that Romanian politicians become true creators of value. One cannot use ideology as an excuse any more. The elites can demonstrate that they are able to put up a common front under the flying colors of national ideals.

There are many theories trying to explain the collapse of communism, but above them all, the real explanation lies in its economic failure. The Western world exported their technologies (they even granted credits for that), but they have never accepted to import the products manufactured according to those technologies. And now, the West is condemning those very technologies, while forcing the Eastern countries to pay for them once again. In fact, the West is forced to witness the dramatic failure of the models they came up with. The West has no other instrument to eliminate the gap, but by exercising pressure. The problem is that pressurising is not a solution, it is only a palliative alternative. Thus, having reached this stage, it is a vital necessity to form a project, to build an integrated European space.

In her post-revolution period, Romania was faced with naive representations on society, which materialized into hasty actions, motivated by the need to respond to various types of protests. The first six years of this decade marked the fact that Romania stepped along the route to reform and democracy. During the 2000 elections, the voters decided to carry on the economic reform, which had been interrupted by a four-year, incoherent, so-called right-of-centre government. The choice made by the Romanian electorate enables us to resume the development of the country as against the utopian myth.

What is Romania's place today within the concert of European evolutions? Deprived of any type of project, divided and almost turned to a state of autarchy, the Romanian society is under obligation to accept a forced march, to burn all the stages left behind. On the one hand, Romania has to provide for a lack of primary economic resources, and, on the other hand, she has to compensate for a trust alteration regarding the economic concept of free choice.

The society of the future shall be an intelligent network, having thousands of nodes. Traditionalist strongholds are deconstructed, undermined by the new solidarity models. The main wealth of a country will be its nationals' ability and ingenuity to become "nodes" useful to the whole, sharing common specific values, and, mainly, the values of mankind. Romania's future can hardly be conceived of if no end is put to the brain drain or if the obsessions caused by the more or less distant past are not exorcised.

The policies according to which the former communist countries are being transformed are arbitrary and extremely complex. Neither the transient needs nor the casual accidents should allow that these countries turn into game-like experiments that may have winners and losers. Already a lot of political conditions have been imposed and they violate the rules of democracy; at the same time, pressures have been exercised upon national sovereignty. What was the result of all these for the Romanian society?

The elites' role is neither to pass judgments nor to give verdicts; their role is to build ideals and instruments to reach those ideals, to create the necessary social environment to renegotiate a climate of communication and co-operation. Ever since the year 2000, the government exercise has been based on different premises, namely the political and economic state of the country which rules out any experiments that the government might imagine. Another premise is the urgent need to identify the optimum solutions so as to turn to account the country's production potential. And yet another one is to maintain a balance between the imperative need to carry on the economic reform and the social stability.

Until the year 2000 excessive weight had been given to the concept of political and party membership, turning it into a serious shortcoming for the administrative system. This is a solution which is seen as unacceptable now, both by the political class and by the civil society. The civil society is no longer able to make their voice heard, while the voice of the political class has been muffled by the roar of their clientele. The Government, the Parliament and all the other state institutions, as well as the political parties have to operate with a view to serving the public welfare, not to fulfilling obscure, even onerous party policies. The Government have been trying to streamline their activity by a better division of their tasks, by becoming more professional and by building up a more cohesive team. Political loyalty is no longer the only criterion to select candidates for executive positions.

The most recent example is provided by the recently adopted property law. After having minutely assessed what is left of all the properties involved, the present government has established the return process of those properties on its natural foundations. The former property, be it returned or privatized, has already reached its limits as a wealth generating factor. Thus, all returned properties have depreciated, while society as a whole has become poorer. Any lasting regulation should not start from the idea of "good" or "bad" property, on the contrary, the approach should be based on the concept of equality and legitimacy of all forms of property, seen as economic effectiveness vectors backed by modern management,

A gap of authority as well as the dissolution of power were generated by the fear of dealing with a strong state. The state has not assumed its role as agent of change. But for strong state intervention we are running the risk of extending in the transition period for several decades. For the present stage, the thoughtless decrease of the state role (the role of the Romanian state, as representative of Romania's general interests) is a counterproductive factor and the consequence is the fact that the national general interests are being seriously disregarded. Market justice is not tantamount to social justice. All citizens are entitled to "life opportunities", thus striking a balance between the idea of stimulating the offer and securing the citizens' rights. Incomes should not be equal, but access to education SHOULD BE.

Could globalization, as temptation to generalize consumption, not by promoting an intercultural approach, but by establishing the dominance of the North-American economic model, be a momentous, ultimate exam for mankind? We do not know it yet, but we afraid of it, so, our fear might keep our reason wide awake... Globalization is a source of repeated shocks to all civilizations. There are areas obliged to adopt this model, depending on the geostrategic interests of its promoters.

Romania has joined the globalization trend by stating her desire to become a EU member. But this desire goes along with a handicap: fifty years of communism and the last four years' inability to carry on the reform. After 1989, Romania brutally switched from Karl Marx to Coca Cola. Her future seems entirely dependent on the electoral will of the nation. Still, this is not enough. Due to a shortage of responsible politicians, whose actions could be held accountable for their decisions, as well as to the vote cast for them, we are on the brink of falling into the romantic trap of the deadly slumber. If, in fairy tales, the dormant Prince Charming was the recipient of a miracle, for Romania's real situation the only possible miracle is the idea of national solidarity around a new political project.

After a ten-year slalom along the transition slopes, after a ten-year period which resulted in living standards under 50% as compared to 1989, when the Romanians took to the streets and had themselves a revolution, the Romanian society think that our country is going in the wrong direction.

Therefore, it is necessary for us, Romanians, to undertake a new course for our future, based on a new project.

Only in this way could we initiate the "battle for the future".

PART I

CHAPTER ONE

CHANGE – BETWEEN UTOPIA AND THE NEED FOR A POLITICAL PROJECT

"Change /..../ deepens the gap between what is thought to exist and what exists in reality, between existing images and the reality they are supposed to reflect"

Alvin Toffler

1.1 A heavily delayed start or looking for the time wasted away

Ten years have passed. Ten years since it seemed unjust and offensive to us to hear that some political analyst considered we needed twenty years to recover; now we fear that prophecy might have been too optimistic. Ten years since we have experienced the collapse of the communist system, against a similar background in the region, that is other communist countries caving in. And also ten years since, harassed by deadlines, chronologies and ultimata, Romania has democratically accepted the power alternation principle. We are still beginners, so, it is not merely by chance or as a simple demagogic tool that Western countries keep on discussing the need to continue and enlarge democracy. There is no perfect, final and permanently consolidated democracy. Especially in the East, democracy has only reached a state of fragile balance, while these last years have demonstrated to the countries in the region, Romania included, how alert we should be when it comes to protecting the rights and liberties we have shed our blood for.

And from now on, what is going to be the direction taken by all those dynamic change processes in relation to the general tendencies of the global system? This is the question on the answer of which depends Romania's future development for the following decades:

The transition decade is immensely important not only for Romania, but also for all the region previously enclosed within a closed world, under the sign of the "total fortress". The expectations were extremely high, and their achievements disproportionately low; such a relation can only reveal the innocence of the initial moment, when the change started off. The last ten years have taught us all a series of lessons which, if forgotten or ignored, will slowly but surely distance us from the objectives we set for ourselves in 1989. To no avail have we been waiting for a new Eastern European "Marshall Plan" and we have been feeding ourselves on the illusion that the "civilized world" will help us despite any obvious interest. More over, we have often been tempted to underestimate the systemic complex changes we were supposed to face, evading the resistance opposed by mentalities, specific attitudes and conflicting behaviors. **We have escaped the constraints of the "Cold War" to join the constraint of the war for jobs and markets.** Doesn't Romania run the risk that, instead of becoming a market economy, she might turn into a mere market for the market economies of other countries?

There is another lesson we need to learn – **that change is a process.** It is not a continuous circuit, but it has stages and phases, it is a sequence of events and gradual solutions. And, besides, no ex-socialist countries have started from equal positions; some of them were at a disadvantage, they got "bad marks" along the road and were unable to set an equal pace in a competition which, by now, has become so very intense. For too long a time, the Romanian society has been stuck within the critical period, the starting one, thus wasting useful time in dealing with adjacent issues: how we change, what is the pace we are able to sustain, who we should penalize politically, how we should build the upper power structures, what kind of relationship we establish with the voters, etc. More than once have we been in a position to pursue a target without having thought about the means to reach it. It was only after 1992, when the Constitution was adopted and new elections were held, that things started to be shaped in a coherent manner, our society acquired a sense of stability and our economy a new project. The democratic system was established and it took the modern parliamentary variant; political and economic processes endowed institutional structures with new value; the idea of joining the Euro-Altantic space has generated a consensus among the political agents of change which has turned into a priority both for them and their supporters. Daring seemed to have become tenacity, therefore there appeared some concrete results. Unfortunately, as far as our foreign image is concerned, we have not been able to fully turn those gradual transformation stages to our advantage. This is the reason why we have not been able to benefit from the Western support to the extent our competitors proved to have the knack to project an image of "prize winners" in their race for capitalism. This very critical item was not rectified after the 1996 democratic alternation to power, although it was said that the economic reforms were going to be much deeper, and the change was to surely bring about the fruits of prosperity for all Romanians to enjoy, even if delayed. It did not happen so; most Romanians started to perceive the reform as a redistribution process, aimed to include only a select few, while handling very limited resources and accumulation opportunities. This idea led to distrust and pessimism, frustrations and discontent.

Romania's citizens felt the need to have a normal political and economic life in this country, so, the result was a majority vote for a social-democratic solution in the 2000 elections. It was not mainly a kind of nostalgia for the previous government or for paternalist solutions, as the results of these elections have been wrongly interpreted. It was a reasonable choice of a team which proved not only to be competent enough to manage social aspects but also serious enough to make decisions and enforce them. PDSR's victory was a victory against the past and a means to place Romania again along the road to development.

1.2 "Shock therapy" and a jump into the unknown

The citizens' will to accept sacrifice does not last for ever, and, obviously, it cannot feed on rhetorical arguments and the promise of an atemporal prosperity. The new government believes it to be a priority to regain the public trust, seen from the perspective of reaching the promised welfare. Overwhelmed by their daily problems, the citizens no longer have the strength to look into the future. The "shock therapy" is a useful change only when all the necessary conditions have been met, mainly those regarding the government activity and their representative character when it comes to measures imposed from the top. The present government has been trying to establish a dialogue, aimed to reach consensus, with the opposition and the social partners, with all those "worshipping" the concept of legality and constitutionalism, thus attempting to rebuild the pattern of social cohesion, heavily altered during these years of profound social and economic changes.

Following years and years during which the miracle of a unique solution has been a dominant feature of all Romanian political discourse, only now do we realize how necessary it is to build a "mixture", somewhere in-between the free market, based on the sacred rule of private property, and some residual forms of public property, gradually transferred to the private domain. Government action needs to maintain its strategic role, that is it must carefully design all future development, direct resources toward those sectors which are worth encouraging and protecting. This very year's budget has special provisions for such sectors as information technology, infrastructure, public works, energy, that is those sectors stimulating economic growth. Next years' budgets will be constructed based on specific programs, while those domains which are considered priorities will benefit both from budget and also foreign programs financing.

This process will no longer underestimate the local capital. Nation-wide objectives, such as infrastructure projects or privatization, shall be easier to accomplish by resorting to the national capital. There are models of economic success for this type of approach. France, Germany, Great Britain, after the war, and, more recently, Greece, Turkey, Spain, Portugal, Korea, as well as Singapore made use of the model of guided economic growth, with a strong state intervention component. In this respect, I would like to mention the declaration made by a Polish finance specialist, as his country was used as example and argument in favor of the "shock therapy": "During the first years we got acquainted with the errors of the market economy running totally out of control; there are specific structures which have to be shaped by the state, and they do not belong only to the domain of social policies" (Brzezinski; 253).

The Government can answer the dilemma of choosing between the shock therapy and gradual policies by setting priorities and being coherent in fulfilling them. The aim of the Government activity is, mainly, to find progressive answers, as a result of clear and objective thinking, faced with the permanent challenges that a world on the move places in front of the Romanian society.

1.3 Epistemic components of a political project

We live in a diversified world, and the diversity of the world – despite the tendency to uniformly globalize economies – is still so great that we cannot really conceive of the world economic or political system as a unit. We are no longer speaking about a world, but about worlds, having various developments and growth rhythms. These last few years, the world has met with unprecedented political, economic, technologic and social global changes. A closed world, the Soviet one, collapsed, opening up to rediscover liberal democracy and the market-generated economic system, as well as all its benefits and gaps. There is a series of new realities, such as the information society, "information economy", recently developed symbolic means of exchange, which, a decade ago, seemed quite distant al least for part of the Romanian society. Today, we are living in a world of communication and information, the main feature of which is to rapidly adjust to fluctuating situations. Information has turned into "money and wealth", while the capacity to operate with the stored information becomes a component of the ability to provide a coherent and controlable course of all changes.

Eastern Europe is not the only part of a world undergoing changes and facing transition. Mankind as a whole is confronted with that moment when the past makes way for the future; truths are still wandering about in this transition period, which also includes frustrations related to an uncertain future. To repeat again statements such as "*L'histoire n'a pas de sens*" now, in the twilight of history, to reiterate them as a way to signal that history is perceived only as a continuous movement to the future is nothing but a way to voice the keen interest for a temporal dimension – the future. The problem is that any human being is forever oscillating between the past and the future, while looking into the past for a *passe-partout*, a master key to open the present, able to find the future in the present lacking vitality or tempted to experience an unlimited regression, when confronted with a seemingly endless crisis. A political project may be a solution to restore the society's optimism. But one cannot imagine void projects, one cannot forecast any possible variants for the future without resorting to the tendencies established by the past. All time-related, cultural and political types of behavior, generated by the awareness that time is pressing are likely to be related to the downstream flow, often evading any upstream relation, any connection with the origins of the problems that society has to face while going towards the future.

Romania is isolated from the real space and time of the world which we are trying to reach. This makes it even more imperative to build up a governance project designed to be valid and purposeful. Its being valid arises from the fact that it has two open windows – one to theoretical and applied extensions, the other one to the need to restructure the reference system, after having meet the requirements of each new stage. To become operational, the project shall have windows to all the changes within the inner and outer environments, to all the developments taking place inside, but it shall also have some degree of autonomy, established by stability and balance. Largely speaking, these could be the epistemic components of a political project, to the extent by which such a project intends to achieve its own legitimacy and also be legitimized by the citizens. Such schemes are necessary to build a modern managing model for all public affairs. Nevertheless, without the capacity to transpose these components into clear, sectorial objectives, no political scheme, no matter its philosophy, shall be legitimized. History has already been faced with a series of schemes which remained mere utopias; some of them finally emerged out of that utopian world, but proved to be if not achievable, then blamable – it was the case of communism and "real socialism" activated to make it possible for the Western myth of the "golden age of humanity" to become real. Toynbee wrote there are two attempts to escape a torturing present: futurism and archaism. It is in fact the very essence of any Utopia: our return to a lost paradise as well as our escape to the fantasy world of a happy future.

1.4 Europe's rhythm and Kutuzov's dilemma

The Romanian political life has experienced a lack of the sense of unity between the doctrine and its political realization. As a result, society has been growing more and more distrustful of the political component, of the publicized schemes and programs, which have remained mere fiction as they could not really be practically verified. Consequently, it is necessary to construct another model having new foundations, such as: trusting the creative capacity of the human resources available to us, accepting differences and rejecting any type of limitation, be it dogmatic, racial or ethnic. We need concrete schemes to build an economy in keeping with the interests of our society, meant to support the majority of the population, not go against them. Therefore, Romania shall update her policies to become instrumental in a more dynamic entrepreneurial culture. The very first measures aimed to make the Romanian economic environment adjust to the requirements of the world business environment are to pass a law regulating the activity of small and medium-sized enterprises as well as fiscal facilities designed to rehabilitate this sector. At the same time, various types of public property are being modernized in response to a more and more liberalized world. Likewise, social justice should not be understood as an imposition, but as a more thorough application of economic and social rights; it should be viewed as the only way to generate stability and prosperity, or, in other words, it is the same as a balance of prosperity, the result of effectively making use of the social costs we had to bear along this winding transition path. The role of the state shall be revisited so that it comply with the rule of law and the legitimacy of all democratic institutions. Only thus shall we be able to outline a valid economic model for Romania. If a fruitful dialogue is established between the political factors and the civil society, we shall be able to create those mechanisms that will enable all communities to reach their aims, in accordance with the constitutional rights and freedoms.

Politics is not a form of contradiction and we should be able to finally understand that we need to create a space where we could come to an agreement and harmonize our economic, political and cultural interests. Long-lasting tracks are the result of an approach based on consensus, so, to gain prosperity and her real time connection to Europe, Romania needs such a track of mutual understanding. On the other hand, prosperity cannot "contaminate" us, it is not a catching condition. We are obliged to build it ourselves, using the resources that are available to us as well as some human resources who have been rather neglected so far.

We also have to avoid falling into new ideological traps. The scapegoat of monetary and economic integration has imposed increased requirements even on the EU member countries, which everybody should be aware of, and mainly those who believe modernity is being forced upon us by means of structures which belong to a past that the West itself has given up. If, in the more or less distant future, Romania would like to participate in Europe's common life, she has to come up with an attractive, creative proposal, not sketchy components of older ideas which we are the only ones to still consider valid. The 1989 Revolution promoted the idea that we should break with dogmatism. That is the reason why, for the generations to come, the reform and the transition as well should not be a series of activities at the end of which we might be in a position to say, like Marshall Kutuzov: "What is the use of having won the victory, if we are left without an army?".

We are witnessing the world covering a highly dynamic period, the motto of which could just as well be globalization, all its threats and benefits included. As far as Romania is concerned, it is an example of a relatively industrialized country, who, within a not very long period of time, was demoted from among the third rank countries, not so much as a consequence of her inability to rehabilitate according to the standards of the post-industrial revolution, but as a result of the fact that the country lacked the necessary means to do that. At present, Romania is a country eroded both economically and socially, while the erosion factors go on digging a structure which needs overall repair works, mobility and solidarity.

CHAPTER TWO

1989 – SIGNIFICANCE AND INTERPRETATIONS

"History is an art
gallery where there are few
original paintings and many copies."

Alexis de Tocqueville

2.1 Moving away from post-factum theoretical approaches

Here are some of them: the years when Lech Walesa, the Gdansk electrician was a hero, the days and nights that Vaclav Havel spent in prison, the symbol called Dubcek, Andrei Saharov's being so well-known, Gyorgy Konrad's spirit, Adam Michnik's courage, Janos Kis' being so noble, Jacek Kuron's tenacity or Milovan Djilas' apostasy. These are but a few names which have behind them millions of people waiting and seeing their "getting out of communism" as their "entering history" ...

To a great extent, the 1989 revolutions established a dramatic and unexpected course for the change of a system which, at least in the early 80's, still seemed stable enough for anyone to be able to forsee when and how it would collapse. Neither "sovietologists" nor outstanding experts in the development and operation of the Communist Block were able to forecast the moment of its collapse, and even less so how rapidly it would take place. It was certain that a regime based on a single party rule would finally disappear, be it merely because of the global race inequality, if not under the pressure exercised by their own "subjects" and the tyranny inherent injustice.

The timeless political myth of the "bright future" was disgustedly rejected by a population humiliated by fear and terror, by having their human dignity and quality trampled upon. It all culminated in a hurricane of discontent which swept away the "tribal" remains of an excessively nationalistic and constraining type of communism.

The history of a whole system and its tyrants came to an end in a very brief period of time, as they died on the streets of the capital cities where, not many years before, the communist leaders had attended meetings destined to show their proletarian solidarity and the people's support to the representatives of a Single Truth: "What perished on the streets of Prague, Berlin and Bucharest, during the endless meetings in Budapest, at your round table and now in your parliament is not only communism, but also the belief in a closed world, governed by a monopoly of truth". (Dahrendorf, 1993; 37)

Later on, analysts and political sociologists have tried to explain the series of causes for this extremely deep phenomenon, while resorting to various types of explanations, gathered into four broad:

The communist regime collapse was caused by the economic failure, and, seen from this perspective the year 1989 was the end point of a soviet type of economy. It is true, though, that, ever since 1970, because of the general direction established by Moscow, all communist countries adopted a very risky policy for their economic development, and resorted to large foreign loans to upgrade and industrialize their economy. The problem was that this policy did not cover the population's consumption needs, it only provided for the need to create and keep alive "strategic industries"; this incurred huge costs and made it so that other branches were neglected, branches that might have created real accumulation rates. At that time, this trend triggered a critical approach even from some economists inside the socialist system, who found themselves caught up in the argument between the "progressive-minded" and the "acceleration-minded" ones, as the former realized how dangerous it was to neglect the development of the consumption industry and favour, at all costs, the socialist accumulation rate growth. The 1973 and later on the 1979 oil price rises made the global economy growth slow down; this phenomenon had an even greater impact on the communist countries, as it became harder to pay for their foreign loans. As a direct consequence of this situation, the domestic interests were sacrificed, and paying-off one's foreign debt was considered to be a national priority, a guarantee for one's sovereignty and independence. The idea proved to be totally wrong, as all international creditors have always been interested in protecting their old debtors and are hardly ever inclined to grant new loans – and this is one of the reasons why Romania has been unable to easily access large loans after 1989.

There is another category of theories which consider that the arms race caused the collapse of communism. It was a phenomenon which triggered huge economic costs that the Soviets could no longer support in order to meet the pressure exercised by the American technological progress. Under Presidents Carter, Reagan and Bush, USA forced the Soviet Union to spend huge amounts of money on high-tech weapons, which precipitated the failure of centralized economy. It also contributed to a sharp decrease of domestic investments and, at the same time, made it impossible for the Soviets to provide economic aid only based on ideological reasons.

The third category of explanatory theories are centered around the phenomenon of "perestroika", as Gorbaciov's policy is seen as the cause of the 'real' Socialist Block collapse. Obviously, without Gorbaciov the revolutions could not have taken place, or they would have looked different and they would have happened later on. It is stated that the Soviet leader operated two unprecedented changes within the communist world: he wanted to change the face of the regime by providing it with transparency ('glasnost') and all by independently, he gave up the **Brejnev Doctrine**, which originated sometime in 1968. After seeing that the Soviet Union would no longer resort to force to block the course of the reform, the communist countries immediately moved on and rejected the monopoly of the single party, while the situation in these countries progressed towards democracy.

Finally, the central theme in the seriers of explanations is the idea of looking into the alternatives to communism. According to this last approach, the mere economic failure or just abandoning the absolute power control exercised by the Soviet Communist Party offers no complete explanation for the 1989 revolutions. The communist country leaders could have held on to their power if there had still been any domestic confidence in the ability of this type of system to meet the citizens' needs for progress and modernity. Indeed, this did not happen, and both the citizens and the new political leaders initiated a process of reidentifying the political and national priorities. The 1975 Helsinki Agreement made the communist countries accept the principle of co-operation in the field of human rights. Via Pillar Three (of humanitarian exchanges), the concept of human rights was introduced, just like a virus, in all East-European countries, thus triggering the internal explosion of communism. The domestic alternatives to communism were influenced by the specific features of each country: Czechoslovakia and Poland adopted the "civil society" formula as opposed to that of "authority" (meaning communist parties). Opinion leaders such as Lech Walesa and Vaclav Havel were promoted, due to their own personal merits as opponents of the absurd communist politics. Yugoslavia played the card of promoting nationalistic figure-heads, while in Romania the change was so sudden that not even the domestic opposition was able to come up with a pre-established plan to build the new system. The consequence was, that, for a very short while, there was a void of authority.

2.2 Finding *de facto* economic reasons

A totalitarian government has only one weapon to impose the individual's total dependence to the state and that is to maintain an absolute control on the economic field. Centralized planning involves distorted economic decisions, such as arbitrarily established prices or predetermined purchasing and contracting parties, in other words the exact opposite of any concept of product and labor value. As such, this system can no longer exist.

One cannot come up with a more comprehensive analysis of the 1989 revolutions unless we take into account the way the four above-mentioned categories of causes are interrelated. Certainly, the economic factor has played an important role, and if we look behind, we can establish a pattern of the communist countries dynamics. The 60's and 70's meant the peak of the socialist system economy, at a time, when the Soviet Union had, indeed, become a scientific and military super-power, able to counter-balance the US, which was indeed the driving force of the West. Moreover, some communist countries had implemented several limited reforms (such as the Hungarian "new economic mechanism" or the Yugoslavian "self-management") which made some semi-private formulas acceptable. Those formulas were quite effective in maintaining the domestic consumption within reasonable limits. The high threshold reached by the socialist economy at that time made it difficult to believe that only capitalism had the recipe of constant economic growth, in keeping with full employment.

In time, that optimistic attitude was trapped – the cheap growth was coming to its final point, the possibilities to build in the areas where the resources were to be found had already been exhausted: there were hydropower plants in almost all areas where they could be efficiently operated, mining fields were no longer that profitable, the infrastructure had reached a satisfying level. Therefore, in mid-70's there had already appeared a risk for underemployment. Faced with this situation, the Soviet Union assumed the responsibility to provide cheap resources to the socialist states industries, thus delivering what may be called cheap economic aid. But world-wide events showed Moscow that they would not be able to do that for ever. At the same time, the labor force in the communist countries carried out a huge quantity of labor for minimum wages, which was a sign that socialist had reached its subsistence stage (the so-called "Brejnev standstill" period). When the workers started to demand more rights, more consumption goods, more food and a better life style the only momentary solution was repression (that is what happened at the mining fields in 1977 and in Brașov in 1987). On the other hand, in those countries where some limited economic reforms were implemented, the desire to gain profit was rekindled as well as the hope to achieve better conditions by working in a more efficient and better organized way. Last but not least, in the long run the contact between the centralized economies and the Western ones had a devastating effect.

Competing with modern structures and a free economy, the communist countries attempted to speed up their retrofitting process and imported technologies, while paying for them with money also borrowed from the West. That money was used to build new industries and production units, which, at least theoretically speaking, should have also provided the means to pay off the debts, by selling their production in the West for hard currency. But things did not go according to the plan. Moreover, part of those loans was spent to cover some medium term needs (not so much of the population as of different industrial branches already faced with difficulties). In some cases, the potential markets disappeared following the collapse of the Soviet Union or a change of strategic direction to the West.

The policy of accelerated industrialization and the emphasis laid on industrial giants (steel-works, machine building as well as petrochemistry capacities) showed their flaws within a closed economic system. Hardly could any new types of consumption goods be manufactured anymore, and it was becoming ever more difficult to pay off the foreign debts, while everything involved huge sacrifices, made poverty more and more encompassing and signaled a general lack of trust in the national currency, which could not buy almost anything anymore (in Romania, for instance, boxes of Kent cigarettes, coffee packages or exotic drinks had become the real currency used to purchase various services or to rapidly access administrative mechanisms). At the same time, ever since 1980 the Gross National Product had started decreasing, while no clear solutions to remedy the situation appeared against the horizon of an excessively ideologically influenced 'light'.

2.3 Cold war pressures, perestroika, and alternatives to a rigid type of communism...

Besides the global energy price rise, there was another increase imposed by the strategies developed by the US and their allies – that of military expenditures. After the thawing period of the 1970's, the Soviet Union and the US joined a mad high-tech arms race, a race involving more and more sophisticated strategic missiles, but which incurred ever greater costs. Even if the communist states had no such 'planning', they suffered from the indirect impact of the fact that the Soviet Union reduced their cheap economic aid.

That was the moment when Mihail Gorbaciov arrived at the Kremlin, after the interlude of the 'ephemeral leaders' (Andropov and Cernenko). Gorbaciov was the man to strike the final blow to a "clay-legged colossus). The Soviet leader brought along not only the concept of economic pragmatism (manifested as the will to reform) but also the idea of political renewal, by creating a 'humane' trend within the communist system. But there was an obvious contradiction between the facade principles of the system and the social reality, which triggered the erosion of the system's popular support. In March 1986, the XXVIth Congress of the Soviet Union Communist Party approved Gorbaciov's moderate reforms, and in January 1987 the Soviet Union Communist Party Central Committee Plenary unanimously voted for the amazing switch towards democracy made by the Secretary General. In February 1990, the Soviet Union Communist Party Central Committee Plenary voted for putting an end to the attempt to abolish all private property and also to the political monopoly of a single party. During the XXVIIIth Congress, Gorbaciov destroyed the very mesh of the Soviet Union Communist Party, abolished the concept of democratic centralism and forbade party organizations to interfere with the state administration.

Brejnev did something that Stalin had avoided – he joined the global competition, but this mad competition made the whole scaffolding collapse the moment when Moscow was no longer able to support the battle for supremacy. The global package of communist ideology had exhausted not so much its resources of attractiveness, but its political and economic efficiency, and Gorbaciov was aware of it.

What was much more important than 'glasnost' and 'perestroika' was the fact that he gave up the "Brejnev Doctrine", that is the doctrine of limited sovereignty and, consequently, withdrew the occupation forces in Hungary and Afghanistan. What Gorbaciov had stated in his December 1989 United Nations speech would be abided by afterwards, therefore the threat of a military intervention carried out by Big Brother in case of any transgression against the real socialism dogma (thus) became history. Consequently, there appeared a favorable background for several topical issues: streamlining the socialist economies, by limited or gradual reforms, rediscussing the political role of the single party and 'allowing' the public opinion to get involved in the major decision-making process. The individual experiences were very different, as, in fact, the "monolithic unity" of the communist world concealed a variety of types. The Czech Republic rediscovered 'the Prague spring', while in Yugoslavia the interest for each national culture stirred the embers of ethnic dissentions and the Croatians renewed movements such as *Matica Hrvatska*, which had existed ever since the preceding century. In the 70's, that movement had drafted an autonomous constitution, causing some of its leaders to be arrested. One of them was Franjo Tudjman, a former general who gave up all military honours to defend a nationalistic cause.

There was another series of additional factors which made it possible to launch protests based on the concept of civil society. The first one was the 1975 *Helsinki moment* and the concern about exercising one's 'human rights', this being a vaguely defined concept which, nevertheless, was instrumental to all reforming movements. When a rather lesser known rock'n-roll group, "Plastic People of the Universe" got arrested in Czechoslovakia, 243 writers, intellectuals and reformists organized an informal group called "Charter 77" in order to protest and demand that human rights should be respected. The "human rights" weapon became a very good tool to be added to the fight against oppression, just like in Poland, where Solidarnosc was supported by a highly efficient Catholic Church, especially after Karol Wojtyla had been elected Pope.

In Hungary, 1989 was more of an "evolution" than a "revolution", as the Hungarian communism had already tolerated strong reforming elements, mainly economic ones and there existed a freedom zone which was still an ideal for Romania. While the secondary economy had been legally admitted in Budapest ever since 1982, Ceaușescu had strengthened centralization even more. The "new agricultural revolution" was an example in this respect, and it culminated in a genuine "chaining to the land" in the systematized villages. It was not possible for any mass movement to exist outside the party, like in Poland or Hungary; the opponents inside kept their voices low, while all the reforming politicians were marginalised and kept under strict observation. It was no longer possible to resort to the dogma as a solution, as long as Hungary opened its frontiers to Austria and the Czech police force refused to intervene against the protesters. In November 1989 the new Cabinet in the Democratic Republic of Germany started reforming the immigration law; Vaclav Havel was released from prison in Prague and the meetings supporting him effectively put an end to the supremacy of the communist party.

But Romania was not going to experience a "peaceful revolution"; she was to live an extremely harsh one. It was not to be an evolution, but a break, not the continuation of a gradually reforming trend, but a violent change. During its very midst there was a brief period of relative anarchy, when the reforming forces had to shape up and find a viable course for the unfolding events. The "Romanian example" showed something else, too: the more decided the oppressing forces are to resort to violence in order to hold on to power within a 'clan', the more rapid the fall of the system is, and the more radical the solutions.

The Romanian revolution was determined and radical, rejecting all moderate, 'velvet' stages which existed in the Central European countries ("The most striking feature of the Revolution is its force, which one cannot oppose, a force which sweeps everything aside." – de Maistre, 1997; 29). As far as the way in which the revolution started, clearly, the popular rallies were the cause of the regime fall. It is, indeed complete opposite idea to that of the "palace coup" supported by some, inclined to find a mysterious explanation in the "theory of the conspiracy".

The only plot involved was the tangle of sufferings, deprivations, despair and social frustration that the Romanians experienced, after a decade of frantic efforts to pay off the foreign debt, which seemed to be the only coherent aim that Ceauşescu's regime had during its twilight period. Ceuşescu's personal dictatorship and the single party rule collapsed together. The concept of collective responsibility for all general political trends had been a very active principle during the thawing period, but now it had just become a void string of words, a platitude frequently repeated in the speeches delivered to be heard only by the rulers, not by the huge crowds of dissatisfied people. The people were no longer ready to give credit to the raving state of nationalistic delusion put forward by a fanatical tyrant, resembling an eastern despot.

CHAPTER THREE

FROM THE REVOLUTION TO CHECKING ON DEMOCRACY

3.1 Revolution and... evolutions

The Romanian antitotalitarian revolution released a miraculous quantity of social energies which dispelled the eternal charm of an anachronistic type of despotism. The people's minds were freed of the absurd limitations imposed by the autocratic power representing the empire of deception, while the cages of silence and fear lost their bars for ever, and those acting as animal trainers a moment ago were violently eliminated.

The power disintegration phenomenon manifested itself during the initial stages of the Romanian revolution, the more so as the Revolution had a very clear program which, among other things, aimed to do away with the communist party, that is the very hard core of the system, as, at that time, it was considered the major reason of the feeling of "fear" we had to deal with for so many years: fear of repression, violence, and even physical destruction for some. But it is true, indeed, that in those hot moments it was not the people who led the revolution, it was the revolution which led the people.

The belief that the revolution was progressing by itself rapidly conceded its place to the need for organization. The need to somehow fill the institutional and legislative void was obvious, as well as the necessity to provide for the lack of authority and public order structures. In such an inflamed social environment, there was no other way to remedy incoherence and instability but by initiating a new type of institution building. Such a process could only aim at building the rule of law, a multiparty society and market economy. Everybody knew that it was not going to be easy, which was quite clear in 1990 – 1992. It was a period of extended protests, but not in parliament, as it would have been only natural, but directly on the street. Taking into account the methods a revolution uses, nothing seems abnormal during this *sui generis* 'Jacobin' period, as every such movement is first of all an attempt to destroy its own creation. Nevertheless, at that time, specific gestures or speeches resounded in a different manner and acquired new significances, thus the social unrest was about to become endemic. The famous **Statement to the country** issued by the National Salvation Front had already dissolved the power structures of the 'Ceaușescu clan' and had established a ten-item program that may be called the platform of the Revolution: a multiparty democracy, free elections, power separation based on a new Constitution, restructuring the economy and the country's agriculture, reorganizing the country's culture and education system outside any type of ideological control, observance of ethic minorities' rights and liberties, pro-European foreign policy, observance of human rights. Still, what was not known was how and by means of which instruments we could fulfill these objectives very rapidly, the more so as there were various voices belonging to the newly re-established political parties who considered that the election would be no solution to this problem, due to the fact that the Romanian voters lacked political judgment.

The transition from the communist regime to the multiparty democracy was two fold, both a political and an economic one. If politically speaking, things went very rapidly, that is as far the institution building is concerned, as well as the construction of the constitution and party systems, economically speaking the changes have been very slow. Still, from the very beginning there was a very clear commitment to the creation of a free market system. What happened after 1990, which includes both the economic and political aspects may be presented in a specific sequence.

Stages of the post-communist transformations

The first period (1990-1992) – the transformation

The political objective of the 1990-1992 period: to meet several basic requirements of democracy, such as freedom of expression, freedom of the press, rejection of the single party and of the centralized command system, accepting the concept of pluralism of opinions as well as political pluralism. We should also add the Constitution and the Election Law, free elections, the ascent of a new political elite.

The economic objective: to achieve stability, to initiate the process of economic opening the rejection of centralism in favor of the market economy, to eliminate all arbitrary controls exercised by the State. Let us add some other objectives as well: to eliminate price control, to liberalize prices, to redistribute agricultural property, to achieve spontaneous privatization.

The second period (1992-1996) – consolidating democracy

The political objective: to move away from transformation to stability, to establish the constitutional democracy as well as new institutional structures, a parliamentary regime and the rule of law, to transfer political arguments from the street to the parliament arena.

The economic objective: to move away from transformation to stability, to rebuild the economy by means of reform, to re-launch production within a free market system, to build the legal framework for property and business, to adopt new management techniques, to initiate the necessary steps to obtain foreign financial aid and to make everything operational.

The third period (1996-2000) – testing the government alternation

The political objective: to consolidate and strengthen the democratic regime, to check the reliability of the power separation principle, to check the power alternation principle by means of the free election test, to develop the political culture and to consolidate the culture of legality, of the Power – Opposition parliamentary game, to consolidate the administrative mechanism.

The economic objective (largely unattained): to establish parameters which favor growth (economic boom), to develop the domestic capital capacity, to make social policies more flexible, to lobby pro capitalism, to finalize privatization, to establish an entrepreneurial culture, to demonopolize the system, to develop small and medium-sized enterprises, to set up a bank system ready to sustain the economic growth.

The fourth period (2000) – the decisive step towards transformation

The political objective: to regain the citizens' trust in the benefits of a democratic government, to make the decision-making factors accountable, to decentralize the administration, to improve Romania's foreign credibility, to have Romania join the Euro-Atlantic structures.

The economic objective: to have sustainable economic growth, to streamline the production structures, to liberalize trade, to re-launch public investments, to develop the IT sector, to carry on privatization.

3.2 Too young, too rash, too naive

A rather naive representation of the initial stage of the Romanian transition generated blurred and disproportionate images regarding what the politicians and the parties should have done, which overlooked the necessity to have all those critical judgments include the difficulties involved in the process initiated in December 1989. This resulted in a series of hasty political attitudes, triggered by the need to immediately meet the requests made by the protesters, even if it was a simplistic, naive and counterproductive approach.

During that euphoric period, the dominant attitude was to wait. The public opinion was waiting for the politicians to intervene, they were waiting for foreign aid, for help to find solutions, aso. The question was asked whether a *slow transition* was preferable to a *shock therapy,* which would have largely involved the consensus of all the political forces, the existence of a very solid entrepreneurial culture, considerable financial aid, and also a political force capable enough to tailor-make this method and to legitimize it, for as long as it remained very rough for the majority of the population. Transition costs grow even more when all problems and solutions are only rhetorically approached, while the social and political costs of such a way of life are extremely high. The newly-initiated transition had no models to follow, there were no preceding successes regarding the change of property type, mentality, behavior, attitudes. Immediately after the Revolution was victorious what prevailed was a feeling of impending emergency, of inactivity and possible failure, all these caused by delays. We were faced with the first period of the change, when there seemed to be enough optimism and confidence that the system would be capable of dealing with the big issues, establishing priorities and setting up major action lines. But there followed the second period, of frustration and discontent, of political passions, of dissatisfaction as to the West which seemed to indulge in an attitude of mere spectator rather than active participant.

The Revolution generation seemed to be living under the pressure of immediacy, of the imperative wish to change or restore what the preceding generations had wasted, thus involving history in an *au rebours* progress. The underdeveloped socialism had proved to be contrary both to what the fathers of scientific socialism had foreseen and also to all human ideals, generally true. Yet, unlike the 'revolution' which had brought socialism about right after the war (helped not by the vocotry of Stalin's version of Marx and Lenin's principles, but by the Red Army), the 1989 Revolution was carried out by the Romanians themselves, and this made it decisive and anti-communist. In fact, the need to modernize and the objectives of a new model cannot be separated from the philosophy assumed at that moment. That new philosophy regarded communism, and rightly so, as the main blocking factor, oppressing the capacity of the individuals and of society to develop freely.

I consider that the period of dissatisfactions and illusions has already finished. Now we are facing a moment when we have to see what our achievements and benefits are after a decade of more or less successful transformations. The country cannot be governed by virtue of a utopia. The objectives are the same, but the future can only be drawn closer if the decision-making factors are realistic and the means are adjusted to present Romania's possibilities to make things real.

3.3 When legitimacy is disputed and regrettable rifts take place

Maybe with the exception of Russia, nowhere else has communism generated such a deep and strong dissolution of the civil society structures as it has in Romania. The main constituents of this process were terror, discord and corruption. Unawares, communism was able to pour into the Romanian society the poison of passivity and ignorance, the comfort of saying 'no' to all initiatives, the non-commitment to projects which, anyway, brought about no benefits, or, at most, permanent risks. Accustomed to always be assisted by a severe but protective 'Paternal' figure, immediately after the state of elation caused by our being free, we were overcome by what Erich Fromm called the "fear of liberty".

None of the major post-Revolution politicians contested the fact that the 'miracle' which occurred in December 1989 was a Revolution. There is no doubt that it was a genuine revolution, mostly carried out by the younger generations. Unfortunately, there was no avoidance of the very winding path. The contradictions did not turn into fruitful democratic or parliamentary debates but into violent outbursts, into ways to let off steam after decades of silence by means of street unrest, into pressures, concessions and swift changes of the situation, into uncapping the ethnic discontent crucible, into a total blame cast on those who, merely days or hours before, had been acclaimed and considered as 'saviours'.

"The man on the street" was idealized, summoned to rally in the name of the people's sovereignty, of historic legitimacy or various other symbols. Inter-ethinc conflicts took place, various social categories were stirred against each other, into opinion leaders emerged, and, in the meantime, Romania was heading in poverty. The democratic institutions could not 'evade' the trap of everyday life in order to provide the order necessary to build the new Romania which would not be ideologically, ethnically or otherwise parted. Obviously, part of the blame for this confusion lies with the government team, with the then prime minister, who rejected all dialogue, especially when it was extremely important. These were moments when it might have been possible to prevent some outbursts of violence in favor of the country's general interests. So much tension could only lead to a climactic moment, that is the well-known and ill-famed 'comings of the miners', which dealt a very harsh blow to Romania's image abroad. The government's means to protect the public order may have been very precarious. It was clear that, if such a new power, already so much contested despite the results of the May 1990 elections had resorted to force, things would have been even more confused. What is very interesting is that, right after the elections, when things should have gone back to a calmer, more normal state of affairs, the exact opposite happened. A real image war was waged and, unfortunately, it turned into concrete, violent actions.

The decision made by the National Salvation Front to participate in the elections on May, 2oth, 1990 caused the explosive indignation of part of the intellectuals in Bucharest, and the Front was reproached that they could not be both organizers and competitors. Yet, the vast majority of the population considered it was useful for the Front to run for office; it was also considered beneficial for the normality of the Romanian society. The success of the National Salvation Front, by a very comfortable election score of about 65%, was highly contested by the then opposition. The opposition parties that had obtained ridiculous scores considered that the elections had been rigged by a team that wanted to stay in power at all costs. Later on, it was clearly seen that the suspicion of totalitarianism did not hold, that the elected power did not turn to any form of dictatorship or authoritarianism. The new governing structure could not give up its prerogatives, however much those groups of interests may have wanted it, irrespective of the more or less obscure area they represented. The will to exercise the prerogatives of power (by virtue of the legitimacy given by the elections) was classified as dictatorial. That was the main stake of the protests which led to the "University Square" phenomenon and to similar events. That was the regrettable moment when there appeared a rift inside the Romanian society. The original sin was the lack of understanding of the fact that the Power and the Opposition are complementary, that they do not represent two Romanias, but only one, for which, given the circumstances, anarchy was no solution. Unfortunately, the political disputes and arguments went on being voiced on the street, not in Parliament, as any democracy would have it.

Despite the above-mentioned difficulties, democracy started being operational. The Romanian Parliament started passing laws, a new Constitution was being prepared, mechanisms were being thought of to stabilize and connect the social and economic situation to the rule of law. Nevertheless, the economic situation was a disaster, production kept decreasing dramatically, the economic chaos seemed inevitable and the gaps difficult to cover. Privatization was immaterial, but the state itself seemed unable to support an economic circuit, if not as a whole, at least its efficient components. Having said that, it was obvious that the social dissatisfaction was going to increase, which did indeed happen. As a result, the Roman government resigned and, later on, the National Salvation Front split up, not long before the elections. Even now, I still consider that the best variant would have been for Petre

Roman to accept, after the September 1991 government resignation (the 'fuse' which goes off when the system is under pressure), to become again one of the leaders of the National Salvation Front and prepare for the elections which were to take place in the spring of 1992. A much more efficient solution, both for Romania and the National Salvation Front, would have been to win those elections and re-appoint Petre Roman as Prime Minister. Anyway, the Parliament became the real arena of the political arguments, and the Romanian politics experienced the natural phenomenon of polarization, while the political competition sublimated the conflicts. Unfortunately, except for very few moments, such as the 1995 Snagov one and the preparation of Romania's NATO pre-accession strategy, the rifts continued to exist, despite all declarations of intentions.

3.4 Difficult beginnings and 'inheritances at war'

The government that came to power after the 1992 elections tried to fulfill their social and democratic commitments, by creating the stable environment necessary to the economic development. It resulted in the first years of positive economic growth, 1994-1996, since Ceaușescu's regime collapsed. But, irrespective of those successes, the gap between Romania's domestic economic progress and the development level of the Central European countries deepened, while maintaining a potential for conflict as far as the social situation in the country was concerned. Nevertheless, after a sharp decrease in her image abroad, Romania managed to become again a credible partner for the regional plans and policies, for the geostrategic stability options that the big powers drafted for the area.

Regrettably, Romania was unable to maintain a steadfast rhythm in the transition process. On the one hand, the Romanian Party of Social Democracy was harshly blamed for the very slow privatization rate which only made it more difficult for us to move towards the competitive space occupied by all modern economies; on the other hand, the governments that succeeded one another after 1996 sped up the privatization process, indeed, but there was a price to pay for that, too. The profit gathered in a very limited area, while the losses spread to the level of the whole nation and affected all the population.

The philosophy that the post 1996 governments imposed on the Romanian economy did not generate either trust or credibility abroad for Romania. The hesitations and the delays depended on a series of outer events, the counter-weight system required by a political coalition difficult to manage slowed things down even more. The reform became a vague concept, an all-encompassing one, ranging from benefits for various coalition participants to benefits for foreign actors who had had a logistic contribution in the 1996 election campaign. Any realistic outlook on things was replaced by clichés and stock phrases borrowed from the Romania – IMF bilingual vocabulary, which the media and various opinion leaders understood quite well. Clearly, a political official, a minister or a politician cannot have a total grasp of all the theoretical and factual data which cover the economic problems. But they have to resort to the experts, to those experienced in economic policies, as they specialize in knowing all the details and are trained to co-ordinate activities of various working groups or data bases, depending on their individual expertise. Thus, one can group together a large number of different types of expertise and set up formulas which should allow the inherent framework and institutional mechanisms to develop. This is the point when technocrats have to be called in, experts who do not only belong to international financial bodies, as was implied by the economic policies of the post 1996 governments.

The successive economic fall shows that the inner logic of those policies was not infallible. All economic policies got entrapped into vague models as well as idyllic images about what the Romanian economy should look like. Indicative of the fact that center-right parties were unable to find the best way to carry out the economic reform was their inability to come up with external evidence to document the validity of the implemented policies, their spasmodic and delayed response to the social stimuli, and also to the stimuli coming from the domestic capital.

The government program stressed the need to make the market mechanisms more efficient but it did not really take into account the administrative instruments, while the idea that the privatization process should be transparent existed only in the political departments of the government coalition. Moreover, being in a 'hurry' to speed up privatization, the law was often broken, which caused the population's even greater distrust as far as the reform was concerned, as long as the unquestionable values of the market system were being compromised. That is why a paradoxical attitude appeared which was well captured by the opinion polls – the majority of the population declared they were pro privatization, but, at the same time, they declared they wanted to work in the state sector.

The gap between the expectations and the results is huge and it refers to the whole issue of 'change', not only to the specific case of privatization. It happened because Romania was the only country where a rift in the continuum of the reform was preferred, which has cost and will still cost us a huge price. Welfare is generated by the real economy, by its growth, not by economic programs based on various kinds of general principles or by resorting to various 'historic' types of legitimacy.

Nowadays, our priority is to regain Romania's credibility in Europe. We are of a clear mind, we are realistic and we realize that we have a lot to make up for, especially in this respect. In fact, to be credible is to inspire trust in all issues having an impact on the community's interests, far beyond the strictly diplomatic level. We have to become credible economic partners, we have to offer guarantees as to how secure the borders are between Romania and the countries outside the European Union, we have to consolidate our legal system and the public order in order to stop importing illegal immigrants to Europe, we have to become a country which generates regional stability. As far as the foreign policy is concerned, the most convincing step would be to honour our position as president of OSCE. A successful presidency would undoubtedly be a useful lobby to regain our credibility as a state. Anyhow, all the priorities that I have mentioned are to be found in the government program of the new Cabinet and it would be extremely difficult to establish a hierarchy. They are rather interdependent issues, applicable only within an overall pragmatic outlook on the Romanian society and on Romania's position in Europe.

Romania's geographic position is an advantage which has been widely talked about, maybe even excessively. There were some tendencies to rely too much on such natural advantages, and this type of attitude is not positive at all. The new Government shall no longer consider that type of advantage so often as before and will try to promote policies which stimulate initiative, responsibility and a serious attitude in one's activity. There are much more isolated countries, the geography of which is rather plain, but they managed to develop by turning to full account their human resources. I believe this to be the type of state which we have something to learn from.

CHAPTER FOUR

GLOBALIZATION AND THE FUTURE OF TRANSITION

"Globalization is not a catastrophe. Globalization offers all countries more opportunities than risks."

Oskar Lafontaine

4.1 The Society of the future – an intelligent network

Within the borders of the former world of 'real' socialism as well as inside the 'democratic and developed area', as the current name of the Western part of the Old Continent is, the beginning of the third millennium is expected to bring about profound changes, the impact of which cannot be assessed yet. It can only be foreseen. We can express the certainty that the present is 'better', which does not automatically entail that the future is safer. The dramatic geopolitical changes, the alterations affecting the objectives of the financial and consumption markets, the technological changes, the transformations of government policies as well as the ones in legislation, in the macroeconomic stability and the capital flows, the changes in environmental policies, all these are but a few of the features contributing to the permanent change of the world we live in. The global society will have some characteristics, such as: intensified economic exchanges, globalized markets, increased speed of information flows and, last but not least, international organizations and multinational corporations having more power than nation-states. This type of society is mainly a "network society" (Castells, 1998; 82) based, to a large extent, on knowledge, the discourse of which relies on the pair "democracy and knowledge" to the detriment of "demos and ethnos". In this global society cognition involves IT, financial services, communication-related activities, education together with applied research. Such an IT society has no center, it only has nodes of different sizes which can asymmetrically connect in the global network. It is an open structure with a tendency to expand in all directions, so the network does not depend on a specific center; it only depends on the global information distribution, later on dissipated into the economy and society.

The continuous transformation 'within the network' shows that mankind is facing a new historic cycle, the end point of which will be not only a new geopolitical restructuring or a reshaping of the international political positions, but also a restructuring of the present power positions of the financial or management nuclei, while restructuring, too, the global resource-related and market relations. Although there have been major changes in the world of capital, one can see that the final destination of profits (the real essence of the market system) continues to be beyond the existing borders, just like the desire to concentrate power. Less than 5% of all the world companies have more than 70% of all world-wide assets and this is the hard evidence that accounts for the steady growth of the industrialized nations. These are the reasons why, most probably, the future may bring about again the temptation to 're-colonize' some countries, but this time the attempt will not be motivated only by the very low labour costs and cheap resources, but also by the desire to 'transfer pollution'. At the same time, the national and government structures will have less and less control over processes and domains traditionally viewed as much too important to allow the interference of any external actors. This will happen not because the national political elites would be less capable or coherent when establishing and pursuing their national priorities. Kenichi Ohmae wrote a book that caused great stir. In this book the author says that we are heading toward a world without frontiers, in which the very concept of national security would become redundant, as all interests will be shaped at the level of each individual, not at the level of the nation (Ohmae; 225).

In a global world, no country can risk becoming isolated without compromising its future, therefore it must integrate as much as possible a universe of games and complex exchanges, where one comes to occupy a good position in the top based mainly on efficiency and 'realpolitik' pragmatism. For a country, to be flexible is the same as to be able to adjust to the global environment, modifying its data bases in case there appear developments or tendencies having possible negative effects. In this type of world, retaliation is still possible, even if in more situation than one no force is resorted to. Here are some ways to penalize an actor considered eccentric: to withdraw investments, to threaten a 'lock out', to deliberately resort to economic suffocation by denied access to loans and technology.

The emergence of the new order will make it mandatory for all societies to have power, professionalism and flexibility to adjust to all organizational changes. These will be the qualities required for all the countries going through the unavoidable transition process, such as Romania.

Trust, Flexibility, Sustainability. I believe that these three concepts define any genuine democracy, define the expectations of the individual who refuses to be a mere statistical figure, a humble taxpayer as well as the victim of a limited administration. Just to paraphrase what I believe to be an essential feature of the period that Romania is faced with now, that is the switch from Marx to Coca Cola, I would say that we are moving away from the period of a TYRANNICAL administration to the period of the modern citizen, free to build up a career for himself anywhere in the world, to have a bi-, tri- or multilingual family and to have his savings deposited wherever he pleases on earth and who can directly access the web address of the mayor of London, New York or Paris to be granted an audience.

So, we, Romanians have to deal with two major simultaneous changes, which require us to put aside everything we knew before and to adopt a new way of life. The good news is that the change imposed by the new economy means more freedom of initiative, of movement, of creation. We have been waiting for a long time to be given this opportunity. What is a social democratic government supposed to do under these circumstances? My answer is the following: to initiate a firm battle, without wasting time, without hesitations and to pursue the idea of modernization so as to fully enter the new world.

4.2 Going from socialism to capitalism: what scapegoat shall we look for?

The need to turn to the market of the East European economies has demonstrated how difficult the adjustment is for the economies that have operated in a chain sequence, based on a single principle and on the ideological party control, especially when it comes to adjusting to the reality of a very mobile and fluctuating world. Let us remember that in Romania's neighboring countries there was some degree of economic freedom, while in this country the political factor attempted to concentrate everything (we should mention just the rural sytematization process and the 'new agricultural revolution') to make sure that no centrifugal tendency would appear and that there would be no possibility to contest the ruling group.

These are some reasons why it has proved difficult to implement market reforms in Romania and to make the effort to adjust for such a 'patchy' economy. There was no assessment of how bearable the implemented reforms might be and this was reflected in the population's dissatisfaction following the heavy recession and a highly eroded living standard. The collapse of totalitarianism generated a state of general elation when a series of wrong steps were stated and implemented, which had negative effects on the Romanian industry, on its capacity to preserve strategic markets for its products. The financial resources that Romania still had were rapidly exhausted.

From the very beginning there was a stormy debate between two schools of thought. One of them supported the idea that the models presented in literature should be simplified and argued that the door to economic success can only be opened by a rapid transition. The well-known *shock therapy*, mainly promoted by the IMF triggered an attack against hyper-inflation, which we all accepted. The major stress was upon rapid privatization, deregulation and macro-economic stability.

The other theory, known as *gradualism,* lays the stress on the need to create the institutional infrastructure materialized in laws destined to protect contracts, to provide competition and to generate efficient corporate administration as well as anti-trust laws and regulations aimed at maintaining a solid financial system. The gradualists are worried about social safety. That is why experts representing such schools got involved in studying the transition countries and comparing various economic systems in order to demonstrate there exists more market economy than free market. Let us examine the country considered to have been successful, namely Poland. After a rapid decrease of the inflation to 20%, a fluctuating rate was allowed to exist during all this interval, and then they continued by implementing a cautious and gradual privatization policy. The situation was similar in Slovenia.

Unlike in these two countries, tough monetary policies were applied in Romania, which resulted in the demonetization of the economy until the present day situation – more than 60% of all transactions are of a *barter* type. Russia was proud of her rapid privatization, but this process allowed an oligarchy to control most of the country's wealth, while the taxes they pay are quite limited. For the very rich, deregulation was a way to transfer a large part of the country's wealth across the border.

The government in power in Romania after 1992 supported the theory of gradualism, having good reasons for that, reasons which proved to be true and were also backed by some successes. Indeed, those successes were not major ones, but they provided social stability and made it possible for the private actors to emerge. They also permitted the return of a property-based system. Gradualism had a series of social and psychological reasons: the effects of fifty years of Marxism could not be wiped out immediately, while the individuals' attitudes and their economic behavior were still indebted to the State inertia. People expected that the government should provide them with everything they needed, so the strikes and social protests confirmed this inherited or induced inertia. **Taking into account the inertia specific to the individuals' and institutions' behavior, the system transformation is a process which may last for a whole generation.**

The opposition shock therapy versus gradualism disappeared later on, as it was too vague to really cover such a complex process and the specific features of each country.

The recession affecting the post-communist economies was mainly due to a massive and premature withdrawal of the State. In other words, it is in fact a crisis of the role of the State itself. The examples offered by Poland, the Czech Republic and Hungary prove that the economic recovery of these countries were triggered by the fact that, later on, the State got involved again in the economy, even if under a modified form.

4.3 The inheritance of the past and the burden of the present

The centralized administrative system that operated in the countries organized according to the Soviet model was based on maximizing the role of the central political elite who had the absolute control over the whole society. Industry, agriculture and services operated as a single national enterprise, controlled by means of centrally taken decisions. For instance, the mass-media was controlled by the way the paper and electricity resources were allotted, going as far as their distribution and the number of staff they employed. The number of copies printed did not depend on the public demand, but on the party directives as well as on the party's cultural and ideologic temporary tendencies.

The total monopoly exercised by the state-party orientated and concentrated the national market tendencies in a mass, all-emcompassing structure. This giant enterprise created the illusion that they had total control (which did not also mean an efficient control) over the production, development and labor force. All type of management responsibility of all economic operations was replaced by centralized decisions. In exchange, those enterprises knew they were protected by budget subsidies or any other material or legal privileges in case their performance was poor as far as exports or productivity were concerned. Economic decisions were imposed by ideological reasons, and these were often wrong, taking into account the economic grounds that motivated them or the access to the world market. The prices of various products, of consumer goods and services were generally established depending of the interests of industrialization – the great obsession of the communist regime. Therefore, a major fact was neglected, namely that capitalism was heading towards another period – the period when services are diversified, they become prevailing, when symbolic means of exchange are being perfected and the Western concept of productivity regulated its price based on the quantity of 'intelligence' incorporated in each product, not on the mere physical labor consumed. That was the immediate effect of the IT revolution, of the new high-tech discoveries, and, unfortunately, Romania had a marginal position in all that.

Some beneficial steps were taken in agriculture, such as large scale irrigation and use of fertilizers, but something else became obvious – labor efficiency was decreasing (I would only like to give an example, the so-called 'socialist group work' which meant that the crops were gathered by the students, the army and the workers). To efficiently manage most collective farms and many state farms as well turned out to be a nightmare, aggrevated by the low export prices. The reason (why) the prices were so low was that it was by all means necessary to sell in order to get the hard currency to pay the foreign debt.

The Romanian national currency was not convertible. The fixed prices did not express a real relation between supply and demand, therefore a 'parallel market' developed, sometimes blacker, sometimes grayer. Neither did salaries express the labor reality, they were generally standardized and did not facilitate performance and positive competition.

Here are some reasons why it is difficult to contradict the analysis made by Lipton and Sachs (Lipton, Sachs; 99) which states the main plague of socialist economies was the never-ending demand for investments, depending on the plan. Nicolae Ceaușescu was also obsessed with ever growing public investments. The result was that the economy became unbalanced, consumption goods that the people needed were missing, thus generating the social tensions which would culminate in the December 1989 popular uprising. Anyway, because of the typically socialist routine, it was difficult to initiate the economic reform. Several factors had to be taken into account, such as the distorted production mechanisms (the planned system and COMECOM had collapsed) and the totally inefficient preceding investment policies.

"Despite the fuss and the noise, no new idea appeared in Eastern Europe" says François Furet, quoted by Ralf Dahrendorf in his book

"Reflections on the Revolution in Europe". Nevertheless, Eastern Europe was invited to quietly wait for the accession train to pass, and later on they were told that the train was not going to stop anymore, or had already passed for some time, so, all those wanting to catch it had better run after it...

4.4 Education and economy

"I think that the supreme moral obligation of the community is to provide education."

John Dewey

One of the most serious mistakes made by Romania's governments during these last few years is that they irresponsibly neglected educating the human capital. Of course, the physical capital is important, but without human resources one cannot speak about development, and especially about sustainable development. Romania imperiously needs capital and investments, but she mainly needs technicians and competent managers, she needs the kind of technical expertise comparable to the Western one. For a country, the power given by its knowledge structure is as important as the power provided by its defence, production or finance. The characteristic feature of the world today is the transfer of power from the 'rich in capital' to the 'rich in information', and the difference between nations is made by the rate of the higher education graduates.

The question we should ask ourselves is **not how we can create wealth, but how we can create the capacity to create wealth.** It is an open question for us, Romanians. If a few decades ago, the human capital was still considered a 'residual' capital, gradually an idea imposed itself, namely that the human capital can explain increased productivity just as well as labour or capital. The human resources investment has a tremendous impact on the economic growth, and the key to this type of investment is education. Once this was discovered, there appeared a phenomenon which is well-known in Romania as well – the brain drain. Willingly or not, explicitly or not, some economic centers have been attracting human capital, thus creating an imbalance in its distribution over various geographical areas. In the near future Romania will have to come up with a very clear policy to create and maintain her own human capital by putting forward attractive offers.

That education is a fundamental constituent of all political programs and projects is clear, be it by only looking at president Clinton's election programs (for the second term of office) or by analyzing the "New Labour Manifesto" drafted by the Labour Party. At the same time, France has been granted her ability to rapidly structure her society and to access modernity by a republican, lay and free type of education. Generally speaking, left or center of left parties are inclined to consider education of major importance.

It is difficult to draft a plan to stimulate the human resources development without taking into account the present and future employment structure, the opportunities offered for professional retraining, the possibility that some social and professional categories still have to become employed, as the economic flow is highly mobile and it presupposes a relatively rapid switch to a new job. One pressing question that all Western educational models are trying to answer is the ability to adjust to a permanently changing environment. Modern education has to meet new requirements imposed by the labour market: to stimulate the students' ability to see the abstract core of a problem, to help them systematize the information they receive, to develop their team spirit and, last but not least, to last as long as an individual is still active, that is to be life-long education.

Unfortunately, in Romania there has been an overall economic decrease during the last years, which led to a large share of the population being significantly deprived of access to education. We live in a country where there is again the risk of having a high degree of illiteracy, compared to the European standards. At present, the

Romanian education system is faced with a major difficulty. Lately, the budget allocations have been totally insufficient and have caused a sharp decrease in the teaching staff's real salaries have generated the discontent of the students and faced schools and universities with the impossibility of paying for their overheads. The anarchy and chaos in education is closely related to the general recession of the national economy during the last four years. One of the consequences is that a major part of the young generation has become marginalized, having a dramatically low level of education and schooling. At the same time, there is an ever-growing risk of generating school drop-out and illiteracy. Another drawback of the Romanian education system is that it stresses too much the need to memorize information and to do theoretical work to the detriment of applied research.

The IT society is a reality to which Romania has to connect. Therefore, a modern education model is vital now, when production has changed so much, it has come to be more and more dependent on the new technologies that bring together information and communication. The service sector, so important for the post-industrial societies is permanently expanding, thus requiring that the education system change dramatically. What has to change refers mainly to the various basic vocational qualifications which train for every day life services, but it also refers to the high qualification levels, for the so called 'symbolic' services, that require the ability to organize and handle abstract concepts. Many professions of the future will largely ask for personal qualities, motivation, enthusiasm, initiative, the ability to work in groups of fluctuating size, all these features being totally different from those required by the mass production process, typical of the industrial period.

It is the fundamental changes inherent in the new social profile which require the permanent expansion of knowledge in order to face the 'demand for mobility' presupposed by the labor market changes. Therefore, we speak about life-long education, in keeping with the fact that periodically some activities become obsolete. Obviously, a degree no longer guarantees long-term employment, and this has to be understood in Romania as well by most of the public opinion. That is why we need an education system ready to train not necessarily specialists, but educated individuals, able to adjust and demonstrate professional mobility.

It is unacceptable that Romania should ignore or underestimate education, which she needs vitally to train the necessary expertise to implement a through reform of the economy and of the Romanian society, while the European Union countries consider education a priority of their government programs. We cannot speak about economic growth and social progress in Romania if we go on underestimating or ignoring the human capital investment. Education is the place where the future of our national identity is being designed, from a European and global perspective.

Jacques Chirac, the French President, was asked about the priorities of the coming millennium and he spoke about "the two pillars of development" that is education and democracy. Referring to education, Jacques Chirac said: "Education is the best way to development. We have to provide equal access to education for both young women and young men, while supplying them with the means to succeed. The new IT technologies facilitate this task now. We should pay attention, though, and avoid creating a new gap between the level of knowledge in the rich and the poor countries, offering the latter the access to the new technologies." (Anthony, Dekkaz; 51).

4.5 The Catcher on the frontier to the future

A country which does not grant science a privileged place condemns itself to a winding, useless, endless road. Progress means science, and the challenges involved by the planet's rapid changing rhythm into a competition market only confirm it. Many Romanian politicians have tried pathetically to sell themselves as reformists, without doing anything to prove it. Moreover, the really important activities for the country are located on a secondary plane, behind their personal interests. Faced with this situation which is unfavorable to scientific research, the new government has drafted a program aimed to take the first and the most important step towards placing that activity in the honorable position it deserves. A country without science is a country without a future.

Human sciences professionals have long been marginalized because they were courageous enough to express their opinions, to see things only in the light of the truth. And contrary to their expectations, the 1989 Revolution did not bring them a better life. Even if they are no longer persecuted, their work is totally disregarded, as far as their salaries are concerned. This situation results in them being no longer intellectually independent, they are obliged to 'create on commission', moving away from a genuine scientific calling. The present initiative aims to be the first battle to regain the former autonomy, to restore the dignity of those who live among books.

The political factors' negligence caused the most dramatic state of poverty of people working in research. If humanist intellectuals have the possibility to protest by their crafty use of language, exact science professionals are more difficult to approach. They live in and for their world, and if society despises and allows them to fall prey to poverty, their attitude is simpler: they resign, keep quiet and leave the country. The main objective of the initiator of this project is to put an end to this unfortunate exodus, which impoverishes and dishonours us. It will demonstrate that the hardships researchers have to face can be overcome and that very gifted young persons can have a decent life in Romania, too.

The present project is integrated in a (possible) key concept which will be the basis of the government's future doctrine and policies: "the catcher on the frontier to the future". It is fundamental and necessary that our contemporary world should head towards the future in a progressive manner, thus becoming aware of the European social-democratic ideologies. The present initiative means the concrete transposition of this idea, it is the palpable proof that demonstrates that it is more than a mere slogan and it may come up with real solutions for real problems. We must understand that we cannot face the present without realistically looking into the future. We do not need false prophecies, we need scientific forecasts, based on existing facts, that have a quantifiable development.

The number of research staff per one thousand persons is below the European level. The rate is about 10 researches per 1,000 employees. Let us compare this figure to France (14/1,000), Germany (14/1,000) and Sweden (14/1,000).

So, the main problem from the Romanian research is qualitative not quantitative. There are enough staff in research, what is flawed is their structure. As an argument, let us refer to the research staff structure and the Romanian research results between 1995 – 1999.

According to the latest data supplied by the National Statistics Commission there are, at present, about 55,400 employees in research. About 32,500 are higher education graduates (and 6,900 have a PhD). Apparently, this should be a positive situation as the rate of research employee is quite enough. But, if we take into account the age groups, we can see that the number of researchers who are within the limits of the peak creativity group is obviously lower than those belonging to age groups when their creativity diminishes.

According to Romania's Annual Statistical Report there are about 11,700 researchers under 40 years of age, while there are about 19,000 over 40, that is almost twice as many. This has a direct impact on the research results. One should only mention the dynamics of published papers during these last few years. In 1995 and 1996 there were more than 25,000 scientific papers published each year in Romania, while in 1998 about 15,000 papers were published at home, and in 1999 approximately 13,000. The difference between the number of papers published by Romanian researchers abroad in 1995 and then in 1999 is also very significant. In 1995 there were 5,351 such papers published abroad, and in 1999 only 3,780.

The state of the research sector is rightfully considered a disaster. The recession started in 1996, but it has to be stopped, otherwise we shall be faced with a process that may become irreversible, namely the de facto disappearance of the Romanian research.

The main problem relates to the high average age in research. Of course, research personalities have to be the main project co-ordinators; they should not be removed from research, on the contrary, they have to have full support in their attempts to carry on the Romanian scientific traditions. The solution is an inflow of young, outstanding researchers, who are more motivated to create and are of the proper age to reach performance in the field of research.

The 'target figure' that has to be reached is a rate of 14 researchers per 1,000 employees. We consider this figure closest to the relevant European standards. This suggested standard will be reached by attracting staff aged under 40 who are now employed by foreign research institutes and also by initiating attractive programs for young people with a scientific calling. To be able to do this incentives have to be as close as possible to a normal level. Researchers' salaries are totally unacceptable, in most cases. If a research market is created, the activity of the persons employed in research will be more and more appreciated, so, this could be a solution to solve the material crisis that the elite exact sciences professionals are going through. This objective is fundamental to try and stop the Romanian scholars and scientists exodus.

The law will grant financial bonuses for each new level of post-graduate studies (MA, PhD, post-doctoral studies). These bonuses will not be subject to taxation. All additional spending, generated by the above-mentioned bonuses, will be tax-deductible for all companies hiring these specialists. Those who want to undertake studies will get state support, that is grants that could be the amount of money an honors student gets multiplied by a coefficient between 2 and 4.

The budget draft will have clear allocations to provide material support for research. The National Science Agency will be set up. The Agency will have wide autonomy to manage its funds and it will replace the existing institution (The National Agency for Science, Technology and Innovation). Encouragements will be given to establish incentives for private companies ready to participate in financing the scientific research. Private companies that will invest in research will benefit from having their research and development spending tax-deductible, and their corporate income tax will be diminished by an amount of money directly proportional to this type of spending for a whole year since the moment when a new product, invention or innovation is licensed.

The companies that do not have their own research departments will be encouraged to subsidize research projects as they shall be granted the unlimited right to benefit from the results of the respective research project, the respective spending will be tax-deductible and they shall be given priority to getting state subsidies. The research teams will be autonomous and will thus have the ability to recruit highly trained staff under 40 years of age. These teams will get the necessary support to be able to contract various projects with Western research institutes. The support will be provided by the state that will offer free consultancy on the Western research market. To complete this law the Party of Social Democracy will suggest various co-operation programs with the European Union and the United States.

Companies operating in what is generically called ‘high-tech’ will benefit from the unequivocal support of the Romanian state by implementing research programs with the Romanian institutes and/or by taking some of them over. The amounts of money invested by these companies in research will be tax-exempted for ten years. When bidding for a research project or when taking over such an institute, the main aim will be to make them operate as efficiently as possible. The state will not collect any money out of these contracts, it will only have the role to monitor the way the contract terms are implemented.

One of the main priorities will be to improve the research institute management. Mandatory courses will be organized free of charge for all those who want to become executives in research institutes and departments, both in the public and the private sectors. The funds to be allotted for that will be supplied by the European Union programs, by sponsors, the budget of the National Science Agency and additional budget allocations.

Each academic center, be it in the domain of human sciences or exact sciences, will be encouraged to develop a research center or laboratory. These new institutions will have a sector-specific budget, managed by the Ministry of National Education, but it will independent from the general budget allotted to this ministry. Thus, new jobs will be created in order to recruit all possible researchers from their student years.

4.6 Waiting for one's turn in the transition tunnel

Dreaming about the past, as a sort of comfort in a world that is changing too fast, triggers a reaction that sociological surveys or opinion polls call the "nostalgia paradox"; in other words, it is a form of collecting oneself by appealing to a specific moment in the past, especially when the present seems discontinuous and closed. After the end of the communist era Romania has experienced this phenomenon as well – it is the "time of certainties" as Vaclav Havel called it. One of the most serious threats against the Romanian society is the temptation to experience nostalgia, which we should avoid, just as Ulysses avoided the sirens' song.

To be able to realistically look into the future, such anti-temporal attitudes are only relevant to the extent to which we are interested in carrying out genealogical studies, not if we want to draft good plans for a desirable future. Seen from a different perspective, such rejection reactions are not caused only by how rapid and comprehensive the changes are, but also by the fact that incongruous, so called 'right-winged' policies paid very little attention to various social groups. These groups prone to nostalgia are those which, in fact, have a limited endurance capacity, mainly as to the negative effects of change.

To overcome the difficulties of the transition it is necessary to have both the state efficient intervention and reasonable social actors. The metaphor of the tunnel is highly suggestive in this respect: if two car columns are blocked in a tunnel and one of them manages to start moving, there may be two consequences. First of all, the motorists in the immobilized column may lose their patience (why them and not us?) and they will try to penetrate the other column, thus blocking the traffic once again. In a happier situation, the motorists in the immobilized column will not lose hope that their turn will come to get out of the tunnel and they will patiently wait for their turn; thus, the situation will be resolved faster. Unfortunately, the Romanians will almost always choose the first variant!

One cannot stop the changes generated by globalization. Everything depends on the way we are able to manage them, channelling them to desirable objectives: prosperity, normality and European integration. The uncertainty caused by the transition has to be envisaged as a need to come up with a functional synthesis; it should not be looked at through more or less powerful or more or less colored political lenses. Borrowing a beautiful German expression, we Romanians need "*Vergangenheisbewaltigung*", that is *a victory against the past*!

PART II

CHAPTER FIVE

POLITICAL WILL AND POLITICAL ELITE – STRUCTURES AND PATTERNS

"The poet's as well as the politician's calling is to look for new harmonies. And all these starting from tradition and heading toward the future."

Jose Augusto Seabra

5.1 From the masses to the public. From the politician to a professional specializing in a political career

Believing that one of the causes of the present political void existing in Japan is the scarcity of ideas of the political class, the Japanese who want to be involved in the public life go back to school. They attend schools training them for the profession of politician. Descendant of the eloquence schools which have rapidly multiplied, this type of institutions educate the national and local elected representatives. The question was asked whether this form of education is a renewal of political culture. These schools are successful in Japan because the citizens are suspicious of the professional politicians. Therefore, the former accepted the idea that, in order to efficiently participate in the political life, they have first to understand how the system works. This way, Japan secures a new political class for the next millennium, a class endowed with the status of an elite.

A new political model is conceived so as to educate people rather than mobilize them by very simple scheming, to help shaping a new type of political culture valid for the whole society, by using a progressive rhetoric, not just a demagogic one. Politics based exclusively on mobilization means, in fact, an attempt to take over or have access to power. Mobilization may be achieved by various means, such as charismatic leaders or institutions that can influence the crowds. But such a public that can be easily mobilized by such means or by similar ones is not able to generate an opinion, they remain masses of people, as Jose Ortega Y Gasset showed as early as the 20's.

Mass politics for which mobilization as well as voting are simply routine matters makes institutions bureaucratic and centralized, and the administration can only cover the desires of the political top rankers. If politicians turn into professionals of a specific career, matters of principle may be neglected in favor of career-related interests. Therefore, I would like to suggest a model in which (to stress) the capacity that citizens and communities have to structure and multiply decision centers. On the one hand, this means more information sources for the community and its members, and, on the other hand, an acquired model of taking political action, including during the elections. Seen from this perspective, state power can only adjust to the many-sided social system, that is by maintaining contact between electoral promises and government objectives and also by abiding by the principle of autonomy that the socio-professional powers have in relation to the political power.

The Romanian society needs to find its balance, so largely affected lately. Only a society that has a good political, economic and social metabolism can provide a high degree of safety. If the huge wealth, income and education disparities are diminished, a high degree of social and political culture may be finally achieved. In a stable society there will be no more childish image fights, there will be no more attempts to find legitimacy by letting the TV screen mediate the relationship between citizens and the governing group. In a stable society there will be a flow of political circulation, while politicians will be promoted and legitimized function of their competence and efficiency when drafting various policies and their capacity to set up decision-making mechanisms.

5.2 Brief presentation of the elite or why should intellectuals be so easygoing?

The role that the elite plays in society is decided by history and also by society as a whole. In Romania, too, the elite was called upon to manage various social and political processes that had major effects on the entire society. Top Romanian intellectuals have often participated directly in the community's life as heads of various social groups, as leaders of movements of ideas or even by being actively involved in the administrative and political decision-making processes. Thus, they have shown their solidarity, have come out of their isolated world of ideas and accepted to be in the front line of the battle for the future. Such a mission allowed them to closely study the specific features of the Romanian cultural model, the best and the worst aspects of the various social groups' behaviors, the way the state and its political life operate.

I believe that the only test of how mature a society is during a period of crisis and of serious tensions, but the historical destiny of our geocultural and political area had the ability to block, at least on the medium term, the normal development of necessary social processes. A major consequence was to block the development of the social and political life. It is interesting to mention that there was a major cultural compensation, as it frequently happened that the great men of this country produced masterpieces, scientific models and social theories that they sometimes sent from abroad to Romania.

Due to the specific social and economic features of the country, it has hardly ever been possible to reward the elite or to acknowledge their achievements. During the communist era, the

Romanian elite preferred to be totally immersed in their personal activity. To be able to express their expertise, a genuine professional performance culture was created as well as a real art to overcome the obstacle set up by the power and the bureaucracy.

For the sake of historical truth, one has to say that even the communist regime understood that they could not exclude any contact with the rest of the world and that they needed large groups of well-trained people to assimilate technologies and carry out an inter-cultural dialogue with the West. There were research institutes, publishing houses, cultural magazines, the public radio and TV stations, schools, the health system, universities – all of them swarming with people whose expertise was confirmed by great international forums. This side of the truth was visible after 1989, when the first officials of the new democracy were persons originating in such institutions.

Romania's isolation, as a means to protect her identity, was not only a way to dramatically reduce her access to self-assertion, but also to limit her knowledge of the relations to the community. The social environment as a whole established a protective behavior which simulated co-operation and dialogue in keeping with the political requirements. But, on the other hand, there existed a specific type of discourse which referred to the individual's social life and which pointed to the compliance with the political side as an imposed exercise, entirely incompatible with the values induced by education and tradition.

To put it briefly, it was the climate of a double existence – the 'home' as the single safe environment and the family as the only trustworthy group. Against this background, the individual was only allowed to escape these spaces which did not permit his development by resorting to culture and by being obsessed with the idea of performance.

As it was only natural after 50 years of suspicion toward the social environment, during the post 1989 period, the public arena witnessed the appearance of individuals who may be characterized as follows: complicated personalities with complex minds, full of complicated theories, but who had a very limited social life, were afraid to meet the others and were highly reluctant to become involved in any social activity. It was in fact a major cultural and intellectual dormant force hopelessly waiting for an opportunity to be socially displayed. Thus, after 1989, a social tension appeared on the

Romanian political arena between all the Romanians' entirely justified expectations (and especially of the elite) and the newly created social offer the tendency of which was to carry out a severe selection.

All these huge dormant social forces exploded in a magnificent burst out, a moment of major social solidarity and, implicitly, of great expectations as compared to the existing possibilities. Consequently, various initiatives were born, some of an elitist nature, some of a socializing one. These initiatives triggered the formation of more or less casual groups, which, following that moment of spiritual joy, spoke about operationality and management. Naturally, a management crisis occurred which was generally produced by a negligent working style; still, such a style only brings about failure against the new social background based on compatible opinions. The most important cause is represented by the performance and efficiency assessment criteria, generated by the difficulties to adjust and communicate. Soon, phenomena such as labelling, blocked communication and intolerance appeared.

The new arena was shaped as an environment with a multitude of unstructured bundles of competences, lacking intercommunication and looking for ways to be acknowledged. Today, the political life is still dominated by an almost paradoxical tension, which cannot be contained; this also happens because, although there are so many major public figures in the Romanian public life, one cannot speak about authoritative personalities that could gather together coherent, united groups.

This is not only a state of fact of a well-determined duration, but the very basic constituent for the future of this society and the continuation of the Romanian elite. What could be the impact of such a structure of the elite public arena on Romania's assessment and perception in the European and international space?

Various types of crises, tensions generated by different approaches, perceptions and solutions to the same problem, such as the Yugoslavian crisis, bring about group or mass-media debates, or even street protests, as an attempt to influence the political decision. This still happens in Romania and it has very serious effects for both camps involved, as well as for the whole society, which is seen from abroad as a hostile, aggressive environment, where just a minimum of co-operation and trust are operational.

I believe it is mainly the role of the elite to clarify this painful aspect, not to pass verdicts, but to create the necessary environment in view of re-negotiating the communication and co-operation climate. This is something that will happen no matter what. It is just a question of time.

I also believe that we can start building the way out of the standstill by taking two things into account: on the one hand, there is a certain tradition of the way in which the Romanian elite gets involved in those situations that are of paramount importance for the future of our society and on the other hand, we have the fact that one should know/assume the values of the world model that is being shaped on the medium and long terms. A past-ridden attitude would be totally unproductive, as, on the one hand it rekindles tensions which are no longer relevant today, and, on the other hand, it confuses and uselessly wastes the thoughts of the generations who are active today and will be so for the following 50 years. In this respect, it would be necessary to re-discuss the Romanian model of identity and the essential values of this space, not because they have changed, but because they have been contested, and evaluated in a more or less honest way, that led to confusion. It would be extremely useful for the whole society if the elite were the first to take this road and offer new models.

5.3 The story of the schism – the rifts in the Romanian society

When monitoring opinion polls one can see that in between 1997-2000 the dominant feeling about Romania's future was the citizens' despair faced with the futile results obtained by a "ruling class" who, in 1997, defined themselves as being "the first democratic power after 50 years". Chaos, ruin, disaster ... these are the words used to characterize the former coalition in a number of opinion polls.(The coalition was made up of the Romanian Democratic Convention, the Social Democratic Union and the Democratic Union of the Hungarians in Romania). The phenomenon was two-fold – a loss of confidence in the values of 'change' and a visible change of opinions. Part of the intellectuals who supported the post–1996 power did not hesitate to accuse them of having brought the economy to a standstill, of having caused recession and confusion, of having led to the dissolution of authority and of the rule of law, of having been incoherent, corrupted and unable to handle the challenges involved. Thus it was proved that the "saviour's myth" is no longer operational. **We will have to get used to the idea that political leaders can seldom modify the political reality, on the contrary, they are the prisoners of this reality and even, sometimes, its product.**

Romania's position became very difficult between 1996-2000, which did not bring any kind of political benefit to the center-right governments nor, by extrapolation, to the political class. The obvious economic disaster was doubled by the sharp decrease of the living standard, by intensified social tensions and increased trade union movements, by a dwindling credibility of the governing group, parties and institutions.

The dramatic gap between two existing realities that never met was to be remarked: the reality of the governing group and that of the remaining Romanian society. This gap became much more visible than the reformist – anti-reformist one or the left-right opposition.

The Romanian voters' lack of confidence in the political class, the politicians and the parties, which some journalists and political analysts considered to be a general phenomenon has a much more important significance, realistically speaking: the value of the election promises or the connection to the political objectives. A promise made during the election campaign is both a contract with oneself and with the other (the voter, the citizen), not only a contract which is distributed simply as a demagogic tool. Even if it is not as strict as a proper formal contract, obviously such an imaginary contract must play a part in establishing responsibility in the relations between the political power and the citizens. Likewise, the reform policy is not a partisan concept (as it was subtly suggested by some of the people in power at that time). The term does not belong to one party because it appeared, as a manifestation of the political will, immediately after 1989; it does not belong to one party as it must serve all interest groups and social structures, promoting the observance of fundamental rights in accordance with the rule of law and the strengthening of democracy. The citizen is the reference point, the regime operates based on the rule of law, while the power serves the citizens, not the other way round.

The social rifts have been growing wider and wider as a consequence of unbalanced economic trends. Under these circumstances, people's trust in the state institution, and their capacity to govern has been constantly decreasing. Deprived of institutions and a stable system of rules, Romania was dominated by uncertainty and lack of predictability for all individual initiatives. The alleviated but unsolved political crisis (taking into account the existence of a 'toxic' coalition made up of six parties representing all possible doctrines) threatened to become a crisis of the regime, creating the impression that democracy had not found its irreversible path yet. **A crisis that seems to become permanent always acquires hyperbolic dimensions in the collective mind, that is why there is a need to have active programs, to rectify the chronic, terrorizing skepticism.**

Opinion polls also showed decreased confidence in the political parties, too, as major actors on the national political arena. It is true that the political parties are a genuine field of power where strong blows are dealt, as a consequence of the relations of competition existing among the social actors interested to use the acquired resources. On the other hand, the suddenly polarized interests may generate schisms. The party elite are not always able to efficiently control the competition games, so the impression is created that they are not able to make decisions. Theoretically speaking, party discipline should limit intra-party competition, but it did not limit the competition within the coalition. Besides the already existing tensions among the coalition parties something else happened – party factions appeared. This influenced government policies and government reshuffles, as each faction was trying to impose their own men and, eventually, their own government ideas.

The center-right power could not avoid experiencing a crisis of authority (the main feature being the fact that the executive proved a lack of subordination in relation to the political decision-making centers). For the system to operate efficiently all subordinates have to accept authority; this should be the first principle, the first norm that the government should rely on. The government should not rely on the protocols drafted by the 'wise men' that, even before the elections, decided what to do, how to do it and to what extent, after they had managed to have the Romanian Social Democracy Party voted out.

The coalition put forward the "power for power" approach and that showed that the 1996 winning parties soon gave up the connection to the political objectives, after taking the power. Thus, some observers of the Romanian political phenomenon stated that the main ground of their actions was to remove the former government, without really having any prior draft or forecast related to what they wanted to do. This motivates the impression that the strategic aspects were neglected (it was not a matter of lobbying or simply winning the power, but it involved the need to establish long term strategies, social and public policies having a shaping impact on the social component). This is indicative of the fact that political factors can easily become prisoners of the power cult. Such a coalition was doomed to failure from the very start.

The result of the year 2000 elections restated the citizens' desire to have a normal social and political life. The center-right forces, worn out by conflicts and inner vanity, while carrying the negative burden of their government were practically wiped out. This time it was no longer a negative vote as in 1996. For the very first time, the voters had the possibility to compare two ways to managing the government, two styles of approaching politics. What prevailed was political experience and maturity.

The social change that Romania has been experiencing after 1989 has been going hand in glove with the need to solve some residual problems of the former regime as well as some new ones. Seen from this perspective, the social democratic variant is valid almost everywhere in Europe, it can establish this type of correlations, if there is open political competition and a multiparty regime.

5.4 Political pragmatism – a necessary but insufficient condition

Another type of conflict specific to Romanian politics is the one between the "moral reference" line and the pragmatic, realistic one. The intellectual forum called the Civic Alliance have identified themselves as an elite competing with the political elite, despising the pragmatic feature inherent to politics, and using as a point of reference an ideal model of the political component rather than a real one. These intellectuals believe that history may be interpreted in a unique way over which they have absolute control; at the same time they have no tolerance for those who do not share their point of view and that is why the philosophy supported by the Civic Alliance has often been rather radical.

Pragmatism is a natural occurrence in political life; it is neither good, nor bad – it simply exists; the same way one cannot say that politics is good or bad (as a reality in itself), it just exists. One cannot cure pragmatism by 'exorcisms', but we can control it, especially if each politician tries to set up some principles for himself as well as for the team he is working with. Pragmatism does not breed corruption (as the Civic Alliance members still seem to believe) because of some outer forces, but because there appear some inner disturbances, within each individual's conscience. It is true that, even if no personality cult exists, there are ambitious people who attempt to apply more subtle varieties of the power cult, within the limits of an adulterated totalitarianism. Politicians and the political class may be blamed for various mistakes and failures, but to criticize a whole reality and to question how necessary some structures are only means that we are still prisoners of the power cult. Power is good or bad, omnipotent or democratic, polyarchic or autocratic, **but it exists as a necessity** for the system to be operational. That the system operates badly under specific circumstances is a different matter.

Seen in this light, political power is but a component of the social power, namely one of its specialized components. What matters is the way it relates to the principles of democracy and law, how it observes the laws, how it makes decisions and how it mobilizes the social body to participate in their own development and progress. To do that, first of all, power must stop being an inexhaustible source of privileges, it must no longer be regarded as a solemn ritual. The antitheses power-opposition; spiritual-temporal; administrative-political; executive-must legislative must be toned down, and assuming responsibility and holding political debates must play a major part.

Positions held within the power structures must be free of any formalism and must be socialized as much as possible, along a normal transparent redistribution process. The political values that the power promotes motivate and legitimize it, without resorting to force. The power is unquestionably limited by the need to have the people's consent for the major decisions they adopt and by the fact that power abides by the law and the Constitution.

5.5 The changes of the political class

"In the political life the mistakes made by one generation are almost always dearly paid for by the generations to come"

Gaetano Mosca

Ten years of sometimes chaotic social and economic changes resulted in a highly polarized economy which is quite unhealthy for domestic stability. Any massive concentration of economic power is always damaging, and as a proof, we should have a look at the way the Latin American regimes operate. Not everything can be subjected to the market economy principles without affecting the citizens (it is the case of the utilities, which are in a state of ruin, although the prices have been constantly increasing).

The reform policy does not depend on one party or another, on one ministry or another, on some leader, etc. **The reform pertains to the Romanian society as a whole.** So, the political action is implemented by the political class, democratically validated by elections. One cannot conceive of another reality without sliding toward models that might avoid the democratic game. The role of a genuine political class is to have the political capacity to assume the decision-making process, to thoroughly know the dynamics of the social environment, to make sense of it and to establish a direction for the future. The political class stands as an example for the rest of the social body, shapes a new way of being, thinking and acting. This is not a "Big Brother" situation, but a means of spreading the change to the whole society.

What the Romanian political class has been reproached with, especially lately, is a very important thing: the approaches put forward by various politicians are divergent. It would have been preferable to harmonize the political parties' interests as far as the major issues are concerned. Each government, irrespective of their political descent, must cover these issues in a way that should complement not destroy the actions undertaken by the preceding governments. Otherwise, the impression is created that we are going through a never-ending transition, a chronological dead end, where truths are nomadic entities, depending on those who have the power. The present government imposes a public image "merging on the horizon", and promotes an integrated vision of a specific future, with strategies and scenarios to appropriate this future.

Any society needs a political class to provide the managing, decision-making, authority and life-continuity mechanisms. Without a political class that co-operates in a professional manner, no modern, complex society can establish its directions of development. Indeed, in politics there are persons who turn the democratic game into something vulgar as well, so they make people lose faith in the capacity and virtues of democracy as a political regime. There are such persons in almost all political parties, especially when the democratic state must be reinvented, rebuilt on the ruins of totalitarianism. To filter out and select the political body requires time, but the Romanian society will solve this problem gradually, by means of the election tests.

Transition is only a 'fasciculus temporum', a time interval that allows the passage from an unstable world to a world built on a new type of solidarity. The value of each time interval depends on the number and intensity of events, accompanied by specific feelings of elation or fear, skepticism or panic. The impression of a never-ending crisis develops a twilight psychology and an apocalyptic tendency, proved by how successful the religious component has become and how many both Christian and non-Christian religious sects have appeared, which all promise an 'instant' solution to the problems of a present troubled by rapid, major changes.

CHAPTER SIX

ELITISM, POPULISM, SOCIAL-DEMOCRACY

"We do not have the time to deal with revolutionary stunts. As we have much more to do to improve society. Just to be opportunistic, we cannot afford to play with violent words or actions."

Olof Palme

6.1 Toward a clientele system

In the preceding section we tackled the issue of political power versus administrative power. Another antithesis is that of political power versus economic power (which, in Romania resulted in turning privatization into a political matter turning both privatization and the executive positions in the still state-controlled economy into political matters). The democratic exercise of the dialogue between the leaders and the competing organizations has also remained a suggestion, never actually applied even when it came to major decisions regarding Romania's future for longer periods of time than a term in office. State power has remained closed to the economic development, although, if the state had been selectively generous to specific economic branches, the country would have obtained great benefits in a relatively short time.

It is obvious that valid politics cannot be supported by recipes provided by advisors and *yes-men*. A balance has to be struck between the political responsibility and the specialists' involvement in a specific domain, whether those specialists are party members or not. Ironically enough, the parties that have proclaimed their anti-communism and their democratic 'clean origin' are the best representatives of the single command principle, of the party directive aimed at maintaining the coalition, while connecting the coalition's political destiny to Romania's 'failed' chances for the future. Having said that, it is only natural to speak about the politicians' incapacity and incompetence, about breaking the political monopoly of the above-mentioned class; but to go as far as stating that "the political class is too diverse and cannot identify with the national interests" is nonsense, while claiming that the press must take the political matters and priorities of the moment into their own hands.

That is the main reason why the present political administration has given up the political membership criterion when appointing various executives. These last few years, the practice of the political clientele has been fiercely promoted, so the quality of the political decisions was affected. The image that the public opinion has of the political class has deteriorated a lot. The political component has started being perceived as intruding upon the social life. The present Executive makes use of the competence criterion when appointing their members, both in the government structures and the local administration. It is a first step to regain the citizens' faith in the Romanian political class.

Modern politics is faced with a gap between the voters and their leaders. The social category support of political affiliation has got eroded, and there are signs showing that there may appear new structures of this type that could generate specific, class-oriented political parties. So, the idea that social position may influence political behavior has lost some of its value; nowadays, one speaks about how volatile the voting process is, as the voters have a tendency to modify their options from one election cycle to another. Unfortunately, in Romania we cannot speak yet about the voters' capacity to cast a 'tactical vote', in fact a reasonable vote, proving that the voter has analyzed the consequences of his vote (for what party I vote, what government formula they will adopt, what kind of government program they have, what are the principles, how it is going to affect me, what job or what life standard I will have, aso). Voters believe that the elections are a means to select governments, when, in fact, they only elect those who will decide who the government will be made up of. A 'more attentive' voter is the one who votes for the candidate or the party that, in his opinion, stands a better chance to come to government.

At first sight, the relatively low degree of electoral volatility would indicate that the Romanian political parties are identifiable and have a clear-cut political outlook, and that voters trust the elected representatives; the more democratic the society becomes, the more volatile it will be, as far as the elections are concerned. This will be even more obvious when the over-involvement of the parties in politics is counterbalanced by serious competitors coming from the civil society. The Romanian voters are not only volatile, but they also reject any partisan ideological project, which is highly understandable after 50 years of continuous political propaganda. There has been a switch from a mass-type of society, forcefully homogenized, to a society characterized by fragmentation and social atomization. Several explanations can be provided for the loss of connections between the parties and the voters: their ideologies have no relevance for the voters' real requests, the parties are poorly organized and eaten by corruption, they appear to be irresponsible as to the voters, unable to recruit young members, unsuccessful in re-integrating their inner factions. In fact, Romanian parties are faced with real difficulties in fulfilling the functions that political parties generally have: to structure the election process, to represent and aggregate the interests of various social groups, to organize the government and to formulate policies. Thus, unavoidably, citizens prefer other types of social movements and alternative organizations, briefly said, the civil society. As compared to the political parties, these groups have the advantage that they concentrate on a single issue.

Whoever studies the Romanian political landscape attentively could reach the conclusion that Romania runs the risk of moving toward the Italian or Japanese model of political class, based on 'clientele' and patronage, which involves 'systematic' corruption. The opportunities offered by the public positions are mainly used to consolidate one's own positions of power. **Wherever there is a lack of stable relations between groups and the accepted models of authority, so, wherever disorganization rules, wherever there are no efficient political parties to represent the society's interests, there exists an environment favoring the growth of corruption. The larger the number of laws for domains such as trade, customs, taxes, gambling, alcohol, aso, the more corruption is stimulated.**

6.2 Political show versus political action

The public discourse that dominates today's media show in the democratic countries is unfortunately becoming more and more populist. The problem is that democracy does not presuppose demagogy, but, first of all, the attributes of political representativeness and responsibility. Political decisions are made by a political elite accountable to the voters, able to rationalize politics and to offer the best variant for the respective community. This does not mean that the principle of popular sovereignty is broken, nor does it mean that a party elite democracy is promoted, which is somehow opposed to the civil society. A political party is only a mediator between the society and the government and by virtue of this role, the party has access to power and can govern. Romania does not need a 'governed democracy' which insists on consensus and participation, but a 'governing democracy' which avoids the 'tyranny exercised by the majority' that can be seen in the construction of public opinion. The most important element of a 'governing democracy' is the quality of the governing act supplied by the democratically elected political elite. A rhetorical appeal to the 'people' creates confusion, generates myths and an anti-elite trend targeting the whole political class. It is dangerous to put forward this point of view, promoted by various media groups or by lesser political organizations that claim to have chosen a 'third way'. To 'idealize the man on the street' or to attempt and hold together the political forces on behalf of the 'people' and their destiny has nothing in common with modern representative democracy.

The deficient way in which institutional proceedings work, the anti-selection for various public positions (be they party members or court intellectuals) consolidate the public opinion's feeling that top politics is an improvisation by means of which some characters create the illusion that they do represent vessels into which the 'popular will' has been poured, that they are the 'nation's knights', the only ones who know the alchemy necessary to govern for the 'people'. The values of the democratic government system were disqualified in the people's perception because of the arrogance and secrecy of the state institutions, the unconvincing answers given by justice, the claims to be a regional leader expressed by a president who was unable to maintain in the ruling coalition a peaceful atmosphere around a few major objectives.

Social-democracy can promote such social reforms that might authorize society to acquire the means to exercise its obligations in serving democracy. Here are some of the fundamental principles that have to be accepted: loyalty to democracy, to the constitutional order of the rule of law, rejection of political violence as a means, of all stunts and theories lacking real support. Romania is no exception to the rule, and social-democracy is a trend that has better adjusted to the period we are going through. It is the expression of a still diverse phenomenon, which can help shape stable coalitions and efficient governments, freed from the constraints of 'tradition'. The discrepancy that exists between the social-democratic values and the economic and financial situation of the ex-communist countries has created a paradoxical situation: the social-democratic parties in power were obliged by the low national budgets to diminish public spending for domains such as health, social protection or education. The right wing parties took advantage of this situation and criticized the budget austerity from specifically left wing positions, which allowed them to win the elections, to the detriment of the social-democrats, the latter being those who had stabilized the economy and had laid the foundations of a growth that could be sustained in the future as well.

The priority of Romanian social-democracy will be to protect the people's security, which has been badly damaged, and assure the citizens that it is possible to achieve a state of peaceful co-existence. Out of opportunism or any other reasons, we can no longer afford to play with violence, be it verbal or otherwise. The main message to the society is that democracy means security, a collective force capable to peacefully change the system.

The concept of equal opportunities is being questioned, social marginalization is showing its teeth, the gap between the very rich and the very poor is still growing. The Romanian citizens have to regain their self-assurance as members of the community, they have to be sure that they can develop their personalities freely, co-operating in the political, economic and cultural life. The state should be a structure providing assistance in a constructive way, it should be able to support social control, and, as Willy Brandt put it, it should be the "legal community of the people which we designate to watch the way security, liberty and justice are maintained". If the citizens are not aware of the fact that the state "is all of us and each of us as individuals", the present political class must, indeed, redefine their objectives and profile. We cannot support the idea that state authority should be totally eliminated by virtue of some utopias which stress market omnipotence, the unavoidable fate that makes the economy operate on the basis of some mathematically calculated forecasts or of some ultra-rationalized, anachronistic and dissocialized models of explaining reality. Romanian right wing intellectuals go on promoting an anti-state discourse, but it is absurd to do so as the Romanian state is completely devoid of authority and has been more than once in a position to be unable to fulfill its natural functions (including the defence of the social order as well as salary payment to public servants). The Romanian mass-media has already used the phrase "dissolution of state authority" quite often.

It is equally true that the state power has to support social control, so the political democracy becomes a social democracy, that is a structure in which there is no theoretical separation between the civil society, the individual and the state. Neither can the state become all-powerful, nor can the individual be endowed with prerogatives which, more often than not, are only theoretical. The entrepreneurial force, the omnipotent neo-liberal god, this Baal that has overpowered Romanian society, is necessary for the economy of competition, without which democracy is not possible. But this does not mean that those who do not have this entrepreneurial capacity or do not want to develop it do not have the right to participate in the political and social life.

6.3 Technocracy does not save Romania

The rules of the democratic game must be specific to all social domains, as this is the only way for the system to survive, even if it is imperfect, but it can improve, unlike the totalitarian regimes. It is based on the real and responsible exercise of individual and collective freedom. In fact, it is the subtle issue posed by the late Sir Isaiah Berlin as to the relationship between negative freedom and positive freedom. To which extent can society provide the individual with a sphere of autonomy within which he can do and be one thing rather than another, without meeting with any constraints? Unfortunately, the economic constraints and the right wing policies provide him with this sphere of autonomy only theoretically. The massive concentration of the economic power to a limited circle diminishes the citizen's power as a reference system for democracy and he comes to depend solely on groups of interests or on pressure groups.

The Romanian society has become obsessed with the problem of the political elites, of the solutions that have to be adopted, of the actors, other than the politicians, who can solve the national priorities. There are two ever-present alternatives: the press which can play this role or the technocrats (the possible government made up of experts). None of these solutions is totally valid. Of course, the press holds a respectable position within the power balance of a democratic regime, it has important social functions (socialization, information, etc.), but the press is far from being able to establish the political priorities of a country. Not to mention the fact that every newspaper, every TV or radio station has its own policy, its own likes and dislikes, and the information they supply has already been filtered and selected.

The second ideal formula, the technocrats' government is not suited on the long term. Generally speaking, such a government is preferred when the elections are near and it is not worth eroding the political parties' credibility.

As a government formula, technocratism is no longer in fashion in the international political practice. It used to be in the 60-70's, when there was this belief that the two systems – capitalism and communism – were convergent toward a utopian synthesis of the perfect society. Taking into account how inefficient the previous coalition government was, there are voices stating that only a government made up of experts can still rationalize Romanian politics at all levels. Implicitly, this opinion makes us think that pragmatism, the capacity to make decisions and rationalization are intangible for the governing group.

From a different perspective, that of the representative democratic value, technocratism is no longer a solution. The technical elite undoubtedly has an acknowledged epistemic authority, but the popular vote has not mandated it to govern. On the other hand, it is beneficial to recruit experts at all management levels, and so reduce subjective attitudes, political and ideological voluntarism, amateurism and ambition manifested by the political dilettantes, thus putting end to absurd and irrational behaviors. An expert can only be imposed by the social and political structures, by the array of different interests and expectations existing in the social environment. The technocratic model is more elitist than the multiparty structure of powers, as it is situated on the margin between the esoteric and the visible. That is why the model to be promoted is the pragmatic one, the only model suited to contemporary reality, as it establishes a continuous, two-way link between experts and politicians, while attracting the civil society into the dialogue, too. This is, in fact, the essence of the 'center doctrine', this is political centrism. Technicians counterbalance the limited, group interests, but they are monitored by the democratic institutions.

Despite the political consensus referring to the need to democratize Romania and grant her NATO and EU access, the concrete results are heavily delayed. The political parties who voiced the consensus could not come up with the necessary understanding to undertake the required political action. It is a unanimously accepted objective, but there is not the slightest agreement referring to the instruments to do it. Political interests and passions could not be contained, so the reform was blocked and corruption flourished. The first victim of this shortcoming could be democracy itself, which people risk to mistake for anarchy and a void of authority. It is absolutely necessary to rehabilitate the democratic institutions by means of clear actions at the macro-social level. But this can only be done by a mature, strong **political force.**

I have stressed the phrase **"political force"** just because it lies at the very center of a very hot and topical debate in Romania. Compromised by their own failures, center-right political parties have perceived the people's disgust for politicians and are trying to give credit to the idea that a technocratic government would be appropriate. At the same time, they attract a series of experts, especially in the economic sector, who could win for them another four-year term. Obviously, one cannot deny the fact that any society needs valuable experts and their decisive impact in finding the best solutions. The problem is whether a technocrat can have the abilities of a politician in a different domain than the one in which he specializes. The politician has that bundle of qualities that allow him to gather a large consensus, he embodies the general option of a group, he is the one who is able to establish the best relations with this group. All these qualities make the politician representative. He is not an expert as the technocrat is, but this lack is supplemented by his advisors. A technocrat only rarely has the abilities of a politician. So, the best position for him is to be an advisor. This is a difficult period, therefore the responsibility for the following term should be politically assumed. The major decisions and the management of a generalized crisis can only be assumed by a political force, and, in Romania, that political force is the Party of Social Democracy.

This Party has the necessary resources to demonstrate that it is modern, fully compatible with the European democratic left. The party has a set of solutions; it has legitimate and acceptable programs for any moderate politician belonging to the European left. The Party of Social Democracy cannot and does not want to deviate Romania from the European integration track, as such a change of direction would be contrary to the party program and to the national interest. Social-democrats have always been the most powerful political force in the country, as a party, which means that one of their major arguments is representativeness. I believe that this attribute will be indispensable to the new political power in Romania. We reject technocrats secretly manipulated who are not representative of the society, superficial coalitions in which parties attack each other and block the reform, or people who sometimes have even acknowledged their inability. The Party of Social Democracy has another alternative – that of a sufficiently strong and representative party ready to assume the responsibility of carrying on the reform, even for the price of tough, unpopular measures, if the case may be. We need a force capable to persuade and attract the society's trust as to how necessary the radical reform is, while maintaining the social tensions within acceptable parameters. Otherwise, all the good intentions will only pave the way back.

The political class may be completed by technocrats, thus combining the managerial performance and the efficient political action. By means of this double association, the Romanian state could return to normality and overcome the tendencies of dissolution trying state authority. Without permanently refreshing the energies of the subsystems making up the social system, we will not be able to reach the standards of social and economic accumulation and revival. Thus, it is necessary to establish a symbolic alliance between theoretical knowledge, which generates guidelines for society, and efficient political action.

CHAPTER SEVEN

POLITICAL WILL VERSUS CIVIL SOCIETY?

7.1 The laws of Chronos and the infant Romanian democracy

Political will is, par excellence, an order-creating force, one of the inherent attributes of political power. Speaking about how successful the reform was in the ex-communist countries, it has been proved that a right wing government does not necessarily ensure the success of the reform. The statement proved true in the case of the 1996 change that happened in Romania. In Hungary and Poland, the economic reforms were taken very far, that is to that point where no return was possible (privatization, deregulation of monopolies, trade liberalization). And this is something that the left of center governments did. It is only the political will that can and should contribute to consolidating the social and political foundation, namely to the founding of the institutions and the laws appropriate to the new social and economic system that we want to adopt. This is a statement that we cannot deny, whether we see things from a liberal, social-democrat or Christian-democrat point of view.

The term of "political" will should not be associated to simplistic connotations. The will to have access to power, the will to maintain power, the intention to change/reform the society or, on the contrary, the intention to block a specific course of events – all these are characteristic features which derive from political will, but do not entirely define it. Political will cannot be achieved or legitimized unless it represents the society's will at a specific moment, which is looking for the common good and the general interest. It is in fact what the political will professes: the will of the City to gain normality, security and prosperity. From this point of view, the meaning of the political will is identical to the one given by Jean-Jacques Rousseau to the term 'general will'. In the opposite case, the society is entitled to democratically replace those who forgot or were unable to fulfill their desires.

Democracy is not a means for various groups to reach their aims or to try and fit in unique thinking pattern to the 'benefit of the public good'. Democracy is nothing more than a 'good society in operation'. It presupposes that one accepts that competition, conflict and compromise are legitimate, and also the fact that we can reach consensus on the major issues, such as the respect for property and for the fundamental rights.

The political class or what we generally call the 'voters' may not have fully understood the mechanism of the democratic political system or the logic of representativeness. Phrases such as 'national interest' and 'public good' lose their value and meaning due to/by excessive use. Thus, we run the risk of participating in the creation of a new 'meaningless language' with words totally devoid of meaning because endlessly repeated. This meaning becomes more and more of a burden in a world that is changing globally, in very rapid rhythms.

A stable democracy, as we would like to consider our country, needs a 'fair' political game, a qualified political class to maintain power alternation, as well as a negotiated agreement between the majority and the various minorities in the state, that everyone should abide by. Another node in the logic of a new democratic system that needs major improvements is meritocracy. This is necessary especially after the deviations generated by center-right coalition. The main objective of the merit system, which does not exclude the use of symbolic bonuses, is to protect power against the totalitarian umbrellas, which appear in the most sensitive social and economic moments. As a rule, in the stable democratic regimes, conflicts are managed so as to reach the compromises necessary to preserve the system. After 1990, the Romanian range had such dimensions and was so fragmented that it generated interpretations based on antitheses specific to any transition process: communist/anti-communist or reformist/conservative. But the media and the opinion polls indicate the existence of a more dramatic antithesis than the first two, the voters – political class one. It is visible in the great number of people who evince a passive political behavior – they do not cast their votes, they do not voice their choice as to the candidates. Is such an antithesis legitimate? Does it hide anti-democratic tendencies? Anyway, the political class is highly controversial, it generated more or less hot arguments in various media, which, nevertheless, avoided going deeper into a specific problem: how can there be cohesion in a society where there is no confidence in the elected representatives? how can such a society maintain the legitimacy of democratic representativeness?

I consider that this phenomenon can be explained not so much by the antithesis politicians – society, as by the unbalanced relationship conflict – consensus, as the value of the consensus is often lower than the conflicts between parties, groups, associations, etc. There is obviously a theoretical, generic lack of consensus referring to what the economy should become, to its rhythm and its progress to capitalism. Only if the consensus is established within the political class, and also between the political class and the other social elite can we identify the priorities of Romanian society: the limits of the public domain, that is the limits within which the state can intervene in the social life; guarantees to protect the citizens against possible abuse committed by the political power, etc. Such a consensus presupposes the existence of mutual trust, honesty, the will to compromise among the present Romanian political class.

To say that there is a conflict between the voters and the political class means to repeat what Marx said, speaking about former social classes. The low election turnover, foreseen or observed during some by-elections does not mean that "the class fight is deepening", although some "knights in shining armor protecting the nation and the common good" have tried to give such an interpretation to this phenomenon, probably influenced by the former interpretations of the totalitarian power. The most favorable conditions to promote such utopias do not exist anymore, even if force might be resorted to. Europe has given up the political myth of the Socialist Party, and also the liberal myths referring to growth. Leaving aside the present context, one cannot build a different reality from the one which already exists. Time wastes the credibility of various ideologies, and the political component is probably the most likely to be eaten by the God who eats his own offspring.

In each society, in the same way we can find political antithesis and political consensus co-exist, the social sources of both conflict and consensus co-existing within the same system. The fact that one segment of the something missing is contested is a sign that new power centers are being shaped, either local or regional. It is a normal aspect in a society that has adopted a multiparty regime. Tocqueville thought that decentralization and activation of voluntary associations are prerequisites for the stability of a democratic system (Tocqueville, 1954; 9-11). That the credibility of the political class (mostly located in Bucharest) is wearing out might be an impulse in this respect transmitted by the society or the local communities which are about to discover the power of 'being' an active, pro-militant, civil society. Obviously, soon, many other power centers will be ready to compete directly with a political class envisaged as centralist.

7.2 The Romanian civil society – reductionism, elitism, partisanship

There may be different interpretations and assessments for the trust granted to the political class, and they are not necessarily of an 'ideological' nature. Some media see the voters as a labor camp which grinds away the credibility of the political class, as they use their own social scheme as well as sui-generis value judgments. Do the voters want a 'new master'? Is it a mandatory or suggested need? Spinoza gave the following piece of advice: "Do not cry, do not laugh, do not condemn, just understand". The present political class may have made their actions too unclear for the voters, they may not have been able to motivate their actions, they may have been too hesitant in some respects, but anyhow it is very difficult to modify mental patterns. Still, care should be taken that the obsession with democracy should not turn into its rejection.

As far as the civil society is concerned, I would like to add a few things to what some people believed it meant for the Romanian post December 1989. Some thought that two very elitist groups, iconoclastic and closed, such as the Group for Social Dialogue and the Civic Alliance might entirely replace the idea of civil society, from a domineering position. The two factions also thought that, if the regime changed, they would be able to have a positive influence. Not even when those they supported obviously failed did the representatives of these civic forums renounce their political obsessions. Can we reduce the civil society to a limited number of voices that claim dominant positions motivated by qualities that we do not deny, but we reject the fact that these qualities are used to the society's global benefit?

The way the civil society is understood and its characteristic features, too, must be reviewed not only for Eastern Europe which just recently emerged from under the dark rule of the Total Power, but also for the Western world as well. Pluralism and the fertile interrelation between state power and the norms and practices which operate in society, without resorting to the state institutions, constitute the traditional territory of the civil society. The foundations and the functions of the civil society have to be revisited in the West as well, especially if we start by highlighting the rather serious domestic problems manifested in the classical capitalist world, such as: social problems, matters related to the need to redefine the status of welfare, the need for responsibility and pro-active civic attitudes, or the replacement of constraint by consensus, etc. A relevant example is offered by the Seattle rallies, at the end of 1999, organized to protest against the activity of the World Trade Organization, and, obviously against economic globalization. Faced with economic and political global actors (IMF, WB, WTO, NATO as well as the multinational companies), various civil society organizations are trying to form conglomerates/corporations in order to reach a world dimension which could have increased mobilizing capacity.

The civil society gathers together sensitive matters and interests, complementary and antagonistic components, individualism and solidarity, democracy and citizenship, constitutionalism and autonomy. Its force to actively participate in the co-ordination or land-marking of a country's progress lies precisely in the fact that it contains these relatively antagonistic pairs.

The civil society is not only involved in rallying the masses for various meetings, protests or similar kinds of movements. This would be a very limited understanding of the functions and role of the civil society. The civil society has to be analyzed by comparison to a series of other concepts, such as: sustainable development, wider democratic processes, modernization, economic growth, social capital and civil commitment, improving the IT environment as well as the mass communication means.

The United Nations see the civil society as a condition necessary to implement sustainable development models: "Human sustainable development is that type of development which does not only generate economic growth, but also distributes the benefits fairly; it regenerates the environment instead of destroying it for ever; it strengthens the population's opportunities instead of marginalizing them. It is the development that grants priority to the poor, increases their possibilities and opportunities and promotes their participation in the decision-making process to the extent that these decisions affect their lives. This development is pro-humans, pro-nature, pro-jobs and pro-feminist" says the UNDP, Human Development Report 1994.

Thus, one can speak about a global civil society or about the global desires of the civil society, among which one can distinguish this desire of sustainable development at a time when economies become globalized, and when, more than once, certain states have been accused of being unable to keep pace with the rapid rhythm of progress.

It seems to be the expression of a universally valid reality that the others confirm, either when they speak about the modern society as a *society of strangers*, or consider it such an alienated society that governments afford to suppress social spending destined to "those who are in fact unknown".

7.3 Public/private partnership – a failed necessity

Those who claimed that they would present the positive center-right variant in Romanian politics and administration forgot (or did not want to remember) one of the fundamental principles of Christian-democracy, the principle of subsidiarity. According to this principle, the state must decentralize the decision-making mechanisms down to those levels closest to the citizens and local communities, to support the citizens' initiatives and when such attitudes or initiatives are very weak the state must stir them up. This is exactly what the first post December 1989 center-right government did not do, although, when they got hold of the power, they did not forget to declare that the civil society had been one of the factors active in setting up the "first democratic power after 1946".

It is necessary that politicians and political parties should conceive the best ways to establish partnerships or alliances with the citizens and the civil society. The poverty level has been deepening against a background of general impoverishment of the Romanian society and it generates social discontent, while it also allows the appearance of a specific horizon of distrust related to the market economy mechanisms, to the fact that democracy is indeed an operational political regime which brings about economic and social benefits. This is an idea shared not only by the social-democrats, but also by all politicians endowed with a sense of social responsibility.

Poverty has always been a public evil and a profound source of discontent. The limitations it creates do not only influence the ability to buy goods and services, but also the possibility and the will to make use of the rights and political freedoms offered by democracy. A secure job, a secure income and a secure health care system as well as a safe environment are components without which no society can survive in the long run. Otherwise, the level of social distrust increases and generates civic indifference, and even passivity.

CHAPTER EIGHT

ECONOMIC REFORM
AND
THE TRANSITION MYTHS

"Bad laws are equal
to the worst form
of tyranny"

Edmund Burke

8.1 The role of the state during a transition period

The transformation of Romanian society after 1989 started out with the economic reform. Despite the lack of a project concerning the change in the Romanian socio-economic system, our country has seen the emergence of two types of answers to the challenges of transition: liberalism and social democracy. Both categories gravitate around the role of the state during this process. The liberal solution is characterized by the maximal value attributed to free initiative, as well as by the idea of a self-regulation imposed by the market mechanisms, in the circumstances of a non-interventionist state. The social-democratic solution has insisted on the gradual nature of the processes leading to market economy, attributing to the state the value of a maximal regulating factor, and that of a balancing instance as to the social costs generated by the transformational process. However, going beyond these reasons, it was obvious that the state was to be the strategist that would orientate the opening of the economy, even though eventually this opening would have to lead to the state's withdrawal from domains and sectors where the enterprising spirit and private initiative are much more efficient than state control.

The revolutionary mood that swept off the ex-socialist states after 1989 replaced the absolutist state, excessively centralized, with a democratic welfare state. Replacing the old type of state with a new one was, however, no overnight action, and was not effected by institutional regulations. After 1989, the ex-socialist countries entered a period of transition to 'the open society', toward a democratic political regime.

The Romanian State was no exception to this process. The revolution in late December 1989 produced an upward rift in the state apparatus. The old state structures were dissolved, and their place was taken, under the revolutionary impact, by a new institutional type of power, based on the principle of the separation of powers within the state, and on democratic governance.

The debate that took place in Romania on the issue of the State's role in a transition period was sterile and practically inapplicable. The involvement of the state is necessary to mitigate the diverging interests of society, interests that inevitably come to be reflected in the act of governance and that demand to be settled. The intervention of the state is the only modality by which we can fight social crises, protect jobs and generate economic growth.

As there was no model to sanction a singular solution, all post-revolutionary governments adopted mixed variants, containing elements specific to both ideological fields. In their turn, the political parties have gradually come to accept doctrinal elements with similar pragmatic characteristics, as regards the economic reform. However, the "identification" discourses, especially the electoral ones, have remained bound inside mechanisms of ideological mimesis. Essential to this moment seems to be the issue of the executive's capacity to apply, in a pragmatic way, either the liberal, or the social-democratic solutions.

In order to render the government's intervention even more fruitful, we need a kind of economic planning. By a kind of planning I mean a coordinated plan, oriented toward the future in view of certain specific social goals that cannot be reached through the market (e.g. education programs, health programs, infrastructure, buildings for the needy and so on). This does not imply total planning, which is characteristic to the communist regime, and which tries to replace the market, but a limited planning that co-exists with the market, merely trying to steer its course when necessary.

The fundamental conceptual error that was made by some of Romania's governing classes in these past years was that of trying to have the state withdrawn from the economy, on account of the country's advance toward a free market system. **Fear of a powerful state led to its extreme opposite, the void of authority.** Economic practice has proved that state intervention is all the more necessary during periods of social crisis, of profound societal changes, and that the state must then assume the role of main transforming agent. Transition, as a moment of upsetting an old order and an attempt at replacing institutions, norms and values with new ones, indeed necessitates a strong state. Generally speaking, transitions are accompanied by a multiplication of social crises and of conflicts among various social categories. Romanian society itself was, after 1989, polarized along several conflicting cleavage lines: intellectuals/workers, owners/tenants, old/young, urban/rural etc., conflicts that were not successfully mediated by the executive, as it normally should have been. This in itself placed the institution of the state in a disreputable position.

However, state interventions can be achieved by law, after serious debates within Parliament and Government, as well as within civil society. A social-democratic Government will avoid brutal, unpredictable interventions. The great number of emergency ordinances, of government resolutions, of contradictory governmental decisions, of modifications operated on laws from one day to the next, all these do nothing but destroy the domestic economic environment. Max Weber drew our attention to the "guarantors of calculability" necessary for investors in order to plan future investments and due profits.

I should like to use this context for a few specifications. By definition, a transition period has a limited duration, while the governing class lends stability and functionality to the new society. System transition represents, in the history of each single country, irrespective of its development status and its performance parameters, a period not only of mutation, but also of clarifications, both strategic, on a global scale, and tactical, on a sector-based oriented scale. In no case can transition be equaled to a 'tunnel' or a time span in which the evolution of society is marked by diffuseness, confusion, hesitation, fear of the direction and finality of change. A correct vision implies that all effectively responsible factors – the State, political forces, citizens – start from the perception and the premise that the transition represents a stage where socio-economic mentalities and ideologies, institutions and policies, social forces confront different, even diverging interests; a stage when all 'social actors' are openly preoccupied with defining the fundamental features of the society toward which we are heading. Debates are meant to strike the optimum synthesis, both acceptable and attainable, concerning the future of society, and to generate processes that would lead to mutations which would render impossible a return to the past. Political and social mutations not only support progress, eliminate immobility and the frustrations specific to the old society, but they also institute social justice for all. Development is re-launched, the state of abnormality – rooted in the old social order – gives in to a stable social and human environment, society finds its balance, political forces become apt to infuse the population with bracing feeling, with trust and hope.

An analysis of the period that we have been obssessively calling, for over a decade, 'transition', shows us that, except for the new institutional framework, which is stable and functional, the other departments of social life perpetrate a succession of political, economic-financial and social support experiences that fail to prove their efficiency, and whose negative repercussions are suffered by the population.

The transition has overwhelmed our society after December 1989. In a ten-year interval – a long one, if compared to the alert rhythm of contemporary civilization – no evolution was recorded that would ensure, in a predictable future, due success for the largest number of citizens. For several years now, political leaders of various orientations, union representatives, intellectual peaks, civil society exponents have had a preponderantly critical attitude toward the transformations already accomplished, and especially toward the chances of success of the economic reforms, meant to conclude, by 'shock therapy', the post-revolutionary transition. The costs of transition are reflected in economic depression, 'influential' underground economy, and an unpredictable course of real economy; they are reflected in poverty, unemployment, the lack of social and community solidarity, in union corporativism, politicianism and clientele policies, intellectual elitism, the deterioration of human conscience and hopelessness.

If we continue this way, we risk extending the transition period to a few decades. In such a perspective, the future generations of politicians and citizens may come to find 'transition' a normal state, the final target of today's governments, and not a final passage to a type of society that would satisfy the population's demands of civilization and its options for democratic governance. This is why it is important, in my opinion, to conduct serious analyzes of the transition process, in order to evaluate its reasonable duration and extension.

Evaluating the duration and especially the targets set forth by the governing class during the transition period is important not only for them, but also for the population, as the population takes on the damaging effects of unrealistic or simply wrong governance strategies. And I should like to emphasize yet another aspect that I find important. Any transition period in the life of a society presupposes testing strategies in all fields of activity.

The more complex the social existence, the greater the role attributed to the political, as an expression of conscious social action, in coordinating and sustaining change. Political action is in its turn influenced by the maturity of political forces, or by the favorable position that the actors of change hold in the political spectrum. On the other hand, the representatives of change do not make up a homogeneous body: barring some general common goals, their interests differ substantially. This is why the modifications operated during transitional periods are usually under the mark of the alternative. The transition implies a diversity of ways of structuring the new society, and the physiognomy of the new society takes shape within a reasonable amount of time. Certitudes are checked by a series of unknown factors, which the political forces are called to clarify and settle by adequate political strategies, entailing the manifest involvement of the state.

By state supervision of the process of privatization I do not mean a return to centralization and restriction on free initiative. On the contrary, I have in mind the establishment of a legal framework, wide and flexible enough to allow for the expression of individual initiatives, initiatives that would not affect the major interests of society, the strategic interests of the state or Romania's economic sovereignty, and that would not obstruct the state in manifesting its social role.

In fact, if we analyze the role of the state and its involvement in the life of society in Western Europe, we shall easily notice that state authorities, though stimulating private initiative, circumscribe it to a legal framework that, once broken, triggers severe administrative or financial sanctions. All the more so, in transitional states the role of the state should be more directly manifest, especially in the economic sectors.

The emphasis placed exclusively on privatization – merely for the sake of privatization – has damaging consequences if it is associated to the liberal thesis of a total operative withdrawal of the state from the domain of economic life. We must not forget that the entire national wealth existing in 1989 was created by the direct contribution of the entire population, which thus has more than a moral right to it. Displacing the production units created or modernized with the material sacrifice of the entire nation, from the state sector into the private sector, without receiving in exchange, as compensation, something equivalent to their real value, means simply disregarding the interests of a vast majority of the population.

The state has, both through Parliament and the Executive, an extremely important role in ensuring the stability of legislation. We understand very well that passing from a centralized economy to a capitalist-type economy presupposes changing the old legislation. But the experience of the last three years has shown that the laws adopted in various fields – both economic and social – in the previous legislature are changed function of the interests of influent parties within the present governing coalition. In this way, the rule-of-law system, that was to mirror the sovereign will of the nation, and to reflect its general interests, is becoming excessively politicized; the rule-of-law is coming to represent, as the word goes, the will 'of the ruling party'. Such a notion contradicts, in fact, the very idea of the Romanian state being a rule-of-law system.

The mobilization by the state of important human, natural and financial resources, based on the state's owning a large part of the national wealth and especially on its right to adopt adequate normative regulations, fundamentally represents the expression of a will to assume its pending constitutional responsibilities: the stability of the national economic environment, ensuring coherent productive and commercial flows, providing jobs for important segments of the active population. The actual assuming by the democratic Romanian state of its pending economic role might also benefit from the expectations of large categories of the population, eager to prove their social usefulness and to free themselves from 'passive protection'. There exist people preoccupied with the observance of laws, people willing to accept the involvement of the most representative bodies of authority in order to impose and consecrate beneficial rules of economic, social and professional behavior. The actual assuming by the state of its economic competences would accommodate the various group and professional interests with the general interests with which they are now at variance, thus generating tensions and convulsions. These are only some of the arguments in support of my claim that maintaining an apathetic, expectant position of our state toward economy and social relations, toward the life standard of most social categories, feeds and aggravates the difficulties of the transition period.

These have been only a few aspects strongly suggesting that the indiscriminating decline of the role of the state in society, as felt at present, is counter-productive and entails a serious offense against general national interests.

8.2 The state and modern society

The multitude of perspectives, specific to ideatic debates and to the confrontation of solutions regarding the relations between the state and economy, can be synthesized as follows:

a. the existence, on the one hand, of the thesis on the sovereignty and omnipotence of the individual – equating to the illegitimacy or evil character of the state's involvement in economy;
b. the existence, on the other hand, of the thesis on the omnipotence of the state, or on the 'tutoring state', correlated to postulating the impotence of the individual of manifesting him/herself as a competitive agent within the economic system;
c. the existence of a 'complementary space', to which the correspondent is the thesis of the selective, balanced involvement of the state, so as to eliminate neither the enterprising natural persons, nor free competition.

The most representative periods of the 20th century – the 1914-1918 war, the Great Depression, the Second World War, 'the thirty glorious years' after the war – have proved that national economies have become substantially dependent on public authority and the competences of state power. In the circumstances of the war economy, the state rendered evident its capacity of controlling economy and increasing national income, of ensuring the employment of manpower, of detecting resources potentially useful in order to preserve the general life standards. During crises and while pressing for recovery, societies go from an economy functioning 'by itself' to a controlled, authority-supported economy.

During the reconstruction years, after 1945, and during the 'boom' years, the state assumed its enterprising role, the role of supporting programs of development, of re-shaping and amplifying world financial flows. Such directions and priorities met the will of those people eager for law observance, for guaranteed, safe work-places, for the certitude that temporary sacrifices will be followed by social policies of welfare and prosperity.

The mutations of the economic system – which was unrelentingly going astray from the ideal of 'natural harmonies' – and those within the realm of social relations and structures, especially mirrored in the social policies of income redistribution, of supporting labour-force employment programs, were accompanied by attempts at theorizing a state with 'positive functions'.

The main liberal analyses, conducted in the first decades of the 20th century and on into the middle of the '70s, came progressively closer to the doctrinal-pragmatic option of social democracy. They abandoned the theoretical constructs of the 'neutral state' or the 'watchdog state', that had driven the governance act throughout the 19th century. The doctrinal projections of neo-liberalism were to be materialized in the theory of the 'positive-function' state, that would preserve its democratic essence and the defining features of representativeness and legitimacy.

The imposition of the 'positive function' state into the role of guarantor of economic stability and protector of group interests, in a consensus with the general-national interests, represents the result of resonant political experiences and attempts, both theoretical and practical, of the main developed countries, West-European or outside Europe. Of the long list of initiatives that consecrated the 'positive function' state, we can mention: the 'New Deal' launched by president F.D. Roosevelt during the American Great Depression; the governance program of the Swedish social democracy in 1932, promoted by the Prime Minister Per Albin Hansson, who claimed that the essential function of the state must be that of creating a political and social order that would guarantee to any citizen the feeling of security in his/her own country; the 'anti-crisis' program assumed by Great Britain authorities, and conceived with the substantial contribution of John Meynard Keynes; the writings in economy and economic philosophy by the French author Jacques Rueff, opened by the programmatic study 'Why am I still a liberal?'; the 'Walter Lippman' colloquium, which took place in Paris in August 1938, and which drafted the 'chart' of the 'positive function' state (a chart that was to be applied, after 1945, in most West-European countries); Belgium's 'Van Zeland plan', conceived around the Second World War; the program of economic recovery of the Bonn Republic, bearing the imprint of the professor and political man Ludwig Erhard, who conceived and successfully applied the model of 'social market economy', etc.

The ideas launched by the personalities and programs mentioned above have materialized, in various ways, into a rich legislation that admits that the traditional aspirations of the 'wage-earning classes' regarding the 'humanization of development' represent one of the necessary conditions of humanizing 'industrial society'. Also, the government practice carefully correlated material demands with those concerned with ensuring a decent standard of spiritual comfort. At the same time, justice, as a goal of the economic process, claimed by the representatives of the un-propertied, crosses and sometimes dominates political discourse in the years 1980-1990.

In the last decades of the 20th century, the relation between the state and modern economy has become, once again, the bone of contention after the rebirth of individualist liberalism, as embodied by Thatcherism in Great Britain and Reaganism in the United States. This form of liberalism, which reached the most different regions of the world, has placed social democracy in a defensive position for almost two decades, and accused it of having encouraged consumerism and having neglected the production of assets and values, of having underestimated the place and importance of production and of having been concerned with re-distributive policies only.

Lately, the Western world has been witnessing the ascension of a principled position denying the nihilist claims regarding the state, arguing that such an initiative would equale turning back history with approximately five decades, and that the political and social experience of the 20th century would become **tabula rasa.** Thus we are gradually coming back to the idea of a 'new alliance', in moderate forms, between the individual-citizen and economy, on the one hand, and public authority, on the other.

The **necessity** of the state's involvement in economy and, in a wider sense, in social life, is supported by a wide range of arguments, of which we will only mention the most representative:

- A pure and generalized market economy has never existed in any country on earth, no matter how strongly rooted may their liberal traditions be. The history of modern societies has recorded, in the last two centuries, predominantly free markets, and not absolutely free markets; which means that, in those economies, the market and its mechanisms had, during certain periods, a decisive role.
- The realities of the last four-five decades have not confirmed either of the options regarding the economies and/or markets controlled entirely by the state, since all attempts of this kind ended in failure. Therefore, history refuted both the theses on the state's generalized control, and those on the completely free market, while at the same time validating a cautious involvement of the state in economy, and even the consecration of the state as an instrument of the industrial system.
- Besides the reasons mentioned above, other arguments in favor of involving the state in economy can be the following: the inefficiency of private initiative in fields of general interest; the complex character of certain issues during difficult times, issues which, through their perspective, solutions and resources, outdo the possibilities of private enterprisers (we have here in mind **collective goods, public goods** or **activities of national interest,** etc.); the 'natural', inevitable qualitative growth in the status of the owner of an important part of a country's wealth, which it (the owner) is called to administrate and capitalize; the state's capacity to correct shortcomings of the market, to reconcile the economic and the social, to harmonize the relation between the economic and the human resources.

The proportions of the state's involvement in economy represent an amply debated issue in economic theory, in the sociology of the state and the sociology of power. Without providing a complete and precise answer, researchers claim that the proportions of the state's involvement in economy must be optimal, which presupposes the total elimination of extreme positions; moreover, the optimal dimension varies from one country to the next, from one period to another. The optimum of involvement is influenced by circumstances and by time, place and space factors.

The modalities of involving the state in economy in order to help it fulfill its economic and social role are mainly materialized in: involvement through public administrations, a procedure that offers and provides collective services to economic actors, without direct equivalent labor conscription on the consumers' side; assuming all responsibilities that befall it as representative of the general interests of the nation, which it mirrors, supports and defends inside and outside country borders; assuming the task of a guarantor of private property and defender of private initiative; direct involvement of the state in economy as a subject, actor and economic enterpriser; elaborating economic programs and policies.

8.3 Social democracy and the Welfare State

The belief that mere ideological solutions can entail efficient governmental action has represented a double trap. After 1996, problems were not solved by the liberal solution, though the amplified effect of social polarization is undeniable. As for the social-democratic variant of democracy, we must take into consideration a wide portrait of this doctrinal family now, at the end of the 20th century. Social democracy, after the withdrawal of the Keynesian models, has been left without a very clear definition (that is why there is talk of the Blair paradox and of the weakness of Gerhard Schroeder's German social democracy). Social democracy has lost some of its initial substance, that insisted on a dynamic capacity to change the system from inside whenever it was demanded by the exigencies of society –

except for the courageous anti-unemployment policies experimented by the Jospin cabinet in France. This was best seen when Oskar Lafontaine's attempts at impressing a social-democratic a line to the government – a line justified by the voters' choice – came up against the relentless opposition of the international financial markets, of the national business community and even of an important part of the German social democrats. It is evident that pragmatics of the Blair type determine the emergence of radical trends inside the social-democratic field, but also the injection of neo-liberal elements in this political trend. **Today there is place a veritable process of turning social democracy into a half-breed.**

The present-day variant of social-democratic pragmatism (Blair, Schroeder) seeks to transform capitalism into a 'mitigated' version. It no longer tries to introduce principles that might modify social disparities, but only to establish a consensus that would save, in the long run, real social cohesion. As for the vogue enjoyed today by the 'Third Way' political line, Lionel Jospin, the French Prime Minister and leader of the French Socialist Party, stated: "If the Third Way means a middle ground between capitalism and communism, I accept it. But if the Third Way means a middle ground between social democracy and liberalism, I reject it".

In my vision on inserting center-left political principles, social democracy is seen as a system capable of offering an alternative to neo-liberal capitalism, making possible the existence of the Welfare State. The Romanian state's attribute of being a 'welfare' state is recorded by the Constitution of December 1991. The specification implies that in Romania a state was projected that, by its initiatives and actions, is called to ensure for all members of society (and not just for some of them) an effective and balanced participation in the benefit of civil rights and liberties, as well as in the results obtained by joint effort. In fact, the qualifier 'social' implied in the notion of welfare was conceived particularly as a corrector to classic liberal essentially political democracy. Liberal democracy, in most of the strongly developed countries, from the economic and technological point of view, has freedom as its core. Or, in the circumstances of underdeveloped or developing countries, 'freedom' would merely be a metaphor, were it not financially supported. In these societies, 'the general interest' takes precedence over the individual interests promoted by liberalism. In the name of a general interest, the state can intervene in order to regulate an excessive private monopoly, in order to stimulate or support certain private sectors, in order to take over the management of the management of either administrative domains of high importance or of deficient ones, or in order to protect the disfavored social categories.

The fundamental principles of the left – freedom, justice (as equality of opportunities) and solidarity – must become principles of action and valid social norms, assumed not merely by the adepts of a certain political party, but by the whole social body. The modern notion of citizenship comprises not only political rights granted to citizens, but also social rights, such as health insurances, retirement benefits, support for the disabled and so on.

Neo-liberalism criticizes social-democracy because it often tries to force the introduction of equalitarian principles over differentiation, innovation and individual profit performance. The principles of social-democratic equity, however, have nothing in common with communist equalitarianism, it being merely an attempt to mitigate unjust inequities. From this perspective, justice must be seen as equity, as equality of opportunities. Correcting the injustice capable of leading to a violent modification of the democratic system must be one of the goals of social democracy in Romania. In the conditions of a hardening of the conflict between labor and capital, here in Romania as well, topics such as economic and social rights for the wage-earners, union rights, unemployment benefits, social services will have to be increasingly taken into consideration.

Moderating the individualist philosophy, acknowledging all through the prism of the market, is a necessity. The individualist philosophy imposes as such the following definition: you have produced an unmarketable product – even though you are dealing with cultural or spiritual goods, that cannot be merely evaluated as any common stuff – and that is bad. Next time be smarter and only produce whatever is marketable. Looking at things in this way means viewing society merely as an abstract concept, reflecting the exclusive inter-relationality of individual activities and choices.

The justice of the market is not the same thing as social justice, as it does not try to offer correctives to these highly individualized and contradictory choices or activities as regards the possibility of a growth of social cohesion. What neo-liberalism emphatically calls 'market justice' is a wrongly interpreted concept, a 'de-personalized justice', as bad as the 'justice' brought about by the totalitarian regimes of the Soviet type. Social polarization almost always leads to the emergence of radical and anarchic trends, and history proves that where the anarchic tendencies in society go beyond a certain limit, it is always the case that the governance act begins to resemble it. The same situation is valid for neo-conservative right-wing trends, which is why the existence of the 'minimal' state is still allowed, reducing it to the position of a 'watchdog', and not that of community strategist in search of a balance between private and public interests. The show of zeal is not accidental in various departments of social research, in the research units of renowned Western universities; these display a vivid interest in studying the 'chaos theory' and its social dimensions. There are certain directions within the world system, that have led us to imagine scenarios derived from the applications of the 'chaos theory'; scenarios that imply 'events with a chaotic potential in the making'.

Social democracy does not restrain 'a priori' individual action, in spite of what certain Romanian political-intellectual elites have claimed. The spirit of initiative is an aspect specific to the free market, but the individual's choice and action take place in a larger context, relying heavily on a given society. The goal of a society is not profit, but maintainance of cohesion, seen as a condition of the society's long-term survival. We, as a society, do not wish to belong to the integrated structures of the capitalist world merely because of reasons pertaining to collective/individual profit, but also because of reasons pertaining to our acknowledgement of the fact that such a belonging will better preserve our balance and facilitate our evolution.

Communism denied the individual in order to focus on structure. Capitalism excessively denies structure in order to focus on the individual alone, which it endows with abstract and sometimes optional characteristics, that are not inherent to human nature. The individual has an existence that is not determined by the 'pure market' alone, he is circumscribed to the larger frame of interpersonal relations, he has the awareness of certain solidarities, and even needs social solidarity, just because he is a human being. Therefore, for social democracy social justice is a modality of action, by which the political is pressuring structure when the structure becomes oppressive and when it, in its turn, pressures the individual by reducing, in spite of its claims, the autonomy of action and the possibility of equal opportunities. To the principle of social policies (assistance, jobs, unemployment support, the right to education, the positive reconsideration of the human capital in productive processes) are related to the principle of social justice. Without extensive access to education, the structural barriers created between people vitiate the principle of equal opportunities. Income must not be equalized – it would be absurd; but access to education does.

A pertinent analysis of Romania's situation after a decade of transition leads us to the conclusion that the exclusivist or imposed solutions risk to reduce system reform to the condition of a system with attractive technicist or ideological, but on the whole counterproductive accents.

8.4 Ideology and reform: an unacceptable solution

In the present situation of Romanian society, it is no longer possible to ground intentions and economic decisions starting from the more or less explicit assumption of a certain ideology. More precisely, the ideological grounding of economic decisions is merely an illusion, a confusion similar to that of identifying reform with change or market economy with the exit way out of the present economic crisis. An ideology can never generate economic solutions; it can offer to the system only the institutionalized instruments of remedy, balance and evolution. In a certain sense, ideology is nothing else but a sum of value judgments which serve to delimit political segments. In other words, it is a label, a means of identification through social-political lenses.

Tarrying within the field of ideological concepts turned the reform either into a standard technical issue, or into a political problem. Romanian society joined this trend because it merely followed the position of all ex-communist countries. The political cared little about the real, specific aspects of change. The governments that came in succession after 1989 had to confront a reality that was too poorly conceptualized and instrumentalized at a political level.

Any ideology, any doctrinal construct should be the proof of a preoccupation with detecting means of streamlining the functioning of institutions within the rule-of-law, with a view to rendering economic growth a permanent process. Or, in Romania, the inflation of concepts such as reform, rule-of-law, market economy is a phenomenon that proliferates to the detriment of a preoccupation with solving an essential aspect: Romanian society produces over ten times less than the developed countries, and the gap continues to widen. The intensive use of these terms does nothing but devalorize them, leading to the appearance of a new 'wooden language'.

Turning 'reform' into an ideological term transformed the purely technical aspects circumscribed to this notion into the elements of a 'compendium': from the moral crisis to the economic one. The notion of reform, insistently circulated by right-wing forces nowadays, had been the exclusive prerogative of the European left between the two world wars. Then, reform meant improving the life and labor standards of the workmen, and granting certain social rights. It is a most appropriate example as to the relativization of the meanings of certain concepts seen from different ideological perspectives. In the same way, derived notions such as macrostabilization and restructuring have become redundant in political discourse. People have come to identify the dimensions of the reform mainly by its preponderantly negative connotations. The daily perception is at great difficulty in telling apart governing parties from opposition parties. In fact, from an ideological point of view, the main political groups pretend to hold the key to valid solutions not only in the case of our economic crisis, but also for Romanian society in general. Moreover, the 'salvation' programs are delimited into fixed periods and stages, as if the external environment and the market variables were to stay the same during the application of their programmatic projects!

The solutions put forth in the ten years of transition did not have a doctrinal support in the true sense of the word. Obviously, some political actors have reacted in a reductionist fashion, actually assimilating daily ideological language to that specific to doctrinal constructs. Such solutions, vaguely, sometimes even contradictorily grounded, were represented as veritable 'economic categories', capable of entailing governance solutions or even actions proper. Last but not least, even in the circumstances of a drastic reduction of the number of parties on the Romanian political stage, the fact of ideological and doctrinal mimesis continues to exist. All Romanian parties display the desire to integrate into the most significant trends of the developed countries. This is the reason why, at the level of the Romanian political spectrum, a tendency becomes increasingly obvious – that of occupying only two ideological fields and of placing them around the classic left-right axis.

We must notice that for the individual as a member of society, little does it matter what doctrinal nuances the political parties choose to assume. What is decisive is the configuration of the mental structures operative in real life. The daily perception of the political is sensitive to the significance of language and concepts. Their redundancy is followed by the impossibility of establishing clear ideological demarcation lines between Power and Opposition. Consequently, the political options of various segments of the population are not determined by the doctrinal contents of discourses, but especially by their becoming personalized and by emotional identification with them. The latest sociological research emphasizes a waning of the identification of the voters with the voted party, while what gains in importance is the image of the political leader or political communication, to the detriment of parties or programs.

The same perceptive mechanism functions within parties, which is indeed disquieting. It is not so much clear options that bring together members of a party, but generation or inter-personal affinities. The coagulation of parties around personalities, veritable 'mentors' bestowing political identity upon parties, and not around ideas, as well as the justification of members' options, form a model whose mechanisms are to be found within the political sphere, as well as at the level of its daily perception. Let us not forget that one of the characteristic features of a political party is its continued existence after the physical disappearance of its leaders. If it is not so, we are dealing not with a genuine party, but with the mere personal clique of a leader. This observation does not take as a premise the quality of the capacity to operate with doctrinal categories, but the specific mental structures as a regime of forming and functioning of political judgment, values, attitudes, and opinions.

8.5 Is reform a matter of state interest?

"You cannot know the intentions of a government that doesn't know them itself."

John Kenneth Galbraith

Romania has witnessed much talk of the liberal and social-democratic solutions as being the main channels through which Romanian society can assume normality and the return to contemporaneity.

The role of the state in changing Romanian society will continue to be the main source of ideological confrontation. Although the issue of the state is important, the way it is approached inevitably leads to answers circumscribed to the exclusivity of political and electoral discourse. Romanian politicians are not aware that, beyond good and evil – translatable here as the political avatars of day-to-day – they must remain above the national interest.

An already classic example in this direction is provided by the typically ideological reasoning that largely influenced the political behavior of parties. After December 1989, the structures of the totalitarian regime were eliminated through the removal of the single party that for half a century had subordinated and assimilated state power for its own a political purposes. Theoretically, the reconstruction of the democratic state could have been automatically launched from the political point of view. The disillusionments that followed were only equal to the initial hopes. These generated both the justifications and the political attitudes that shaped, along years, the relations between parties, when political pluralism was to a large number of Romanians a vague notion, almost always associated with freedom. The quick passing from a dictatorial regime to a political system with a great number of parties, most of them of dubious political quality, merely shows the insubstantiality of the change process as regards the accumulation or distribution of power. The great number of parties is not necessarily translated into a democratic system characterized by political competition, but can simply be a symptom of the fragmentation, chaos and insecurity felt by a society unprepared for change. Very few political leaders had an experience of the pluralist game, and those who had it – the 'survivors' of the historical parties between the wars – were guided by the idea of a restitutionist 'revanche', without having a clear perspective on who was really guilty. Of course, the first guilty body had to be the governing one. This amplified the ideological contestations of the type 'reformist/communist', 'democrats/neo-communists', 'European/ national-communists' etc., all these antitheses having been compellingly introduced and having invaded a great part of the energies that could have been employed in quickly solving matters of public interest. The peak of such a contestational crisis was represented by the 'University Plaza' phenomenon, a core not of the 'new generation', but, as was eventually seen, of coagulating the political Opposition and building the populist alternative, the Romanian Democrat Convention. After November 1996, it became apparent that this movement was merely a political strategy exclusively relying on the idea of 'change' at any cost.

The entire political spectrum agreed – at least this is what one can gather from their statements – to the idea that the new state structures had to be built in conformity with the general rules of liberal democracy, dominant in the Western world. The Democratic Social Party of Romania considered that the process should unwind starting from the premise of certain legislative acts that would ground the functioning of the new rule-of-law institutions. Not even this minimal goal, envisaging Romania's acquiring of necessary democratic standards for its integration into the Euro-Atlantic organizations and, after all, into normality proper, not even this, then, managed to capture the consensus of the Romanian political class. From the point of view of the center-right parties, the respective process was at that time unsettled by the perpetration of the old structures. But this was later on proved to be a mere populist claim.

Apparently, the two options might give one the natural feeling of being confronted with different political opinions. In fact, a reality independent of the political will of the parties instituted and legitimized one point of view as the 'Opposition', the other as the 'Power'. More important is the fact that, despite the same reality, both parts ignored a fundamental aspect characteristic to the structuring process of any institution. The mere elaboration of the functioning laws of institutions is insufficient for their effective structuring. It must be doubled by their acceptance and by forming the daily behavioral automatisms of conforming to rules, of developing a participative culture of the citizens in public affairs, of creating civic education, briefly, or materializing what the specialized literature called 'political culture'.

Two interesting phenomena then developed. On the one hand, reality refused to conform to the wishes of the parties, and the Executive found itself powerless as to the rules that this very reality, tacitly and autonomously, seemed to establish. On the other hand, political parties identified and defined the situation in an exclusively ideological frame, as a mere governance crisis, limiting its solution – as was natural – to the strict rules of the democratic political game.

At least until now, Romania did not witness regime crises; the governmental crises were related to the contestation not of the democratic regime, but of their efficiency, or to the disputes within the parties forming a parliamentary majority. **Exclusivism, specific to hyper-ideological grounding, always leads to intolerance and to amounting politics to the vicious circle of politicianism.**

In the 21st century, the problems of societies will no longer be settled by unifying ideologies, but by ideologies capable of adapting to the globalization of the international system. It depends on whether globalization will be governed, or governments will be circumscribed to globalization. Practically, this is the essence of the differences between social democracy and contemporary socialism, and economic neo-liberalism.

Unfortunately, Romania lies at the periphery of a world where, over a decade ago, the technological revolution deeply branded industrial relations, social co-existence and societal relations as a whole. The gaps widened during an anti-progressive governmental office (1996-2000). Although at world level there is an explosive capital circulation (1.3-1.4 billion dollars every day), the Romanian space is closed to or avoided by this flow; the strategies that have operated until now are not efficient enough to ensure penetration. We must understand that economy and society work as a whole, that when one of them gets sick, the other follows suit.

Social democracy is also a political practice, and in Romania the programs of those parties that assume their belonging to this family must transpose this responsibility in real terms. Social democracy puts forth a political and/or economic doctrine, a particular way of thinking social order from the perspective of equity, social justice and solidarity.

The problem of the Romanian social democracy relates not so much to the priorities or the purity of the doctrine, but to establishing some common issues as regards the intended model of society. Instead of an essentialist definition of democracy, it would be more useful to see which of the variants submitted by parties within this political area is more valid from a double perspective: economic-social, domestic-foreign.

The course steered by transition has led not only to polarization, but also to a degradation of the free development of the Romanian society. A democratic regime cannot function in the absence of a decent life standard for a majority of citizens. The priority of a social-democratic governance is consolidating democracy by improving the life standards of the population. So far democracy has not been deeply employed, in the sense of transforming the state into a genuine juridical community of the people, capable of watching over sustained security, liberty and justice. On the contrary, democracy has become a rhetorical instrument, manipulated in propagandistic wars, in 'sovereign' appeals and ultimatum-like phrases, such as 'we are more democratic than you'. In parallel, the Romanian state found itself deprives of any powerful organizational structures, and when this truth was uttered, there followed accusations of etatism, authoritarianism etc. State power was no longer submitted to any kind of social control, being in effect divided into lots distributed among coalition parties. As a consequence, the second goal of a social-democratic governance must be a new, better order of society.

We can hardly explain or justify the fear felt by some as to the public control of economic forces, when this does not mean either nationalization or centralization. Privatization represents an important means of improving the degree of co-interestedness, of stimulating initiative and the spirit of enterprise, of enhancing management quality and accountability, in order to use with maximal efficiency the natural, human and material resources of society, and in order to sustain actions of re-structuring and technological improvement. But **privatization cannot be seen as a goal in itself**, as a miracle solution or panacea to all economic and social problems.

It is urgently necessary that we return to privatization on economic principles, that would ensure, through a transparent and coherent process, the correct employment of the stock capital of commercial firms, the increased efficiency, the development and modernization of national economy. The way important economic targets were privatized in the past few months – SIDEX, Banca Agricola, Oltchim – proves that the process of due sales can be accounted for at the decisional level of the state.

Private property and market economy are absolutely necessary tools, but they must not be used to create differences that might entail potential social conflicts. Utilitarian individualism is not the true, viable goal of transition. Social democracy is not characterized by the wish for equality, but by the attempt to reduce inequality to a level acceptable by the population. The principle that lies at the basis of social-democratic action is that of protecting those disfavored in contractual relations such as employer/employee, owner/tenant, producer/consumer etc. This is why social democrats must provide a community project of social order and prosperity, by which the community of citizens should live free of the servitude of selfishness (competition-based or group selfishness alike) and of the servitude toward any totalitarianism of political power.

The Democratic Social Party of Romania must more clearly redefine itself pragmatically, historically and nationally. Its major strategic goal is that of accomplishing a post-nationalist Romania. **Post-nationalism is defined by focusing its political discourse on a civic and global nationalism, consonant with the spirit of the Constitution and the democratic notion**. Eventually it will resort to imposing the concept of the Romanian citizen as an integrated, post-nationalist and anti-ethnic concept.

It is essential to make it clear that a social-democratic government can pull Romania out of its stagnation state. A government that would reintroduce the streamlining of politics, expertise and efficiency (in policies, in selecting political staff, in projects and initiatives etc.) is what Romanian society needs at this moment. **Political power is lacking substance if it does not rely on information and professional competence, and implicitly on the people who possess them.** Only thus can we establish, relatively quickly, the most appropriate strategies of coming out of this crisis.

Social democracy defines itself as a pragmatic-reformist trend:

- it is pragmatic, i.e. it establishes a continuous and reciprocal relation between political people and experts (specialists, technical people etc.);
- social-democratic reformism can be defined as the capacity of the system to be modified from the inside – without violence – whenever social exigencies demand this. Reformism must be also understood in the sense of a permanent actualization of the energies and possibilities of society to transform itself.

A center-left policy implies fulfilling the aspirations of a real social dialogue, of reassessing technical functions to the benefit of society, of rationally countering group interests and partisan political voluntarism by the efficiency of the governance act. **It is certain that Romania needs an intensive development of capitalism, in parallel with an internal socialization of capitalism.** A social-democratic policy will attempt to preservation of the equilibrium between the dynamics of market economy and preserving social cohesion. It is just as certain that Romania needs a social modernization based on community projects. But this modernization is impossible without economic growth. The reform must be understood in the sense of a permanent actualization of the energies and possibilities of society to transform itself. It will aim at building a concept of security of the individual, the Romanian citizen, by implementing four criteria:

- minimal economic security;
- social security – the capacity to predict the short- and medium-term future, from the point of view of the social, judicial and administrative situation;
- national security – the capacity to establish a direct relation to the central and local authority;
- regaining the authority of those state powers competent in the field of justice.

PART III

CHAPTER NINE

POLITICAL PARTIES BETWEEN IDEOLOGY AND POLITICAL CRISIS

9.1. Sterile disputes and calamitous outcomes

Political discourse has, no doubt, its own logic, itself prey to ideological inertia, but also constrained by the presumed finality of political acts. This type of discourse operates with arguments and projects that must not be synonymous to stagnation, but on the contrary, to flexibility, movement towards the future. These projects are based upon analyses which imply defining the goals to be reached and formulating the lines of action that will allow one to reach the targets set forth.

The effort of "saving", "delimiting" of fighting for "identity" benefits from the advantage of drawing upon a pool of sufficient resources. Its permanent refill potential comes above all from the political capitalization of people's expectations, generated by the ruthless processes of transitional realities. It is well known that the simplest dichotomy of the political spectrum was constituted upon an imaginary abscissa of the "left-right" type, involving from the very start a one-dimensional cleavage as prerequisite of assuming a political identity.

Going beyond the superficial commentaries that frame the political actors within these two categories, we must say that the degree of structural completion of the left and right depends on the political behaviors and attitudes of the citizens, on their amount of political culture, as well as on the influences of political "acculturation" and the capacity of assimilation of certain foreign models. The left-right axis is the result of a long process of codification of the political; a process laden with symbols, thus facilitating the decoding, by the citizens, of the political stage. The identification of individuals with this pattern offers certain symbolic gratifications. It is known that at the origin of this perspective on politics lies the France of 1789, where the representatives of the aristocracy to the Constituent Assembly sat to the right of the presidium. It is generally believed that the political right tends to be rather conservative, stressing the nation, family, state and tradition. All of these are incorporated into the principle of gradual social engineering (the reform "without commotions", as a 19th Romanian conservative politician was saying).

In post-revolutionary Romania, the left-right cleavage has reappeared after the reinvention of the multi-party democracy; however, some political analysts prefer to define the 1990-1992 and 1992-1996 intervals rather as a communist-anticommunist, or reform-antireform cleavage. Consequently, the left-right cleavage was subsumed to this approach of reality. Generally speaking, everything left of CDR was categorized by some as "neo-communist" or anti-reformist, anti-modernist, whereas to the right of it there could be nothing relevant in point of political projects, at least not in the period around 1996. After the alternation to power took place, the Romanian political scenery could be perceived in its entire complexity. The differences grew blurred, and even turned to be uncertain when the first prime minister of the new government was an ex-union leader, and a party that declared itself to be left-center, the Democrat Party, became an important pillar of reform. Doctrinal clarifications as regards the direction of governance were never a priority. The coalition parties made the headlines, above all, by working to satisfy the governmental algorithm and by placing party members in key positions. Confusion and dilemmatic attitudes persisted with these parties, affecting the overall situation of the country in terms of financial, budgetary and economic policies.

For all the pro-reform discourses, meant to save the coalition, the economic decline kept its pace, so much so that we could speak about a certain stage of "stagnation in decline". Much like in Brezhnev's time, political discourse was extremely mobilizing, always optimistic and calling masses to consensus, with the eternal promise of a somewhat better future. All CDR-USD-UDMR governments proved to be extremely careful in their wording, in order to handle with gloves the partners in the majoritary coalition. This method of accepting the arbitration of the Executive by the political council of the coalition, diverted the direction in which Government's interest should have been channeled: economy and social equilibrium, capitalization and development of private actors, fortifying the capitalist nuclei capable of extension. Consequently, the crisis of Romanian society amplified, as an outcome of a "reform at ease" type of attitude, totally unjustified by the Executive's rhetorical recourse to the fact that "Romania is an ungovernable country". This phrase regarding the Romanians' governability is contradicted by the fact that in the first two years after 1996 there were no major social movements, radical disputes or endemic violence. The true issue was who governed and how, and if the balance sheet of the 1996-2000 governments is a negative and failed one, it leads us to think that, during this interval, we were only presented the appearance of governance, one much more interested in being politically correct and aligned rather to the international financial organizations, than to the electoral promises of 1996.

9.2. The year 2000 – Evolutions of the Romanian political system

Political parties are real cornerstones in the functioning of democratic regimes, as they bring forth leaders and mobilize the public support these leaders need in order to accede to the governmental apparatus and the control of the social system. Unfortunately, under the heavy burden of economic hardships, opinion polls have lately disclosed a shift of trust from the area of political parties and the political class, towards an area of ambiguity and distrust in these (almost 50% of the subjects distrust political parties).

We are thus to a certain extent falling back on the theory according to which political parties in Eastern Europe are weak organizations, floating somewhere in the sphere of inside-party private interests (of factions, camps etc.) Considering the fact that the Romanian electorate draws its information from TV and radio stations rather than newspapers, magazines, public debates and active exchange of opinions, and considering the fact that lately television stations have primarily emphasized the conflicting aspects of politics, it is only natural to see it reflected in the level of trust placed in political parties.

Another idea introduced by spin-doctors (and by small parties in search of popularity) is that "big" parties are disconnected from the real interests of the electorate. From this angle the new political elites, derived from the transition from socialism, are impotent, driven exclusively by personal ambition, their political vehicles (parties) merging or separating not on the ground of competitiveness, but of vanities and of renegotiating key positions inside the organization. This theory is largely adopted by journalists, themselves guided by certain interests, but also by self-taught political analysts.

All important Romanian parties have gone through internal crises and fractures, either total or partial. One outcome is the fact that the political transition will be longer than anticipated. There are and will be successive gradual openings and concessions, first between the parties now holding power and those in the opposition; eventually, the concessions and openings, and political compromises, will take over the area of actors with resembling doctrines (social-democrats, liberals, Christian-democrats, socialists). Only the coagulation of the great political families will be able to generate superior organizational power, coherent and unitary governance programs and stable government coalitions.

The much-too-harsh competition between parties seeking to cover the preferences of a large segment of the electorate on the basis of platforms that are ultimately much alike, is a factor that essentially increases the instability of the regime, allowing for "toxic coalitions"; these *can* govern, but not efficiently. This situation lies at the core of the legitimacy and representation crises, and of the stability crises of the Romanian political system. They might send us to the Italian evolutionary model, based on clientele networks and the fragmentation of the political spectrum.

Romanian parties can be generically classified as follows:

- Parties justified by the revolutionary platform of 1989 (as source of legitimacy);
- Historical parties – Romania is the only post-communist country where these parties acquired a major significance and political role;
- Other parties created after 1989: ecologist, of agrarian orientation, hybrid (based on cultural and interest groups);
- Anti-system parties, ready at any time to criticize both power and opposition.

The refusal of politics, or the anti-political politics, has as its representatives groups of intellectuals that reject the deficits of political parties on grounds of moral deficits. They promote action modes based on models of successful collective action, but the competition they represent for parties is limited in range. In Central and Eastern Europe the period of umbrella groups, of the civic activism type, has disappeared together with the very inclination for activism, rallies etc.

The coalitions of parties from politically and doctrinally related areas will emphasize continuity. Coalitions seeking to make up political poles will bring back together factions and the initial group, by a process of rediscovery of common grounds. Instance of personalization must be downplayed in the process of structuring the social-democratic family. All pole variants take into consideration the "volatility" of the vote.

The structure of the Romanian political abscissa:

PRM ←——————————————————— → UDMR

UDMR (The Democratic Union of Hungarians from Romania) and PRM (The Great Romania Party) are parties that belong to the anti-system category, as they are difficult to integrate in the "left-right" game. UDMR is a party built on ethnic criteria, whose political agenda is exclusively dedicated to representing the interests of Hungarian ethnics in Romania. PRM does nothing but mirror, in its actions, the political activity of UDMR.

The center of the abscissa is an imaginary construct, having as reference point the party holding power at the respective time.

(0)

PSM PDSR PSDR ApR PD PNTCD PNL UFD

It is easy to notice how political parties tend to cram in to the center of the political abscissa. The interests of the parties seeking political identity by relating to the political center are completely different. First of all, they are trying to draw the discontent citizens from both sides of the political spectrum, especially from the two main political blocs, PDSR and CDR. Secondly, the parties in intermediary positions might benefit from the advantage of having wider opportunities for political alliances, by negotiations with parties situated both to their right and their left.

On the center-left side of the Romanian political spectrum, the year 2001 is to bring an important clarification. The PDSR-PSDR merger will not only consolidate the main political force in Romania, but will also consecrate the ideological legitimacy of the resulting party. The extreme fragmentation in the social-democratic area is practically over once the Social-Democratic Party is born. Both as political weight and as doctrinal substance, PSD marks the beginning of a coagulation process of Romanian parties around the three doctrinal blocs: social democracy, liberalism and Christian democracy.

9.3. The attraction of extremism and the ideal of cohesion

In the generalized crisis situation of Romanian society, the fact that parties seem to exclusively channel their attention towards ways of diminishing their adversaries' credibility might generate unwanted side effects. This attitude leaves room for radical or extremist solutions. The political personnel is selected, through vote, by a social body which presumes that they will bring about benefits and fulfill certain services for society as a whole, not merely for some particular parties. If promises are consistently disregarded, it may happen that public representation in its two forms, political and publicized, should enter a crisis process whose effect is a weakening of the legitimacy of the democratic government system. This lies at the origin of the extremist threat, which appropriates legitimacy even before legitimacy is granted to it by the electorate.

Extremism is a phenomenon that appears as consequence of an unjust distribution of wealth, of an ill-oriented patriotism, of fear. This fear is not indissolubly related to an external enemy, but to an uncertainty as regards the future, the social situation and survival chances. Extremism denies social complexity, always suggesting simple solutions, judging the world in Manichean terms ("them" and "us"), and being very vociferous. Extremism is what it is because it has no doubts: it already knows the answers and is sure of them.

A reform that leaves behind a huge majority of population to stand the losses, an obscure privatization process, can only force the affected population to adopt a different game, with other stakes and even with the acceptance from the start of a "voluntary servitude" (in the sense given to the phrase by Etienne de la Boetie), if this is to reduce their uncertainty and discomfort. There is no doubt that extremisms represent residual ideological forms which ultimately favor another political group, even if it is one with authoritarian tendencies. Relevant here is the example of Romania between the wars or even of pre-Franco Spain, when, against a background of political degradation of multi-party democracy, relatively minor political groups came to impose themselves as mass political parties or movements. Economic, political and cultural turmoil might provide a solid basis for political radicalization, which is evidently in disagreement both with the standards of modernity and with the parameters of the rule-of-law.

Discerning the danger of losing political credibility in the eye of the public, there appear groups of politicians who gradually become aware of both the inevitability and the necessity of modifying the present structure of the political spectrum. The political significance of the activities performed by these groups is marked by a few characteristics. These groups are not very large, and lack influence even in the parties where they originate. That is why these politicians are unable to bestow major political significance on their actions or attitudes.

What brings together the members of these groups is first of all their belonging to a certain generation. It is characteristic for generational factors to display relatively unitary mental and behavioral automatisms. These groups can in their turn coagulate new political structures in a very short time. And this may prove to be the beginning of the launching proper of an inside-party political re-structuring.

However, there persists the notion that party restructuring is primarily determined by ideological reconstruction. Far from denying the importance of this last aspect, we find it insufficient as concerns the finalization and materialization of the intentions of informal political groups. By adopting ideological arguments, these groups would do nothing but re-enter the mechanism of conceptual and political disputes within their very party.

Bearing in mind the fact that parties represent the actualization of citizens' opportunity to organize or join organizations function of certain motivations, we can say that each party survives for as long as it is politically meaningful for a definite sector of society. It is a significant example that in Italy, the two parties that had built the democratic regime, the Christian Democrats and the Socialists, have practically disappeared from the political stage, just as it happened in Canada with the Conservative Party, which from the position of main government party had come in 1997 to hold no more than two seats in Parliament.

Romanian political parties still fall short of fulfilling their attributed functions. They do not contribute with new people and ideas to the renewal of the political system, through mechanisms of recruitment and selection of their own members for leading positions. There continues to function the system of promotion based on personal connections and clientele. There are no programs or policies for government, but at best generous political offers taken over from the West and impossible to apply here. Thus becomes explainable the lack of training of Romanian parties for the act of governance. They do not ensure the connection between the represented and the representative, as there is a great distance between parties and their social basis. The very political legitimacy of the existence of parties is at stake here. Romanian parties do not integrate in the system various social groups, as they are first and foremost interested in satisfying the interests of their own clientele. Instead, there functions a perverted system of legitimating their own existence, the interests of private groups being metamorphosed into those of society at large.

No political party escapes moments of internal frictions or fractures. These may occur because of the impossibility of competition between programs, but they also certainly occur because of the maladjustment of some politicians to the idea of party. Beyond "party discipline", a term with negative connotations for those who underwent the Party-State regime, we must not neglect the fact that it is necessary to have cohesion inside a party.

It is to be presumed that the structure of today's political behavioral types will undergo gradual modifications. In the near future we shall witness the theoretical reshaping of present-day ideological concepts and of the political discourses on which the main parties fundament their programs and solutions, with a view to solving the crisis of Romanian society. We may also assume that in a while there will be a shift towards the model of representational parties; it is known that at present the model of Romanian pluralism is one of integrationist parties (emphasizing the mass of members). Today's Romanian parties are not mass parties, as they lack an essential feature characteristic of this type: the capacity to mobilize voters. Mass parties rely on a culture of participation, while Romanian parties almost entirely lack the capacity to mobilize, even their own electorate. Romanian parties tend towards an intermediary model, on the one hand that of professional corps party, on the other being preoccupied with drawing the largest number of voters possible.

Relevant in this case was the evolution of the Romanian parties' declared positioning on the political axis: left, center, right, plus all the possible combinations. The "localization" on the axis – the axial visualization – was more of an intentional affair, publicly spoken, to which were added the meaningful biographies of more or less charismatic leaders.

As yet, Romanian parties do not have a clearly defined social basis. They are more preoccupied with drawing voters from all segments of society, rather than seeking the loyalty of social groups with specific interests. No wonder there is no identification of the electors to the parties they vote, and there is a huge rate of fluctuation of electoral preferences from one party to another. Usually, Romanian parties adopt programs with general, consensual goals, avoiding peremptory pronouncements in contradictory matters. Gradually, at pace with the advancement of the reform process, of private property and the differentiations of social-economic status within Romanian society, there will appear real political partitions that might restore the political continuum on the left-right axis.

9.4 The temptation of the closed system and ideological conservation

Immediately after 1989 there were no doctrinal constructs to answer to popular perceptions and behavior. The essential motivation of the appearance and structure of the multi-party system consisted mainly of sets of intentions and vaguely grounded doctrinal goals. We must also take into consideration the difference between the essential biographical data of the parties' "initiators". The blueprint of these characteristics still exists, engaging a series of consequences on the evolution of political groups in Romanian society.

We may note here the birth of a phenomenon that tends to generate sets of premises common to the attitude of big parties. We are referring to the reduction of the political life of society to one's private playground. "The rest" is incoherently treated as "civil society", and treated in an abstract, undifferentiated way. The reductionism signaled here constitutes the premise of minimizing the political significance of certain social "gestures" of maximal importance. Without an opening of the parties towards what we generically call "civil society", the democratic political system risks de-legitimating itself even before it has truly begun to function. We cannot succeed in building political institutions without amplifying political participation, unless we want to find ourselves once more in the dilemma of the "substanceless forms". And the main means of amplifying the political participation of citizens is represented by the activity of political parties. On a larger scale, the task of parties will be that of reconstructing Romanian society function of three main coordinates: democracy (seen either as a value, or as a more efficient modality of managing the social), the idea of nation (accepted as a community or as a social contract), and change (perceived as survival or modernization).

The apparently chaotic actions of the unions, of the economic decision-making cores in the integrally or mainly state-owned factories and of those in the financial-banking system have a clear political stamp, unnoticed by the other parties. Romanian parties seem thus to remain in a state of conceptual inertia, fueled by a not-so-distant post-revolutionary past – a time when both unions and the quasi-autarchic behavior of economic decision makers, followed in the wake of political initiatives generated by the ratio of forces between parties. At present, these ratios rather tend to be inverted.

The influences exercised by economic decision-making cores and by union cores are intensifying. It is obvious that political parties cannot situate themselves wholly outside the influences of this process, be it merely because they are governing or envisaging governance. In Romania, too, there appears the phenomenon of lobbying around political leadership by various social formations thus constituted into veritable pressure groups. These groups have as their main goal the redistribution of the social product in favor of their members. In order to achieve this goal, they get well organized, and when need arises, they may even merge, thus making up redistribution coalitions. The proliferation of distribution groups and coalitions endanger society by way of distorting efficient resource allocation, diminishing economic growth, hindering technological progress if it directly contradicts their members' interest (e.g. the unions). When faced with this phenomenon, it seems inevitable that Government must assume enhanced powers as mediator between diverging interests within society, and that there will be a growth in the complexity of social regulations, resulted after arduous negotiations between all social parties involved.

Consequently, relying on the analyses made by their respective departments, political parties can resort to a series of reactions when they notice that "the rules of the game" lie too markedly on one side only. The response of the parties can entail at least two types of political answer from the interest groups involved. One type of answer is mostly concerned with the preservation of the conceptual and ideological identity of the main parties. This direction of evolution in political restructuring can be mainly interpreted as an effort of the temporary leaders and of the groups that support them, to maintain and reproduce the decisional positions they hold. Unfortunately, it is only too obvious that sometimes the main "instruments" used are demagogy and gross populism. The typical result is politicianism, denounced as the main negative aspect of the distortion of a democratic system. Evidently, this method, though potentially successful on a short term, must soon be abandoned, both because of the strains inside parties, which tend to amplify, and because of social pressures. The only real counterweight to "politicianism" is represented by the extension and deepening of the democratic political culture of the electorate.

The second type of answer will circumscribe the evolution of the parties' restructuring to a direction mainly determined by interests subsumed to real economic processes. This will imply the minimization of actions with an ideological or quasi-doctrinal signification directed at the economic field. The extension and optimization of interpersonal interest-based networks will tend, most definitely, not only to go beyond the field of present-day decisional nuclei within parties, but also to replace them. This direction of restructuring may generate, at the level of certain groups within parties, the extension of interest relations to economic decision makers, union leaders and representatives of the financial-banking system. Initially, those relations will not be subjected to the determinations of any ideological space. However, to them there will be gradually added political motivations. These will precede both ideological motivations, and any other type of motivations as well. It is worth emphasizing that the debut of the Romanian multi-party system involved an axial vision centered not on a cultural dimension (all important parties assuming the rules of a pluralist game), but on an economic dimension (considering it either necessary or obsolete for the state and Government to intervene in the games of the free market).

9.5 Politics – the art of the possible and the utopia of pure ethics

Romanian society is strongly marked not so much by an economic structure of a "Stalinist" type, as by the lack of utilitarian principles in selecting political personnel. But the problem of the "moral elites" in politics is not extremely important. The finality of the political act is ascertained at the social level; this is why politics must not be judged according to the criteria of morals or pure ethics, but to those of instrumental rationality. Has the decision/political act X or Y served the interests of the community (or of the largest part possible)? In the case of an affirmative answer, it means that, from the point of view of political morals, everything is fine. In politics, judgment is made function of the established goal and of achieving or not achieving it; the intermediary route is less relevant.

Nevertheless, politics has a morality of its own, i.e. a practical morality. In today's Romanian politics, the meaning of moral conduct would be better limited to merely respecting the rules of the game.

Romania can no longer afford a political apparatus with excessive costs, having at top level a small number of people who conceive and distribute positions on an exclusively political line (and the whole suite of rituals: publicly vowed fidelity, symbolic penitence etc.), thus overestimating the importance of certain numeric rules. We must do away with the regulations which state that no one is promoted unless he/she is a party member but, on the other hand, joining the party does not automatically guarantee promotion.

Certain representatives of the "anti-political temptation" place from the very beginning the political elites in opposition to the intellectual elites or, on another scale, stimulate a dispute between "the professionals of power" versus "the professionals of conscience", speaking about "the intellectuals' resignation" in front of political disputes. This type of lament must be overcome, especially since the politics of the "new model" necessitate the co-operation with those elites that have a most solid knowledge capital. We are living in an era of computerized information, of symbolic exchanges, so that neither at the organizational level nor at the level of decision-making can the political person do without counseling, without the delivery of data by an apparatus of technicians and experts. A cultural-technical elite co-opted in the elaboration of the political act can contribute to unblock economic mechanisms and to shorten the "route to prosperity".

We must not forget that the political elite is indissolubly related to the optimal functioning of the mechanisms of which it is part. Consequently, we can consider this crisis of Romanian society to express the reality of certain dysfunctional or partially functional elites. Post-revolutionary Romania has not yet undergone a "circulation of the elites", though the limits of the present political elite are obvious. Nevertheless, lately there has appeared a process of contesting the Romanian governing elite; this might be a prelude to the inevitable changes to come. It is necessary for us to understand that we need a political class, and generally speaking elites, that should help in the consolidation of the democratic state, a state limited in its attributions, but strong within these limits.

The importance of optimal selection should dominate all fields; still, in the life of the Polis the classification must not be made according to the remuneration of a few stars, but also with a public and moral dimension. Unlike the others, the political man must place himself at the service of modifying reality, improving inter- and intra-communitarian relationships. From this point of view, modern leftist thinking valorizes to a great extent communion and communication, taxing imposition and subjugation of any minority led by hegemonic "unique impulses". The political man is not a philosopher seeking the metaphysical essence of reality. Politics is an art of the possible, of accomplishing the possible by compromise and dialogue in favor of social goals. It is not the entire society that is looking for the essence of reality; but almost the entire society is interested in how it lives and what its standards of thinking are.

That is why we find it interesting that Romanian intellectuals of considerable merit have tried to impose themselves on the prominent political stage – an attitude that is understandable when the political elites are not numerous, but that is improbable to bear out for a long time. That the insertion of the intellectuality into politics should bring along a bonus of "moral value" to this "artful leadership of the human flocks" is a highly disputable question. To really believe that would mean presupposing, from the very start, that politics is either a-moral or anti-moral, which would not constitute a very constructive departure point. Morals in politics deal exclusively with the finality of the political act, not the morals of the distance covered. Consequently, we must not look at the political act in intermediary terms, but in its finality. The presence of morals in politics cannot be rigorously judged in a Franciscan manner, but rather pragmatically, with a tinge of Jesuitism. In politics, the moral principle has value through its social effects; if it were supposed that all governments should be moral, not even theocracies would stand the tests of rightfulness. We cannot practice politics following an exclusively ethical handbook, which does not mean that politics should turn into voluntarism, or an irrational, arbitrary or scandalous behavior. Ethics involves imperatives destined to set man at ease with himself, building a comfortable environment in his relationships with men and Divinity.

The criticism brought to political power by the intellectuals is worthless when intellectuals themselves come into politics and there is nothing left of the idealism and enthusiasm previous to "going into politics". A good example here is the failure of the parties built on the foundation of intellectuals' associations (in Romania, the Civic Alliance Party). The most important thing the intellectuals should admit is that in politics, and this is all the more valid in democratic regimes, the primordial thing is the politicians' career and calling. Without a degree of respect for the specialization of functions in society, intellectuals can easily be drawn to the temptation of Messianism.

Instead, politics suggests structuring inter-human relationships in terms of power, in the sense of a criterion of optimal ordering, of community survival. We must make the distinction between the political, seen as a system, and politics, i.e. the daily political activity of groups or people. From this angle, the political cannot be involved or compromised in the conflicts between various social forces (that belong to politics), as it belongs to the structural level of society. Political power is nothing but the most specialized form of social power; it does not pursue, or should not pursue, anything but the preservation and evolution of the system on a competitive scale. Carl Schmitt was of the opinion that politics itself can reduce its motives and actions to a relation of the type friend-enemy, emphasizing the fact that a particular community is a political body only inasmuch as it has enemies. Here the adepts of Aristotelianism would say, not without hypocrisy – indispensable to social life – that politics is an objective force inherent to human nature and society. **In morals you must act fair, in politics you must win the game.**

To round it up, the most realist position that the political and intellectual elites should adopt within Romanian society is that of an acute "communicational pragmatism".

9.6. The political pact: a solution, an opportunity...

The mitigation of conflicts while building democratic institutions, when these would not resist pressures from the political environment, necessitates a pact to be signed among social elites. In order to avoid transforming the political pact into a deal among several groups interested in taking over the power without an electoral competition, it is necessary to establish, from the very beginning, the targets envisaged by the political forces making up the pact, as well as the time limit in which these targets are to be reached. If we have a procedural conception of democracy, and not one of the "popular democracy" type, the political pact among elites does not threaten democracy, but on the contrary, offers guarantees in order to consolidate it.

Launching a process of configuration of certain political wills, together with stopping the crisis in Romanian society, might represent natural consequences of the political pact. This would constitute not only an opening of the process of structuring political pragmatism, but it would at the same time represent its very defining element. The issue of the political pact is that of reshaping the political behaviors and attitudes of the parties, and this cannot be reduced to a mere political show-off.

The idea of a political pact is not a novelty in the stands of leaders or political groups. Sometimes, the issue was so superficially presented, that it appeared that its practical application would only depend on the goodwill of the decisional cores in various parties. Goodwill, though necessary, is far from being sufficient.

Concerning the political pact, there may be issues that on the one hand are not explicitly formulated, and on the other hand surpass, at the present moment, the capacity of the parties to formulate an answer. For instance there can be aspects relating to the inclusiveness of the pact: parties, unions, various discrete structures of civil society; or to its content: goals or normative acts in a certain succession, together with the political modalities through which this succession is to be launched and finalized. The main difficulty of constituting the pact would consist of the identification of the political elites making up the civil society partners. A too great participation of the organizations of civil society would considerably dilute the content of the pact, due to the multitude of interests at stake. Selecting just a few organizations of civil society would raise the problem of their being representative of the social body they claim their own. All this, because Romanian civil society is still an atomized, non-coagulated space.

As regards the political pact, the intellectual elites have not yet specified the structure of their motivations, or their approach of the issue. Even in the conditions of applying the idea of a political pact, Romanian society will only record a superficial political show. This would be valid even in the case of a maximal efficiency of the relations between the political and intellectual elites. Unfortunately, there are no premises for Romania to reach the situation of Spain after "Los Pactos de la Moncloa". The phenomena generated by putting into practice the substitute of a political pact would lead to an aggravation of the relations between the two elites. Compromising the idea of a political pact would in fact equale failing, on a long term, the opportunity of solving political crises in this way.

A political pact between the main political and social forces in Romania, negotiated for a few years' time, would mean solving the greatest problem of a democratic system: the incapacity of conceiving a long-term societal project in the circumstances of permanent political struggle. It is a deficiency all the more marked with negative consequences for the states – like Romania – attempting to go from one type of social system to another considered to be more efficient. Pluralist democracies, under permanent pressure from the electorate, cannot elaborate long-term projects, and not even projects for a period of time going beyond the electoral calendar.

CHAPTER TEN

POLITICAL ROMANIA – THE GAME OF SUBSTANCELESS FORMS

"Political ideas are those adopted by men who do not have their own"

Frederic Dard

10.1 Ideological discourse and the carousel of political parties

In the Romania of the 1990's, parties adopted names by which they attempted to legitimate their belonging to ideologies already consecrated in the political space of Western democracies. The appropriated ideological discourses tried to reproduce notorious topics, circulated and attributed to their "homologous" parties in societies with democratic traditions. This was also characteristic of political groups whose names could not be directly linked to certain ideological features.

Romanian parties ignored certain aspects specific to the behavior of those Western political families, which they had adopted as models. This situation was particularly possible because of the fact that the "doctrinal history" of a particular ideological type of identification is permanently brought up to date by an intellectual elite, not necessarily a politically militant one. Political parties and the groups that directly influence them benefit from "radiographies" of the state of society, analyses that can easily be transposed into synthetic, daily language. To this type were circumscribed the main political directions lying at the basis of electoral competitions. The goals were, generally speaking, targeted with a view to certain sectors of society, and not its entire apparatus. Electoral competitions had as their "bone of contention" several well-delimited aspects of society: budget, education, foreign policies, health etc., but this did not mean cutting down the populist promises.

The attempt of autochthonous parties to "align" to established democracies consisted mostly of a superficial transformation of the sector-based targets into general targets, essential for society as a whole. The ideological results and the political language specific to electoral competitions – products of a less publicized doctrinal work – were identified with the very doctrinal contents. We can even say that at the origin of the liberal and social-democratic "solutions", in their local variants, lies in fact a confusion that continues to fuel political phenomena. This situation, however, leads to direct consequences on the evolution of Romanian society at large. This is why the main concern of parties should be, for a while at least, the formation of a strategic electorate. This electorate should be taught how to regard the vote through the formulation of judgments, and not from the perspective of emotional responses or electoral promises. It may happen many times that political parties influence the social environment in which they activate, rather than being themselves influenced. Until now, Romanian parties were not preoccupied with forming a clearly structured, stable electorate; they addressed, mostly during the electoral campaigns, all potential voters by means of mass media. This pretension to representing the interests of the entire nation, a claim that clearly reminds us of the model of the unique party, as well as the adoption by the entire political spectrum of the values of free market and political liberalism, led to the loss of the political identity of Romanian parties in the eyes of the people.

As regards the organizational party structures, hierarchy is quasi-sacred. In fact, parties tried to reproduce most of the doctrinal principles of the late Communist Party, principles that were never really applied. The most visible effect of this attitude is the persistence of the system of "integrationist" parties (mass parties, with numerous membership) to the detriment of a representational party system, much more flexible and much less costly.

The evolution of all parties' structures was marked by obsessions of the type "internal democracy", "eligibility of party members", "democratic relationships between territorial organizations and the decisional core", the 'oligarchization' of leadership etc. All these led to a general instability of the party system, by endless division into fractions – dissensions which are characteristic to Romanian parties. Internal party stability can only be obtained by strong, centralized leadership, in control of local organizations and that is able to select candidates for eligible positions, to integrate various internal factions and to mediate between various interest groups within and without the party. Thus resulted unstable hierarchies and party structures, as well as politicians maladapted to party integration (especially among those without experience, originated form the Romanian Communist Party). The outcome of these situations constituted, from the point of view of organizational maturity, factors of dysfunctionality which still continue to be strongly active at party level.

It often happens that Romanian parties display organizational paradoxes. One of the formulas would be that in which territorial organizations promptly react to the command of the decisional core only in exchange for advantages at the level of party hierarchy, or in exchange for major political options, such as alliances or mergers with other political groups. Another formula would be that in which local and often personal or group interests have priority over the interests of the party they belong to. Within one party, political attitudes and behaviors of the decisional cores might sometimes determine, at the level of their own hierarchical structures, different significations of the same political attitudes and behaviors. Typical for such a case is the way in which territorial organizations perceive and process at the level of the informational background the messages of certain "political shows" launched, by means of mass media, by their own decisional cores. At this level, party supporters are often mistaken for alleged members of the respective party. The essential difference between the two categories consists only of the fact that, whereas party members have facilities in acceding to power structures, party supporters do not enjoy this advantage.

The differences signaled out have entailed, and continue to do so, a series of consequences in the field of consolidating Romanian political parties. Above all, we must notice the consolidation of a mechanism of ideological mimetism, functioning inertly, though organization has nothing to do with ideology. At the level of political parties, this is still generating mental and behavioral automatisms relatively independent from what has been going on within Romanian society. Another consequence is the illusion entertained by political parties concerning the true capacity of the Executive to make coherent decisions on economic reform. We must emphasize the fact that, in most situations, the true capacity is completely different from that imagined at the level of programmatic intention.

10.2 The doctrinal paradox: beneficial imperative or necessary compromise?

I expect the political scenery to witness, soon enough, significant political restructuring. First of all, there will start off processes of doctrinal configuration within the liberal and social-democratic ideological areas. Today there no longer exists a system that answers all political problems. There are no longer books or programs that provide all explanations or solutions. The answers must be invented or discovered. Herein lies the difficulty of today's politics.

At the level of concepts specific to the liberal type of ideological discourse, there may occur an inclusion of the idea that it is necessary to have state intervention with the purpose of accelerating the process of capital concentration. This process displays a tendency of focusing mainly on unproductive domains, which is generative of crises. Consequently, there may be necessary eventual corrections and the clasification of notions claiming the selective intervention of state institutions. These attitudes would be mainly determined by the efficiency of certain financial levers at the disposal of the state. The action would be oriented, coherently, towards redirecting capital from the profit-making commercial areas towards those directly productive or those of consumer services, of maximal social usefulness.

A similar situation, in principle, would occur in the case of the concepts specific to the social-democratic ideological discourse. This type of discourse might gradually accept, either the idea of restraining the prerogatives of certain state institutions, or that of radically transforming these state institutions. This would occur as a consequence of the present type of implication of the state in the management processes of structural economic readjustment or the management of privatization. It is enough to recall the amplification and extension of both bureaucratic networks and corruption. The complex processes of allotting resources, the impossibility of checking on their efficiency, to which one must add the influence of the perverse effects that would occur, all these lead to the delayed effectiveness of the productive processes integrated to the competitive market system. For this reason, it is possible that this option should necessitate the direct state intervention in favor of types of economic activities, whatever the type of capital, on condition of promoting new technologies or effective forms of managerial behavior. Thus can be determined the formation of sector-based policies, initiated by the Executive, with a view to unmediated support for private enterprises.

Once included in political discourses, the paradoxes signaled before will determine, even irrespective of the will and programmatic intent of the parties, modifications in the daily perception of the political space. These will function as pressure factors both on the streamlining of political parties, and in the area of the relations between them. They will therefore have direct consequences on the setting off and support of the reorganization of the entire Romanian political spectrum. **There exists here a marked tendency in all democratic systems, i.e. that of doctrinal resemblances between parties and consequently of losing their political identity.** This situation can be given several explanations. One of these would be the globalization process that all economies are undergoing, a process entailing a dramatic shortage of options for national governments. Another explanation could be found during electoral campaigns, when, in their attempt at drawing undecided voters over their side, parties bring their political discourses so close to the others' that they ultimately tend to overlap. In this case we are dealing with what electoral sociology calls "choiceless elections".

The possibility of transforming daily perceptions into other types of mental and behavioral automatisms presupposes, at the same time, enhancing the degree of acceptability and credibility for new alliances and political games. This aspect should prove significant for parties, i.e. it should make them more sensitive and determine them to proceed to conceptual reshuffling, even in the circumstances of some kind of inertia of ideological discourse or of the explicit desire to oppose it. In any situation under crisis, the most dynamic elements (not necessarily the oldest) learn how to incorporate the threat that lies at the basis of new kinds of "games", in an apparent indifference towards systemic turmoil. Gradually, or concomitantly with the increase in the political participation to the system, new political and/or social forces will enter the political stage. This pressure coming from the outsiders will force the 'traditional' political parties to settle deals among themselves, even to form political alliances, in order to maintain the positions they fill within the system.

In a certain sense, most Romanians found themselves, after 1989, to be immigrants in an unmapped land, in an environment where changes and mobility sought to impose themselves as main 'protective' factors in front of the new challenges. This is why one must understand that interactivity is the most important dimension of political communication and of social behavior. The Romanian political stage has been divided into two camps, along simplistic cleavage lines, as it happened in the beginning with the line between communists and anti-communists, and later on that between reformists and conservatives. Between the two sides, the political dialogue has been fractured from the start by the intransigence of the participants, or it has been carried out by means of mass media. Any communication that took place so far between the Romanian political parties, characterized by the reciprocation of accusations, irreducible positions adopted by the participants and the lack of arguments, has been rather an example of how *not to communicate* in a democracy.

10.3 Ideological discourse – a secondary discourse?

At present, the process of political shake-up is going through a difficult period. The solution to this state of fact depends largely on the goodwill of the parties to take significant action in this direction.

Romanian political parties have always invoked the shaping of a set of fundamental goals as being priorities of a normal evolution. This was done in a more or less doctrinal way, using means which they sometimes sought to 'ideologize'. Gandhi used to say that the end is never superior to the means; post-revolutionary parties have tried to impose a certain direction to the social dynamics in relation to their own programmatic ends. It is not a risky overstatement, that the Christian-democrat ideology is, within the Romanian political field, the exponent of a minor political trend, in terms of programs and applicability of ideas perceived in a certain way in traditionally Catholic environments, and differently perceived within Romanian society.

A preoccupation for breaking out of the relatively inert regime of Romanian politics would imply a genuine doctrinal reconstruction, following communication between political and intellectual elites. Thus would be founded a new type of ideological discourse, in which ideology would no longer preserve the memory of 'indoctrination' or 'officialization', but would become socialization, temperance and genuine search for consensual indices. This would entail significant changes at the level of perception and everyday behaviors, which behaviors, in their turn, would become factors of constant support, but also of influence as regards the changes within the political field. From this perspective, the problem of doctrinal reconstruction is essential, if only the process is not mistaken for the more superficial aspects of ideological discourse – itself a 'guardian' of serious issues merely within the playground of electoral images. We must also admit that, within the rule-of-law, in which democracy – viewed institutionally – functions at normal parameters, the confrontations circumscribed to the political field can be largely associated to a normal type of game, carried on according to specific rules regarding the ratio of forces at the government and oppositional levels.

Seen from the perspective of its conditions of development, the political game has different consequences at the general level of society.

Within societies marked by transition and underdevelopment, its effects are completely others than in the cases where transition has been consumed, and development is a constant and visible process.

After the fall of the communist regimes, two fundamental problems came up and stayed on within the respective states: coming out of economic underdevelopment, together with the materialization and consolidation of the institutions of the rule-of-law and civil society. So far, there seem to have been used two ways out of underdevelopment: one specific to the European area, the other peculiar to the Asian regions. The relation between democracy and market economy is today subjected to heated debates within economic and political environments. Empirical evidence so far seems to justify three conclusions: there is no example of a democratic state which does not exercise a system of market economy; there are, on the other hand, enough examples of states practicing market economy and, at the same time, authoritarian types of government; when market economy advances, there inevitably appear pressures to democratize society.

In the case of certain Asian countries – South Korea and the four states from the South-East of the yellow continent – the first of these problems found its solution by exercising forms, more or less acute, of authoritarianism, or authoritarian modernization at the level of state institutions – a phenomenon also visible in Japan. The countries of South-Eastern Asia are characterized by a particular form of capitalism, a state capitalism. The problem of the democratization of society can only find solutions if the essential aspects of economic development are dealt with. It is in the nature of capitalism to secretly nourish and perhaps to start out the democratic forces. Capitalism inevitably gives birth to a middle class. As it grows in number and importance, it will have political claims against the authoritarian regime. From this point of view, there are 'signs' which can lead to the idea that China, too, will follow in the same track, in slightly different forms. Therefore, it would seem characteristic to the Asian model to settle the two types of problems in consecutive sequences.

The European model, characteristic to countries such as Greece and Portugal, has as its main coordinate the simultaneity of the two solutions. The simultaneous settlement of the two fundamental issues imposed itself in the case of Eastern-European countries, as well. The explanation to this approach consists in both their geographical location, in the proximity of developed countries, as well as in the relative similitude of their cultural models. We are here talking about a certain sense to be found in the construction of political will in all these countries. Their political diversity is already 'limited' by the European model mentioned before. This political will may or may not be 'politically charged'; this aspect is irrelevant. What is important is its existence as such, within the limits imposed by the model. In fact, when discussing the chance of solving these problems, we might state that, in reality, this is largely just an equation whose terms boil down to the present-day characteristics of Romanian society, and to the problem of developed countries.

For Romania, the number one priority after the fall of the communist regime was, and I am confirmed by any retrospective approach, building solid institutions that, on the other hand, were to replace the old ones, and on the other hand had to mirror the values of that type of society we wanted to accomplish. By institutions I mean judicial, administrative and habitual systems, which shape human relations within a given society. The institutions were to be followed by a set of laws and rules, clearly formulated and obeyed by all. What we have today is a tangled legislative system, which needs urgent simplification and clarification. The principle that has to inspire us in this action is not that of Ulpian, '*Lex dura est, sed scripta est*', but '*Lex dura est, sed certa est*', the law being grounded on the authority conferred by the institution of the state. Failing these conditions, Romanian society is still dominated by uncertainty and unpredictability, deficiencies especially resented by those who are engaged, or intend to be engaged in economic activities.

The main political parties are convinced of the 'truth' of certain realities colored by partisan lenses, and act accordingly. Until now, at least, there are no signs leading to the idea that the main political forces might have the capacity or intention to modify this perception. Symptomatic for this is the transformation of ideological and moral categories into economic categories, or the other way around. More specifically, out of categories belonging to economic doctrines have been deducted, by simple operations of association or symmetry, principles of political conduct, ideological stands and even moral grounds.

The inertial regime specific to the ideological realm is characteristic of the crisis through which the main Romanian parties are going, a phenomenon amplified by the irregularity of the circulation of elites within these parties. The alchemy of ideological confusion sets under doubt the competence of the largest part of party elites. Party elites are perceived as the 'space' in which there comfortably function the decision-making cores of the parties; mass media have a major role in disseminating this partially true idea. There are other opinions that equate party elites to the party's founding members, or at least to its 'genetic nucleus', even though, at least at an informal level, the groups in search of re-formation of the political action programs are actively contesting the 'founding principles'. It is quite clear that the beginning of the 21st century will impose on the Romanian political class a clarification of the initial conceptual systems, in the sense of more accurately defining the terms of ideology, doctrine, political doctrine.

There is a high probability of turning into a permanent state the ambiguous and confusing functioning of parties at the level of the relation between, on the one hand, their political and moral-ideological attitudes, and, on the other hand, the issues concerning economic solutions. In other words, there is a high probability that the parties carry on with their ideological inertia, which will have a direct consequence: ignoring the limit between their own specific attitudes, and the moral and political reasons. Romanian political parties will be confronted with the following option: they either restructure their attitude towards reality under the pressure of their ideological stand, or they adapt their ideology in order to justify, after the fact, their attitude towards reality. At present, parties are still going through the first stage. No doubt, sooner or later they will be forced to adopt the second variant, thus risking to massively erode their credibility in the eyes of the public.

Locating a political formation to the 'left' or 'right' of the political spectrum will remain, under these circumstances, a mere declarative intention, an attribute of the political show, in which what is at stake is the electoral image, and not the doctrinal substance. The conclusion is self-evident, considering also that ideology represents the first stage in a process of assuming an identity on the political stage. Romanian political parties practice what George Orwell called '*doublethink*'. On the one hand, they preach total adherence to the ideology they represent, on the other, parties are aware of the fact that everything their platforms contain is untrue, or, at best, ideas inapplicable to Romanian realities.

Ideology justifies the difference between parties by situating them at different lengths from a reference point. Through ideology, members and supporters of a certain party find their identity in a certain existing cultural model within the social and political realms of society. The model is that which has the capacity to offer, at the same time, the motivational set of options in favor of a certain party; the problem is whether these options are, some of them, strategic or emotional.

Beyond all spectacular theoretical reasons, ideology does not have the force to settle efficiently the fundamental problems confronting a certain society. It can, at best, create the illusion of remedying them. There can be no serious project of social development unless it takes into consideration its degree of applicability and its appropriateness to the means owned by society at that particular time. **This is why, compared to the identification and solving of real issues, ideology is merely a secondary discourse.** Sometimes there is a false feeling, that a certain ideology died out or remained merely as a political label. In reality, there were merely radical modifications to the main components of the discourse, these equating with an adaptation to the call of reality.

'Left' and 'right' constitute only the fundament of existence and identity of political parties, which is completed with the option for defining certain moral attitudes and values. Against this evidence, political formations in Romania continue to make efforts to identify, within the mentioned fundaments, the justifying arguments of doctrines as 'carrying' solutions to the economic realm, and the realm of society in general.

However, we must keep in mind an unpredictable element: the intellectual elites. The intellectuals, as a social group, are subject to an irreversible decline, visible in all post-communist societies. The communist state used to support them by subsidies granted to creative unions, cultural journals etc. Now all these are gone, and this has given rise to the intellectuals' feeling of uselessness and to their 'repression' in building ideologies understood as unitary systems of belief, claiming to explain social reality. The issue of the moral fundaments of ideological options – and, from these, of political options – is, or should be, the object of theoretical reconstructions, discussions and even disputes, which is a preoccupation specific especially to the intellectual elites. The Romanian political right has a thematic agenda dominated by the subjects imposed by the intellectual groups close to the right: de-communizing Romanian society by a law of lustration, giving up national prerogatives to the detriment of a hypothetical integration into the 'civilized world', disregarding certain social groups, which lack 'democratic political culture' (such as the workers or the civil servants apparatus).

Within the realm of Romanian politics, the intellectual elites have not confined themselves to sympathies towards a certain orientation, but have also become involved, sometimes effectively, in the party structure. The model of the intellectual doubled by a politician is no longer contemporaneous, it being rather a residue of European romanticism. It is highly possible, however, that the intellectual elites get 'swallowed' by politics from the moment they assume involvement in a non-specific domain. This phenomenon might be motivated by the fact that, in the attempt to restructure the political stage, parties cannot do without at least part of the intellectual elites.

One of the most frequently debated issues in Romania is that of 'post-communism'. This problem was developed by a large part of the intellectual elites from the political right. It is also the reason for which the decision-making cores of political parties have adopted this issue as a fundamental doctrinal element, and, whenever necessary, as electoral issue. It is essential here that parties "ideologized" especially the conclusion, ignoring the demonstration.

It is very much true that the type of political power set in after 1989, even though it did not constitute a supporting factor, it did not impede on the continuity of the system of connections and clientele. Sometimes, the phenomenon was even amplified.

In 1989, in the whirl of accusations and unveiling of everything pertaining to the communist regime, we did not realize that the opposite of communism is not anti-communism, which sometimes resembles it very much, but tolerance in social relations and within the rule-of-law. We fell too easily prey to the temptation of evading a communism with a Bolshevik face in favor of an anti-communism with a Bolshevik face. Romanian society was thus transformed into a public fairground, and public life turned into a public court of law, where personal revenge was extracted under the guise of morality. Thus acting, we did not take into consideration several factors.

First of all, we did not take into consideration the example of the societies which opted for forgiving the past and refusing collective guilt, such as France, Italy and Austria after the second world war, Spain after 1975 or South Africa after the apartheid. Then, we did not operate the distinction between types of collaborationism: those who collaborated out of conviction, those who collaborated because of their specific profession, those who enjoyed collaborating with the 'Securitate' and those who simply practiced denouncement. When the Law of Lustration was to be applied in the Czech Republic, the European Council protested that human rights were thus violated. It is not irrelevant that in the countries where the Law of Lustration was radically applied – the Czech Republic, the former Democrat Germany – today are very popular those parties which openly claim their origin in communism: The Czech Republic's Communist Party ranks first in public opinion polls, and the German Party of Democratic Socialism managed to accede to the German Parliament, the Bundestag, though it only collected votes from the former East-German counties. The only explanation is that the citizens of these countries do not rejoice in revenge, or the public vendetta. In a climate dominated by this kind of disputes, people will come to wish for the peace and quietness ensured by the old regime. Between these two dangers, excessive labeling and 'where are the snows of yesteryear', one feels the need for a vast political project that would map out a direction for society.

Another overlooked truth was that the reconstruction of the country could not be done without the civil servants apparatus of the old regime. Kurt Biedenkopf, leader of the German Christian-Democratic Union and governor of the Saxonia-Anhalt county (belonging to the former GDR), admitted to the fact that, in order to reconstruct Germany, the administrative and civil servants elite of the old regime was needed, just as Western Germany needed the Nazi administrative apparatus after the second world war.

'The moralists of transition' did not understand the fact that there could not be judges while those times are still so close to today, and while there is an emotional involvement of the accusers. Only a temporal distance large enough will allow for a proper understanding of the events of that particular period. Facts must be weighed carefully, placed in their historical context, and the interpretation must take place by intellectual distancing, but also by empathy with the others.

Finally, we must not forget that the personal act of remembering, the personal conscience, always have precedence before the public anticommunist summons, dominated by vanity and appearance. Throughout the final period of the communist regimes, the social climate was full of lies, conformity and daily compromises. No one could escape this state of fact. No one was merely a victim, all were co-responsible. The line that separates the guilty from the innocent goes through each individual.

An outlook that aims at replacing one utopia with another only leads to a repetition of the state of facts which generated the fall of the initial utopia. This statement is all the more valid for Romanian society, prey to the simplistic ideology - supported by the intellectual groups of the political right – of passing from integral communism to integral capitalism, without taking into consideration the people's ability to adapt to this change.

The topic of restoration can be interesting for politicians as well, when chosen as a subject of intellectual debate or journalistic confrontation. However, in no case can it ever constitute an essential issue of the crisis of Romanian society. Essential are the modifications of the institutional patterns through which any individual can more clearly structure a certain political option, knowing that this presupposes processes of evaluation, valorization and adherence to a scale of values.

The democratization of decisional mechanisms, of the social control over political power, setting off the 'ideological dialogue', all these are a challenge, among others, to the doctrinal actualization of social democracy. We even see how the Blair-Schroeder line tries to establish a formula of the type 'The Third Way' in the sense of a social democracy (the term as such is not foreign to German social-democratic thinking). In these circumstances, the chance of restructuring the political stage by means of a doctrinal reconstruction, which at the same time would generate a political will able to entail coherent changes within Romanian society – this chance, then, must go beyond good intentions. The relations between the main parties, of 'political families', must find the path of constructive dialogue, in order to mitigate the antitheses overly emphasized in the 1990-1999 period.

The recent political history of the parties deeply affected their behaviors and relatively disordered attitudes. Here are equally included the incapacity to coherently conceive and build the transformation of Romanian society, and the organizational consolidation of parties in the shape of organic political groups. The reference point is no longer merely their own hierarchies and structures, but also certain significant segments of civil society, without which the parties' modern evolution would be impossible, if we see parties as mediators between society and state power. The reform process can no longer be the exclusive responsibility of the political elite. Civil society will have to get involved, more than it has done so far, in promoting social change. By civil society I mean unions (which should have a wider role than that of placing claims), the Church, intellectuals and the local public government. In order to act, civil society must mobilize itself, but this process is, most of the times, very difficult. **The intelligence of a party consists in evaluating and, when necessary, capturing and channeling the dominant stream of opinion in the desired direction.**

Today's social structure is in full transformational process. Different segments of population are far from having concluded the outline of their political attitudes and behaviors. Here are included the coordinates characterized by relative stability, on which parties can count in electoral confrontations and with whose help they can carry on 'institutional' relations. Emotional reactions are still dominant in the configuration of electoral attitudes and behaviors.

Also interesting is the beginning of the formation of rule-of-law institutions, and of those that regulate market economical relations. These should function as institutions, not as interpersonal relationships. The shaping of institutions is not over when their formal regulations are elaborated. It is necessary to allow for a period of time in which people get used to, and accept these regulations. The reassessment of property structures is still at the beginning, and the enterprising behavior is not considered as natural as it happens in capitalist societies. This is why it is with difficulty that we can state that, in the following years, autochthonous political trends – liberal or social-democrat – can detect their real correspondences to their peers in the developed European countries. This does not mean that any ideological transposition, meant to reproduce consecrated formulae from other political realms, is considered useless from the start.

One first signal as regards the changes that affect the West-European political field was set off by the dispute between the pragmatic and the ideological approaches. The theoretical disputes – in which the West-European intellectual elites are involved – are partially taken over by the Romanian intellectual elites. As a consequence, we are witnessing the affirmation of perspectives which announce more or less spectacular upheavals of the relation between pragmatism and ideology. In all appearances, this relation would come to characterize, in the near future, the political behavior of parties, especially since 'absenteism' and volatility set one thinking as to how willing is civil society to assume the 'participative culture', in the sense that the political class gives to this phrase. After long years of silent acceptance of the abuses of the communist regime's discretionary powers, the post-Decembrist period meant a heated contestation of both Government and opposition, in a climate of total confusion. It did not take long, and Romanian society moved on from too high expectations from the political system, to a generalized pessimism as regards the possibilities of coming out of the economic and social crisis, and to lack of trust in the political system as a whole. Instead of assimilating elements of political culture, the population started to judge politics cynically. The estrangement of people from politics is a process with potentially negative consequences for Romanian democracy, which is still *in statu nascendi.* **The society demands clear political answers to the complex problems of transition; Romanian parties are either incapable of providing these answers, or, if they do, the answers prove to disagree with reality. It is a vicious circle that has perpetrated itself for the last ten years.**

Ignoring the problem of the underdevelopment of Romanian society by the Government is counterproductive for the destiny of the reform. Likewise, mirroring the issue of the other political areas and personalizing those of Romania, by the intellectual elites, in a discourse with obvious spiteful accents, is simply damaging for the medium-term evolution of our country. Mirroring the forms of institutionalized democracy is a sensitive spot of transition, but a decade is not enough to change the inertia of a world for which political culture had a different sense than in the open societies.

CHAPTER ELEVEN

SOCIAL DEMOCRACY BETWEEN HISTORY AND FUTUROLOGY

"Political life means nothing
without ideals, but ideals are meaningless
if they are not connected to real possibilities
of application."

Anthony Giddens

11.1 Democratizing society – a work of political architecture

No doubt, one of the most widely accepted and most obvious directions of the evolution of humankind is that towards democratization. A civilized humankind is one increasingly democratic, in which the field of human rights extends more or less suddenly, but always surely. Whether we consult authors on the political left or on the ideological right, the necessity of advancing towards democratization seems evident to all. In fact, one of the criteria which delimit the main cleavages between left and right pertains to the gradual nature of democratization. Should we extend the domain of rights and liberties as quickly as possible, or should we be more careful, in order to avoid the possible perverse effects of this reform? This is the dilemma that makes for the delight, but sometimes torture as well, of political debates in the most developed countries. Obviously, this is a mere nuance in comparison to the acceptance of the process itself.

This agreement, that leveled a series of differences and polemics between left and right movements, is a product of the modern epoch. If there was advancement towards democracy in the previous epochs, it could not be recorded as such. There are too many digressions, deviations or even periods of regression, for us to be able to talk about a march towards democracy from the darkest ancient times to this day. Only in the modern epoch can we perceive a relatively constant evolution that has not been too often interrupted and not too severely retarded. If there were degrading regressions – the totalitarian regimes – these either could not be implanted in the geo-political area we are discussing (the Occident), or they did not last long (the fascist and Nazi regimes).

The buds of democratization were visible in antiquity as well, and their metamorphosis into leaves and fruit will doubtlessly continue well beyond the year 2000. However, this relative framework will allow us to better understand the context in which democracy started to be convincing and winning. More important than tracing the history of democracy is to search for a work tool that will enable us to identify unequivocally what the process of democratization really means. The definition that I have somewhat announced at the beginning of the chapter postulates democracy as the extension of social rights, liberty and equality. A complete democracy is that in which the largest number possible of social segments and groups – be they however small in membership – receive rights that are equal to the majority's. I feel bound to warn you here as regards a possible confusion: I am not talking either about utopia, or about the aberrant equalitarianism of the extremist, anarchic-libertarian left!

Everything that I intend to discuss as democratic evolution will be perceived with reference to the moderate left and right, not to their totalitarian deviations. Or, the moderate left is equalitary, not equalitarian, as it happens in the case of its extreme. The moderate left sets as its goal not the abusive uniformization of the entire society, but hindering the appearance and the deepening of certain social inequalities that might have repercussions on the democratic stability of the state. In trying to place social democracy on the axis of political orientations, we can tell that it is best situated under the heading that we might call 'the moderate left'.

In general, the right-wing parties have made a real electoral banner out of religion, presenting themselves as watchdogs of a life led in faith. The left was, and continues to be discredited, in polemics and electoral campaigns. Simply because the modern fathers of the left were most of them atheists, their heirs have been subjected to permanent attacks on this issue – as if atheism were an ineluctable golden standard against which all recruitments of members and theoreticians are made. It may be that the adepts of the radical right do not see it, or it may be that they do not want to admit it, but the truth is completely different: one of the strongest ideological influences on the left was Christianity. This is, in fact, the first stage we shall dwell upon, within our brief excursion into the history of humankind's democratization. Some of the basic ideas of Christianity were recuperated and integrated into one of the largest pools of leftist thought of all times: equality. Christianity was the first major religious, political and intellectual revolution that postulated equality among people and fought with concrete means in order to help it come true. The cases of Athenian democracy or of the Roman republic are rather insular and ephemeral, with no quantitative weight and without historical continuation. They have remained mere metaphors, symbols against which the Renaissance and the trends after the 15th century measured themselves. Unlike these, Christianity was the one that constantly pleaded for the idea of equality among a people, further developing it and carrying it on into modernity.

The conception according to which all men are equal before God was not to remain within the realm of theology only. The temptation of transposing it into political thought was too great, given the inequalities of Western society. Far from remaining faithful to this essential tenet of Christian doctrine, the clergy constituted one of the main sources of social inequality throughout the Middle Ages. However, people did not give up the claim that they are equal before God here, on Earth, as well. At the political level, the first rather ample movement that took over this idea and based its very action and existence on it was that of the British so-called 'levellers'. Without becoming truly important in numbers, this trend took over the topic of equality from Christian thought, transforming it into material for the later leftist ideologies. Many of their ideas were too utopian to be applied at that time, but it is essential to keep in mind that they announced the explosion of leftist doctrines that was to take place with Jean-Jacques Rousseau.

From a chronological point of view, the history of democratization and of the substantial extension of human rights begins together with the French Revolution of 1789. It is a more appropriate example than the American Revolution, as it is mainly concerned with social conflicts – whereas the former British colonies were fighting for national freedom and emancipation from London. In France, however, almost everything was carried on at the social level, at stake being the replacement of absolute monarchy with the Republic and the adoption of a Constitution that would ensure human rights. 'Liberty, equality, fraternity!' is not a mere slogan; it faithfully reflects the leftist origin of the entire political thought behind the French Revolution. L'Ancien Regime, which today we do not hesitate in placing within the purest political right, was a state system totally opposed to the revolutionary ideals of 1789. The pre-revolutionary society was strongly stratified vertically, on a most strict hierarchy. This hierarchical system was characterized by the fact that hereditary origin was almost always equivalent to the social environment in which the individual was condemned to live the entire life.

In this historical moment of the 1789 Revolution were the right-wing and left-wing defined. Evidently, these designations of political fields are rather arbitrary and metaphorical, if we take into consideration the fact that they merely referred to the spatial positioning of the two rival factions in what we might call the ancestor of the French Parliament – the People's Assembly. Beyond these designations, however, we find extremely interesting political realities, perfectly mirroring the primordial and ubiquitous duality of politics at all times: that between conservatives and reformists. It matters less whether we call the antagonists of this duality by metaphors such as left-right, white-black or old-new. What is more important is the dichotomy between those who desire change and those who oppose, more or less radically, the idea of social transformation. It is essential to remember that one of the strongest manifestations of the conflict between left and right happened during the French Revolution. In fact, 1789 was the first concretization of this conflict in the modern epoch. And perhaps even more important than the concrete dimension of this confrontation – revolution, fights, arrests and executions – is the intellectual aspects of the polemics. I am saying this because the French Revolution launched the first modern intellectual debated between the traditionalist-hierarchical right and the reformist-equalitarian left.

The setting up of the First French Republic determined the coagulation of reactionary, aristocratic forces which sought to regain the privileges lost during the 1789 Revolution. Having at their disposal considerable financial and political resources, these forces benefited from an important international lobby, and were supported by many other monarchies which thus felt their own legitimacy to be threatened by the French precedent. Also, the elevated education of this class of aristocrats dispossessed of their assets made possible the appearance of a group of intellectuals very well instructed and capable of representing the interests of this group. Their ideas were constituted into genuine systems of philosophical and political thought, and these can be considered the first pages of the modern right-wing library. In truth, we are dealing here with an interesting, maybe paradoxical situation: each ideological family started developing in a hostile political regime. The first seeds of leftist, equalitarian political doctrines have sprung in full monarchic absolutism – an undisputable right-wing regime. On the other side, the theoreticians of radical conservatism did not make their presence felt as a compact group until after the regime they were defending had been overthrown and replaced with a more equalitarian one. Only then did they realize the extraordinary force of this weapon which ideology represents, from its most prosaic forms (electoral propaganda) to its most elevated manifestations (the systems of philosophy and political theory). Until then, the aristocrats had lived with the false impression that the exercise of power and the possession of political levers within the state are enough to preserve the status quo which favored them. Only in a left-wing regime did they realize that they needed legitimacy, in order to face up to the challenges of their political adversaries. Or, the first source of legitimacy lies in structured political thought, in elaborated doctrines.

Many contemporary political environments, some even from Romania, circulating the statement that liberalism is and always was a right-wing doctrine. This stereotype, through which I believe they merely seek superficial, circumstantial legitimacy, is strange to say the least. When carefully researching the history of political doctrines, it is obvious that liberalism was not born, but became a right-wing trend when it was practically pushed in this direction by the emergence of leftist movements (socialism, collectivist anarchism and eventually communism). At the moment of its emergence, when the authors thought to have pioneered liberal thinking created the systems that laid out the path of this doctrine, liberalism was left-wing. In spite of the enormous variety of movements and trends that claim their origin in liberalism, there are a series of constants which allow their integration in the same category. Among these, two seem essential to the issues we are now analyzing. One of them defines liberalism as a doctrine of freedom, and the other pertains to the attachment of this ideology to equality before the law.

In comparison to radical conservatism, built as a reaction against the French Revolution, original liberalism is an equalitarian philosophy of liberation, and therefore undoubtedly belongs to the political left. The liberal doctrine has various sources, from the empirical philosophy of Locke to the Enlightenment, from James Madison to Jean-Jacques Rousseau, from Montesquieu's essays to the economical doctrines of Adam Smith and Jeremy Bentham, from the liberals of the 19th century (John Stuart Mill and Guizot) to contemporary neo-liberalism (F.A. von Hayek, John Rawls, Karl Popper or Francisco Vergara). If we carefully observe those liberal sources already existing in the 17th-19th centuries and that influenced the French Revolution, we shall see that these are the main doctrines contested by the reactionary intellectuals. They represented that political left completely opposed to the aristocratic conservatism and which became the main political adversary of the right wing at that time. Liberal ideas were targeted by reactionary polemics, no matter what shape these took. From the mystical

Catholicism of Joseph de Maistre to the fundamental Catholicism of Donoso Cortes, from the aristocratic hierarchism of Louis de Bonald to the ulterior writings of Hyppolite Taine and Ernest Renan or the moderate conservatism of John Burke, all reactionary literature formulated a vehement criticism targeting democracy, liberalism and equalitarian ideals.

This polemics between the left and right continued throughout the entire 19th century, until the period after the First World War. The only modification interesting to our topic is the passage of liberalism to the right side of the political axis, following the affirmation of socialist and social-democratic trends. The equalizing and radical democratic accents that these movements assumed have been the essential factor that pushed liberalism to the right. Socialism was a new kind of thinking, and yet fully mature when the question of universal vote was raised in the European states (with the exception of France). Practically, the universal vote is the first great conquest of the process of democratizing European societies during the modern period. It is eminently the result of leftist political and philosophical thought, and of the pressure of the masses, then at the beginning of their political participation.

The universal vote can be considered a signal that triggered a chain reaction of extending rights and liberties. Only after the introduction of universal vote can we talk about the power of the people in real terms. Despite all perverse effects caused by the emergence, in political life, of masses inexperienced in the democratic practice, the universal electoral right was a groundbreaker for other liberties. No doubt, right-wing parties of today no longer have the inflexible tone of the conservatism of the early 19th century, as it now fully accepts the value and necessity of democratic reforms. However, evolved democracy, as we see it in the developed countries that hold this political tradition, is the product of leftist efforts and ideas. If we consider the electoral representation of the two great political tendencies, the above statement is even more clearly confirmed. Right-wing political ideas defended the interests of the privileged social categories or, if not, the interests of the middle class, then still in the making. These social categories had no interest in changing the social order based on hierarchy and stratification, as this would have entailed the annulment of certain privileges held by them. It is not erroneous to state that right-wing movements were born and preserved, to a certain extent, as elitist movements. On the other hand, left-wing ideologies have always identified with the interests of the many, quantitatively superior, but hierarchically underprivileged. These masses were the ones that took an interest in reform in the sense of equalizing opportunities, and left-wing thinkers were those who theorized this necessity.

To conclude this brief historical excursion, it is most important to keep in mind that the democratization of a society is an incontestable token of its degree of civilization. This process is not finished by far, and it still goes on to this day. We may even say that this is a perpetual tendency that will never find itself exhausted. In society there will always exist tendencies to accumulate, to monopolize privileges de facto or de jure, to usurp, one way or the other, the right to equality of opportunity. We have to understand the process of democratization as an act of political will and responsibility, rather than as an immanent law of history. Only the constant effort of left-wing parties was able to transform this process into a genuine evolutionary symbol of Western civilization. It is likely that in the future it will take the same effort from the political groups and elites that desire the extension of human rights and liberties, as well as the social equality of all. Social democracy came out victorious, loosely speaking, in its fight with exacerbated elitism and social oligarchies. Today we can say that it will be one of the main actors involved in the battle for the future, as it has accumulated a considerable capital of legitimacy, force and prestige. The entire Europe is dominated by this political-intellectual family. In order to win the battle for the future, social democracy must remain constantly a leading representative of democracy, of the extension and equalization of human rights.

11.2 Romania and the social-democratic option

Why do we plead, today, for a social-democratic Romania? How can we speak of the future of social democracy in Romania, as long as there is no local tradition in this respect? This is one of the questions often asked by those who think that Romania's political history has exclusively relied on a right-wing tradition, and that our country should remain faithful to this path. The argument seems to me highly superficial, especially since it is not entirely true. It is true that modern Romania was preponderantly inclined to the right, and more so during the last decade of the inter-war period; but that does not mean there were no left-wing political tendencies.

However, this aspect is not as important as one might think. At any rate, it is not reason enough to abandon a social-democratic path of development. Neither does Romania compare to the centuries of experience accumulated by Great Britain, the United States or France in the field of democratic tradition; still, that does not mean that we must give up the dream of having a consolidated democratic regime. Tradition, as we have so often seen in history, is not the most important factor of decision as concerns the opportunity or undesirability of a large-scale social transformation. If it were not thus, we should be condemned never to reach the democratic evolution and stability we are craving for today, and there would be no point in raising the issue of a battle for the future. The lack of experience and tradition can be compensated where there is political will, responsibility and consistency. These are the arguments we must rely on in the future. We must not fall prey to that cynical and resigned pessimism that has conquered a good part of the Romanian public opinion and implies gloomy, even nihilist perspectives on Romania's chances to build a solid future. This attitude had led to nothing good, and never will, except maybe for metaphors and literary essays. It is rather a small thing on which to build the future of a country. I am not saying we should trust in a cloudless, carefree future, because things are not so. The future is unknown, and therefore all the more interesting. It depends on us whether it will come close to resembling our ideals or it will bring about nothing but disappointment.

What does it mean to win the battle for the future from the social-democratic perspective? I think that the most appropriate sense we can find in victory, from this point of view, is the capacity of adapting to the permanent renewal of essential evolutionary tendencies. We have seen that the tendency of democratizing society is in a perpetual evolution, that rights and liberties are continually extending their domain, against restrictions and authoritarianism. In those geographical areas where this tendency is missing, civilization lies at a very low evolutionary level. We can only consider to be fully advanced that society capable of facing up to the extraordinary challenge of democratization. Allowing individual and collective rights to evolve freely, without repercussions on state order, seems to me an ideal worth following, though highly exacting. Both the political class and civil society need to make colossal efforts in order to reach this goal. Still, before any concrete effort, there must exist an a priori quality indispensable for this commitment: the will to mature democratically. No one can hit the road to anywhere without first setting a precise destination. If we know from the beginning that our destination is democratic maturity and development, then we can set out.

It is in this context that one must understand the opportunity of Romania's option for social democracy. It is evident that this doctrine, together with its ideological 'fathers', was the one that accompanied and determined the process of democratization of civilized societies, and that this doctrine was the propeller of this historical process. In order to face the battle with the future, Romania must connect perfectly to this propeller, to get to know it and use it for its own ends. It is crucial that Romanian society become aware of this necessity now, while it is not too late. And I do not have in mind merely the threat of the country's economic and social destabilization, but, maybe more pressingly, the risk of people's apathy and lack of interest in the democratic values. It is inadmissible that the appetite of Romanians for these values, strongly manifest in 1989 and immediately after, be altered by a mere historical accident, such as the 1996-2000 governance. This is why social democracy is called to restore the process of democratizing Romanian society, and to mend the errors committed in the last years. As guarantor and propelling force of democratization, social democracy has the duty of pulling the country out of this crisis, or at least of dealing with the domains where the crisis is most acute. Not having a rich experience of democratic practice, Romania needs to be carefully trained for the extension of rights and liberties, for a wider power granted to the people. How will this initiation be effected, and what exactly will it have to rehabilitate?

For lack of honest and impartial civic associations, social democracy will have to assume the role of educator in the process of assimilating democratic values. Social democracy has the necessary legitimacy and force to fulfill this ideal. Moreover, I believe social democracy is most necessary for Romania, as our country lives at present under the burden of striking social inequalities. We need to educate the citizens with a view to the social-democratic morals and philosophy. The corruption of late, often lurking in the darkest corners of the government, has determined the dramatic impoverishment of a majority of the population, to the profit of a category that we can no longer call financial elite, but rather 'the Mob'. The members of these groups have not earned their present positions, but took possession of them through thievery, to the detriment of public and private property. Their emancipation from among the masses and their lack of scruples, which both characterize them, gave birth to a most serious threat: that of setting up a delinquent oligarchy. Any oligarchy is undesirable, and all the more it is so with a mob-type oligarchy. Before it is too late, Romanians must do something so that their country does not become a battlefield of various clans and illegal organizations. I see no other solution but an education inculcating the equalitarian imperatives of social democracy. This is the only doctrine that postulates the necessity of social equality. Supposing all right-wing parties of Romania were made up of honest and well-wishing people, their accession to power would be almost just as inappropriate at this time. A doctrine that allows and even pleads for inequality is not able to put a stop to the unjust inequalities that have proliferated like the plague. Social democracy is the only ideology capable of rejecting this plague, of turning allergic to it.

I have tried to justify here, briefly as it may have been, the opportunity of a social-democratic option in Romania. In the present-day crisis, this option becomes rather an imperative. It is the only solution that, if applied now, would allow the successful launching of Romania towards the march for the future. Reducing social inequality, educating people for civic and economic involvement, filling in the void of ethical and political authority created by governance errors – all these are aspects that make up and accompany a process of democratization. This is what the gist of the battle for the future comes down to, and this battle need not be concluded with one winner only. Romania could be one of its laureates, just as the states already developed in this respect. If our country will manage in attaining this goal, then it will have come to the ideal situation in which a state can afford to extend the domain of individual rights and liberties, to emphasize social equality and justice, without at the same time losing in authority or efficiency. Social democracy is a solution worth taking into consideration, as it brings together all values necessary to the fulfillment of such a desideratum. In the particular case of Romania in the year 2000, this doctrine is more than an alternative.

CHAPTER TWELVE

A PLEA
FOR A SOCIAL-DEMOCRATIC ROMANIA

"I am
an idealist
without illusions."

John F. Kennedy

12.1 The premises of transformation – in search of a middle class

Democracy and modernization cannot exist in the absence of a positive perception on the evolutionary perspectives of society. If this premise were correct, then Romanians would be irremediably doomed to fail. Today's Romanian society is more fragmented and unequal than ever before. The number of people condemned to live in poverty grows incessantly, while the distance that separates rich from poor and town from village continues to widen. Jobs diminish in number, income stagnates, and expenditures on education, health or apartment building fail to compensate for the shortfalls of these domains. **Romanian democracy is threatened by the precarious state of national**

economy, by the apathy of a population too concerned with earning the daily bread.

The economic reform has begun by liberalizing prices and foreign trade. The first consequence was a steep increase in prices. The commercial balance quickly deteriorated, industrial production dropped, and imports overwhelmingly surpassed exports. In order to fight inflation, the deficit in the balance of payments and the rising external debts, Romania had to adopt a policy of monetary austerity that had as its main goal the reduction in public and private expenditures. The restriction on demand only emphasized the recession that our country is going through. The real income of the population lost real value, while the queuing of people to buy various goods, a typical phenomenon of the communist period, became a mere memory.

All these economic transformations led to modifications in the structure of social classes, following criteria such as status or income. The number of workers is decreasing, their workplaces are precarious, and all in all they are the social category most exposed during the transition to market economy. The new production technologies imported into Romania clearly separate qualified from unqualified manpower. Unqualified workers will be most exposed to unemployment in the future, and their impoverishment is a real threat to the whole society.

Peasants, though increasing in numbers throughout the last years (in Europe, Romania is the country with the highest percentage of manpower employed in agriculture), cannot manage to go beyond the limit of subsistence, and face numerous problems: the fragmentation of agricultural land to dimensions that make it non-profitable for exploitation, the unaffordable price of agricultural equipment, the shortage in public utilities in the rural area (running water, gas, telephone lines etc).

The intellectuals and the public servants also had to suffer during these years. Following the restriction on the state budget, their salaries were limited, and inflation dramatically decreased their purchasing power. Moreover, after 1997 there appeared the issue of staff reduction in education, health and public administration. Except for the health and administrative departments, where there still functions an informal, out-of-pocket system of payment, the rest of Romania's intellectuality is going through a process of impoverishment that distances it from the status of middle class which it holds in the developed countries.

Then who forms Romania's middle class? Or rather, is there a middle class in Romania? As it happened with the Latin American countries which took abrupt steps towards capitalism while 'burning the stages', Romania as well is witnessing a process of social polarization between a quantitatively small 'elite', with a high living standard, and the large majority of the population, stuck within the limits of impoverishment and whose income is permanently nibbled at by inflation. The identification of a middle class is difficult when there is an underground economy of approximately 40% of the GDP. If the middle class were to gather together people with a high social status, then it would include the technical and humanist intellectuality. However, in a society where material weight is increasingly important when valorizing an individual on the social scale, such a criterion of defining the middle class becomes outdated.

Not many things can be said about the rich class of Romanian society, simply because information on it is largely missing. How was it formed? What were the economic mechanisms that prompted it into being? How legal were its activities? All these are questions to which we have no answer so far. These 'profiteers' of transition tend to constitute a class of fund holders, living on interests, rents, passing on their fortune to their inheritors and thus creating a class of privileged people, apart from the rest of society.

During the last two years, the process of forming a social-democratic electorate was concluded. A contribution in speeding this process was made by the center-right government that led the country during this period, and that, by the measures it took, displeased a large part of the population. If until 1996 the leftist electorate could not be precisely identified, at present it can already be configured. In my opinion, its ranks include the following social categories: budgetary employees, retired people, the unemployed, a great part of the rural population and of the industrial workers. What these social categories have in common is the demand for measures that belong to the political left: increased budgetary expenditures, maintaining subsidies or price control. We may even say that **in Romania, too, there appeared the conflict between capital and manpower**. At the same time, PDSR's movement toward the center by promoting a modern, European discourse – which, beside circulating the traditional leftist topics, will also approach the values necessary for Romania's accession to the EU (human rights, minority rights, tolerance, cultural plurality) – will gradually effect the attraction of intellectuals to this political area. Unlike in other countries, Romanian intellectuals moved preponderantly to the right, mainly due to the diffusion of an anti-communist discourse which has dominated the political stage ever since 1990, and also because the intellectuality sought social legitimacy by opposition (a largely artificial one) to workers. **As the intellectuals' economic difficulties grow, they will unrelentingly turn to social democracy.**

Though the leftist electorate of today's Romania is a numerous one, it is at the same time volatile. Even if there come accomplishments that improve its situation, the expectations of the social-democratic electorate are too high to be fulfilled in one governmental mandate. People's dissatisfaction with the country's economic situation, their demands for a real social safety net, all these might be channeled to the parties professing a nationalist-xenophobe discourse, in the absence of a credible social-democratic alternative. The extreme-right parties, with their political offer combining anticommunism, order, the strong state, Christian values with social protection and the demand to restrict the free market, are targeting the electorate of the social-democratic area and represent a real threat to these parties. Topics such as national identity, localization or the opposition to globalization impose on the political agenda of Romanian parties, to the detriment of topics pertaining to the classic cleavage between work and capital.

For a social-democratic party it will be very difficult to keep the distance from the temptations of a populist-nationalist discourse that still collects votes, the more so as it addresses a volatile electorate, without strongly rooted political sympathies. **Only the emergence of a new generation of citizens, a post-nationalist**

generation, would allow Romanian social democracy to focus its endeavors on the configuration of its own electorate. This electorate will no doubt come from the new cleavages visible after the transformations specific to transition: traditionalist nationalists versus the 'cosmopolitan' modernizers; anticommunists versus those claiming their origin in the old regime; those who stood to gain and those who stood to lose from the transformation of the system. In a not too distant future, we shall no longer be able to discuss the existence of compact social classes, such as 'workers' or 'peasants'; social groups will coagulate according to different criteria, which will force PDSR to adapt its message to this change.

Romania, too, will witness a clarification of the political stage, mainly along the cleavage line separating political forces openly oriented towards Western values, from those preponderantly supporting nationalist-religious values. As with the countries of Central Europe (Poland, the Czech Republic, Hungary), where the center-left parties were those that managed to carry out the most serious reforms with a view to modernization – in the sense of an '*aggiornamento*' of political culture –, and while right-wing parties pose as defenders of traditional values, so will this model prove its applicability in Romania. Social democracy, perhaps with a liberal component, will ensure Romania's integration into modernity.

12.2 The stakes of the social-democratic governance project

Forty-five years of communist domination distorted the ideas lying at the basis of social democracy: the search for general solutions that would solve social problems; supporting the underprivileged social categories through the action of a party that would formulate and represent their interests; the intervention of a democratic state as economic actor capable of offering solution. Another topic of social democracy that we must recall is that neither neo-liberalism, nor economic nationalization constitutes an efficacious way to economic development. A credible and efficient reform program will have to go beyond the rigid separation between the economic, social, political and foreign relations, bringing them together in a synthetic vision.

A social-democratic governance program will only have chances of materialization if it relies on a stable political coalition and deals with the main social groups. Unfortunately, the social support demanded by a large part of the population meets a state whose capacity to intervene and mediate various interests was drastically reduced. Contrary to today's fashionable ideas, social democracy does not think that privatization is a goal in itself, or a *factotum* that would automatically solve all of Romania's problems. There are domains of activity, which necessitate privatization in order to render their activity more efficient, or to bring in an infusion of foreign capital and know-how. However, there are other economic branches that need to remain under state control, either because they are monopolies (the railway system, the electric power system), or because they represent activities of strategic importance for Romania (the defense industry, the national system of petroleum transportation, the system of radio-communications etc.). I consider it urgent to establish clear demarcation criteria between the two spheres of property, so as to no longer allow for state monopolies to be privatized, or for state-controlled economic activities to be preyed upon by private tick companies.

Transfers to population (retirement benefits, unemployment benefits, support for nuclear families) have an increasingly lower value, though they represent the same percentage of the budget. The increasingly lower taxation base comes from the ever smaller taxes paid by trading companies, the state-owned ones being debt-laden, and the private ones often yielding to the temptation of the informal circuit of economy, prompted by the 'accomplished' fiscal politics of the government.

For the stage of development in which Romania finds itself at present, there are still reformist measures to be taken in order to turn the heritage of the old communist system into a modern form of market economy. If in the Occident the difference between a social-democratic and a liberal party is made by the proportion of state's intervention in economy (varying from 20% to 40%), for a country that has just abandoned economic planning it is difficult to adopt such a criterion. Also, the Romanian left must avoid repeating the mistakes of the Western left, which has become the defender of corporate interests of various social groups to the detriment of others (for instance, of unions to the detriment of unqualified workers, who are not organized into associative structures).

We must go beyond the exclusivist vision of neo-liberalism. Taking up the distinction operated by the French Prime Minister Lionel Jospin, between 'market economy' and 'market society', we accept market economy (which is nothing but an instrument designed to create prosperity), but reject its extensions into social life. The state must regain its internal sovereignty. A state is no longer sovereign when a private power has a capacity superior to the state's to define the interests of society. This capacity has nothing to do with the classical debate concerning the degree of state interventionism in economy. I am referring strictly to its existence as public power mandated to apply the democratic will.

In other words, the issue here is the reorganization of the state as an 'actor' endowed with resources that will be firstly invested in encouraging private initiative (especially small and medium enterprises). **The solution will consist of decentralizing the relation between public power and private initiative.** Thus would obtain a flexible structure, supported by public and private funding, which, because of decisional autonomy, will be able to ensure the connection between the government and small and medium enterprises. Based on this support, those enterprises will be able to consolidate themselves and integrate into the global economic network. The state's intervention in support of the SME's or the elaboration and imposition of anti-monopoly legislation are measures pertaining to the logic of the market. But in no case must we allow the discourse preaching the privatization of the public sector to serve as a pretext for the privatization of the state!

As the process of economic reformation moves on, the role of social democracy will become increasingly important. **The immediate**

objective of a future social-democratic government will have to address diminishing the dramatic proportions of unemployment. There is already chronic unemployment for part of the population, in other words, the period elapsed between losing one's job and finding another is prolonged indefinitely. The general causes leading to unemployment all over the world are the decrease in productivity, high bank interest rates, and technological progress. In Romania, the main sources of unemployment are represented by the process of de-industrialization of the country and the prolonged economic decline, set off particularly in the early and late years of the 1990-2000 decade. The real figure of unemployed people is difficult to approximate; among those listed at the unemployment offices there are many who work in the underground economy, or who have gone from industry to agriculture – not to mention the increasing number of people with handicaps and of people with disability pensions. The government set up projects of public works in infrastructure and apartment building, which are largely responsible for absorbing the laid-off labor force throughout the restructuring of the industrial system.

Among all social investments of the state, education is the only one that can ensure a job in the new globalized society. The social-democratic imprint in this field is constituted by the support granted by the state to the children and gifted youngsters coming from poor households, that are incapable of supporting them. The support can take the shape of cash grants during the educational years, and is justified by the fact that a child coming from a poor household or the slums will have from the very start lower chances of receiving good education and, eventually, a job appropriate to his or her abilities. The issue here is **a fundamental stake for a social-democratic party: the equality of opportunity for all members of society.** Another urgency of the Romanian educational system is the connection of the educational process to the practical aspects of society; many times, the gap that separates the knowledge accumulated by a graduate from the demands of the working force market is very wide. In this context, the role of applied research in the educational process must further develop, and this concept can be stimulated by research grants from the state to priority domains. We appreciate that the 4% granted to education out of the GDP is no longer sufficient, due to the alarming decline of Romanian economy; the percentage must needs be increased to 5-6%.

A serious educational project cannot be limited to a compulsory eight-grade public education. We need public mechanisms to ensure an extension of the educational process (by means of modern educational systems, such as distance learning and electronic courses) to the entire population. **Only with citizens endowed with a solid educational stock, will Romania be able to proceed to sustainable development.**

In the developed countries, only public investments have decreased in the past years; as for the rest, interest rates to public debt, transfers/subsidies and governmental expenditures have all risen, in this precise order. In Romania, the first three expenditure categories have diminished their real value, and only the interest rates to public debt have increased. An urgent matter for a social-democratic government will be the increase in public expenditure and the transfer of benefits to underprivileged social categories, and the decrease in governmental expenditure and interest payment to public debt.

State intervention is also necessary in a capitalist state, in order to correct possible abuses of private power, such as the tendency towards monopoly, negotiable sale prices, the violation of ecological, health, social protection or other norms. From this point of view, **the state is nothing but a mediator between capitalism and democracy.** However, the interventions of the state are operated legally, following serious debates in Parliament and Government, as well as with civil society. The great number of emergency ordinances, or contradictory government resolutions, the modification of laws from one day to the next, do nothing but ruin the domestic economic environment. Max Weber, a leading theoretician of the capitalist system, drew our attention to the 'guarantors of calculability' demanded by this system, especially for the investors to be able to plan future investments and ensuing profits.

Income inequalities are becoming, for Romania as well, a pressing matter. The economic circumstances are prompting into existence a gap between the large part of the population, which sees its own situation worsening from day to day, by means of rising prices, unemployment and the diminishing real value of their wages, and a small group of people with high wages, which benefit from the high interest rates in order to multiply their fortunes, while at the same time turning into ostentatious consumers. To these main inequalities, other types are added:

– between qualified and unqualified manpower
– between the income of those working in the service sector (IT and finances) and those working in the industrial domains
– between the degrees of development in various regions of the country
– between men and women as regards opportunities on the labor market.

The social-democratic answers to these challenges lean toward progressive income taxation, and taxation of interest rates and financial operations.

Education also offers a better social protection for the citizens of the country, by preparing them for the exigencies and opportunities of a labor market which has radically changed compared to the communist era. Great attention should be paid, in the future, to the increasing discrepancies between regions. In order to avert social dissatisfactions that can lead up to demands for territorial autonomy, we shall have to study the possibility of transferring funds from the more developed areas to those facing difficulties, as well as setting up special areas that would offer financial facilities to investors.

As time passes, the task undertaken by the Romanian social democracy is that of ensuring a smooth passage, as far as possible, from the old, anachronistic society, to a social and political system adapted to modernity and globalization. The direction and framework of Romania's evolution for the next years will be established by Romanian social democrats, starting from the principle of a more equitable distribution of the benefits and costs of the reform process. The market alone will be responsible for allotting the resources in the economic process; but the state will ensure that the needs of those social categories most affected in the past ten years are converted into solvable demands on the market.

Another priority for a future social-democratic government will be that of governance accountability. We shall have to allow for the popular initiatives envisaging the impeachment of a high official, the initiation of referendums on various issues of national interest, and the obtaining of a genuine independence of the judicial power from the Executive. Without the autonomy of the judicial power, there will never be a proper distance between the supervisors and the supervised. The implication of the people in the political and administrative life is most important, beginning with drafting and applying the budget or various laws. Only by this type of measures will we be able to stimulate the citizen's trust in the institutions of the rule-of-law; to the items mentioned above, we could also add a law against corruption, as well as the notable optimization of the activity of Parliament and the local government institutions. Instead of today's state, we shall impose a stronger, and at the same time more democratic state. Democracy will be consolidated through institutional reforms that would prompt the birth of political and economic institutions connecting representational democracy and civic participation. The state-civil society partnership can yield important results in achieving major projects of Romania, such as investments in infrastructure, education etc. The private companies that assume financial contributions in these projects will be able to benefit from certain fiscal stimuli (especially the reduction of profit taxation).

We still have in front of us a long way to go before we reach normality. The practice of democracy and market economy starts to take shape in Romania. But the thorough democratization will have to be endorsed by a diminishing of social and economic inequalities within Romanian society, by a state capable of intervening in support of the small and medium enterprises. I feel confident that, by gradual, but cumulative changes at the institutional, economic, social and political levels, social democracy will decisively contribute to the legitimacy of the democratic political regime in Romanian society, and to lending a humane figure to market economy.

12.3 Remember the future!

Capitalist society is also transforming, prompted by the progress of informational and communication technologies. The avatars of this transformation consist of the globalization of production, of commerce and the 'financialization' of economy. At the same time, on another level, Romanian society is evolving and developing new aspirations, in keeping with the fast-changing world around us.

Nevertheless, in order to successfully come out of this stage of profound transformations, Romania needs above all a positive image of the future, as now it is still under the negative imprint of a 'commemorative syndrome'. With energy worthy of a better cause, we have acquired a peculiar taste for anniversaries, centenaries, bicentenaries, retrospective celebrations or posthumous vengeance. These are so many collective reflexes betraying a certain incapacity to prefer the future over the past, the project over the memory. Already in mourning for the future, Romanian society continues to take refuge in the consoling familiarity of the present.

The efficiency of the market economy system can no longer be questioned: it creates competition, favors innovation and creativity. However, we must admit that the market cannot entirely supply for the functions of the state. It privileges short-term profit making, distorting the functioning mechanism of public services, such as health and education.

The laws of the market do not yield what in a sociological jargon is called social optimum, as the principles they rely on impose the law of the strongest, excluding any kind of solidarity. The globalization of production and commerce has led directly to the logic of an economic concentration to which we owe the establishment of international companies and financial organisms that are as strong as states. In order to preserve the general interests of the citizens, public administration must build the mechanisms of democratic intervention.

In our days, it is clear enough what governments should do to promote prosperity. Macroeconomic politics is no longer left-wing or right-wing, but correct or incorrect. Center-left governments are those that eliminated, most of the times, the deficits inherited from the political right wing.

From this perspective, I believe that the role of the state is fundamental. We cannot conceive of a reduction of the state to the position of regulating instance. It must continue to take on its fundamental tasks: the guarantee of equal opportunity for all, pursuing the general interest, social cohesion and the new social rights.

When I say 'new social rights', I am referring to the aspirations apparent in all modern societies. The demands for individual freedom, autonomy, personal and collective security are interdependent with the effort of identifying new landmarks and lifestyles in society. People's desire for fulfillment and participation can no longer be dissociated from the need for social solidarity. In other words, **the amelioration of individual evolutions and the collective interest must be reconciled.**

This new social bond can only be the product of an intelligent policy of the state and its public services, a sine qua non condition for the establishment of an environment favorable to economic development. Even though Romania cannot afford to neglect the criterion of budgetary balance, we must be aware of the fact that this is not the only criterion on appreciating good governance. We can no longer squander what little resources we have. Each leu collected from the population must be well spent by the state, as only thus will the citizens acquire the certitude that the state works to the benefit of all. **It is compulsory that the reform of society begin with the reform of the state.**

Still, this is just a foundation. Above it we must build a modern economy, whose raw material should be the knowledge, capacities, abilities and intelligence of the people. Within the frame of the economy of knowledge, education for all, based on knowledge accumulated throughout the entire life, and not just in school, is becoming a priority – both economic and social – for a modern nation.

There are domains of economic life in which the rules of market economy (that is, of the money selection which these introduce) cannot be 'acclimatized', but only administered through the public governments' services. It is true that the level of public services offered to Romanians have been degrading for quite a while. This does not hinder me from considering that the solution can only be a reconfiguration of these services so they ensure equal and qualitative access for all citizens. I have in mind in particular an extension and adaptation of the public services menu (education, health, culture), to the rural areas as well as to the new slums around cities, genuine ghetto neighborhoods.

Nevertheless, any public power, however well conceived and designed, will be unable to reach its targets in the absence of a forceful restatement of the authority of the law in our society. The legitimacy of the law has no equivalent, as it is grounded in popular sovereignty and universal suffrage. Without the law, there can be no equality or social justice. The law is the guarantor of the preeminence of general interests over private interests. Any process of social transformation can only begin by instituting a set of laws in its support – and I would have to say, looking back at the ten years that have passed since the 1989 revolution, that this set of laws seems to have been missing in our transition. Reducing the role of the laws, limiting their field of action, abusing ordinances which have compromised the entire legislative body, all these do not equal to increasing liberties, but to reducing collective capacities for progress and change.

The solution that I find appropriate to a restoration of the state's authority in the Romanian society is the articulation of the law, which offers a direction and a frame, and the contract, which offers solutions adapted to social and economic realities. Thus, I see as possible a better administration of economic evolutions that would profoundly transform our society, raising the educational stakes as required by modern economy, for example, or increasing the staff numbers or of qualified professions. However, we cannot exclude the reverse situation, a marginalization and impoverishment of an important part of the unqualified labor force (unemployed, workers by the day, peasants lacking material means to work their land). A new political contract proposed to Romanians can only start from a special attention to this social category. The increasing growth of inequalities between wage earners and those with a high income erodes social cohesion and calls for an urgent remedying of the situation. We cannot neglect the middle class either (which to this day has not been configured by sociologists, in spite of numerous references made to its existence), the one that carried the bulk of the fiscal effort during the last four years.

Mending social inequalities also implies satisfying the citizens' aspirations to a better quality of life. This presupposes ensuring each individual's fundamental right to security. Whether this means physical integrity, the security of one's family or assets, the citizen has a right to live in a protective environment. Daily security, health and food security, environmental protection, the right to communicate freely are just as many national priorities neglected so far. Entering the path of European integration, but also the demands of our time, will make it necessary to rethink the act of governance, which will no longer be limited to economic management.

Romanian social democracy will have to take into consideration, and more seriously so, the issue of the family. I am here referring to the support given to the traditional notions of family. The familial cell ensures the link between generations, it is the place where values are handed on and the first space of solidarity. The responsibility of a social-democratic government will be that of allowing each family to assume its fundamental functions.

Romania will become competitive in the new international division of labor when its citizens benefit from a high level of education. In spite of the 'alternative reform of education' promoted by the Minister of Education, Andrei Marga, I am still convinced that the priorities of the national system of education are completely different. The amelioration of young people's professional formation, not just in theory but also stimulating their social mobility, is one of these priorities. The social gap between those who are able to work with the new means of calculation and the rest of the population risks being widened, it having the potential to become a more acute form of inequality than the classic one between labor and capital. A consolidation of the priority of education in our country, while at the same time rethinking the methods and trying to mend the new types of inequality based on knowledge, represent a priority on the agenda of a social-democratic government. An improvement of education is essential from an economic, as well as moral point of view. Depriving a child of the possibility of acquiring education is denying his competence to 'fight' the others from an equal position. We cannot build a genuine national community unless we combine responsibility and duty. This is indeed an agreement within modern civil society.

Nevertheless, we do not need education only, but also to encourage enterprises and small businesses, new structures and methods of handling business taxes so as to stimulate progress and reward enterprisers.

The internationalization and acceleration of communicational ways have unsettled the traditional political data. At all levels, local, national, European and worldwide, citizens receive a considerable amount of information, form their own opinions, expect answers, want to be part of the decisional process. Each feels the need to participate in these different decisional and initiative cores, trying to find new kinds of social participation. Social democracy is the one that can satisfy this democratic exigency by initiating reforms such as the decentralization of decisions and the renovation of public life, going as far as a mixed electoral system (proportional vote, combined with uninominal vote) and a limitation of cumulated offices, from the president to the local political officials.

***

We live in an era of global-scale transformations, one of the most dramatic and unpredictable in the history of humankind. Hardly does a month go by, without an important discovery in the field of science and technology. In 1990, two American futurologists, John Naisbitt and Patricia Aburdene, published a book entitled "Megatendencies 2000". There was no need to make predictions for a very long period of time – almost ten years. However, there is a word completely missing from the book: 'Internet', the phenomenon that today is changing our lives. Our world is moving at amazing speed, and continuous change is one of the things than humans stand with most difficulty. No wonder that the era we live in was called 'the age of fuss', or, as in the title of Francis Fukuyama's latest book, 'the great divide'. I think I am not exaggerating when I say that we are in the middle of the greatest economic, technological and social revolutions that humankind has witnesses ever since the beginning of the industrial revolution, two centuries ago.

Globalization has brought about not only economic progress, but also a multitude of fears. We live in a world where our workplace can disappear because of a decision taken thousands of kilometers away, in a board room; a world in which family ties, the town and the country are under constant pressure and threat. It is a world in which the living standards are rising, we can afford to travel and we communicate in ways of which our grandparents never even dreamed of. A world at whose center lies a paradox: though there is more individual freedom, there is also more interdependence. We can do more; still, the nature of globalization affects us most. We buy and consume more, and this is an issue related to the personal choices we make; however, the opportunities we have and the quality of life depend more on the choices we make together: good schools, environmental pollution, safer streets or, at an international level, world trade agreements. Therefore, the changes take place quickly and are a source of apprehension, saturated by opportunities and dangers.

The problem is as follows: do we model change or does it model us? Do we control it, or do we allow it to overwhelm us? The only key to modern day politics is this: how can we cope with change? To resist it would be useless, to let it happen would be dangerous. Therefore, a third possibility is to cope with it. But this can only be done if there are rules, evaluations, in order to find the answer to the question: how and why did we adopt a certain strategy to cope with change? In this regard we must settle an apparent older conflict between new and old, between the adepts of the modern and traditionalists. These latter ones deplore the disappearance of old habits, valorize the greater stability of the past and underline the disorder characteristic to these times. The unconditional adept of modern times sees the opportunities, rejects the prejudices and old hierarchies of the past, is eager to take advantage of the material benefits brought by everything modern.

As for politics, it is fascinating that both camps include left-wing and right-wing supporters. A traditionalist supporter of left-wing politics has a hostile attitude towards world finances, and a traditionalist supporter of right-wing politics is afraid of equality. The adepts of leftist politics who support modernity are too easily overlooking the threat to family life; the adepts of right-wing politics who support modernity believe in the supremacy of market forces. The solution to this conflict lies in applying traditional values to the modern world, and eliminating outdated attitudes. For this, however, we must rediscover the essence of traditional values and we must allow them to guide us in order to face the changes.

PART IV

CHAPTER THIRTEEN

ROMANIA IN THE CONTEXT OF GLOBALIZATION

13.1 From the ideological war to the clash of civilizations

To design a nation, to plan and impose through political means and economic, social, and cultural action the direction of its development, necessarily means to relate that nation to the world. Such a premise requires a separate analysis of contemporary tendencies, of international theories and policies that model, through force or consensus, the fate of the states of the world and, thereby, the fate of human civilization.

International political thought seems to be currently dominated by two paradigms: the first emphasizes the contradictory character of international relations and the trend toward atomization and conflict; the second one points to a major change of paradigm, marking the transition from the conflicting state to that of harmony and integrated development, dominated by rationality and progress. Both theories find powerful arguments in the world around, arguments which prompt their adepts to design and put into practice international policies with global or regional character.

The first paradigm, insisting on the conflict-ridden relations between states, ethnic-groups, cultures, religions, civilizations and economic, social or political-military interest groups has been recently formulated by Samuel Huntington's in his influential study of 1995, *The Clash of Civilizations*. The study circulated a theory aiming to explain and predict the evolution of the world starting from a traditional doctrine that grounds international relations in the principles of conflict and balance of powers.

What is Huntington's essential point? He argues that, after a 19th century dominated by national conflicts and a 20th century dominated by ideological ones, the causality of conflict reached a deeper substratum in which the values that define a civilization are those that oppose people to each other and urge them to accept death with the sole purpose of imposing those values to others. If during the Cold War international tensions and even armed conflicts (such as those in Korea, Vietnam and Nicaragua) were the expression of conflicts between distinct social classes, social orders or ideological views, the Huntingtonian outlook interprets conflicts such as those in ex-Yugoslavia as well as other millennium-wars as the product of frictions among dominating cultures – that is, as wars between Western civilization and other, distinct civilizations. A new geopolitical outlook is thus born, which instead of parting the world on an Eastern-Western or Northern-Southern axis in Cold War fashion, institutes new boundaries that follow the more or less stable and precise demarcations lines of religious and cultural areas, ignoring the (sometimes artificial, it should be said) state frontiers.

What prompted the passing from the Cold War theory of ideological conflict based on the binary logic of a bipolar world to the Huntingtonian clash of civilizations is precisely the need to generate an explanatory framework for the conflicts of a multi-polar world. If, indeed the tensions in a multi-polar geopolitics – rather than the antagonisms between civilizations – explain today's frictions and conflicts, then we have to agree with Graham Fuller's remark on the Huntingtonian theory: "The clash of civilizations refers neither to Jesus Christ, nor to Confucius or Mohammed, but to the question of the unequal distribution of world power, of world wealth and of the influence of certain states. The culture is the vehicle through which conflicts are expressed rather than their cause" (Fuller; 154).

Globalization as a political option was not born at the end of the second millennium. Rather, it existed as a tendency as far back in time as the age of ancient empires. It is a somewhat cyclical process that dominated the evolution of the world. What makes modern globalizations special is its intensity and, if one may say so, its globalism: the phenomenon of modern globalization does not admit of virgin islands. It is global and all-encompassing.

The technical and economic substratum of globalization is the one responsible for its irrepressible force. One may say that a millennium-old tendency aiming at the regrouping of humanity in a global village has now gotten all necessary conditions to pass from dream to reality.

13.2 The informational fast food

There are two categories of globalization theorists. One group proposed it as a solution for world development and world peace (Woodrow Wilson, Nicolae Titulescu, the founding fathers of the European Union, one the one hand, and the Marxist doctrinaires of proletarian internationalism, on the other, all come to mind). The other group signaled the emergence of the phenomenon early on and pointed to the fact that globalization is a real tendency, independent of the will of political factors, which brings together risks and advantages that cannot be ignored. Alvin Toffler, Marshall McLuhan are representatives of this second group who have identified as the decisive factor in the acceleration of these processes the unprecedented globalization of the circulation of information.

The event that has had probably the most dramatic impact upon the explosion of globalization was the end of the Cold War and of the bipolar world. The tearing down of the Berlin Wall was symbolically the destruction of the barrier raised by ideological antagonism against the unifying force of globalization.

Globalization has its roots in the North-American model of economic expansion. One may say that globalization is, from this perspective, a process of dissemination of systems of organization, production and trade that the great American monopolies have first created at a national level and then internationally.

Globalization is said to have been born as a tendency after the crisis of 'fordism', when a hyper-specialized and hyper-integrated economic system reached the limits of growth. From that moment on, the option in favor of flexible systems of production and markets became the new entrepreneurial vision as a manner of improving the access to new resources and new markets. The increasingly abstract character of relations of ownership and of business management is typical to globalization. The so-called shareholders' culture de-individualized the system of ownership and made it independent from the origins of capital. The freedom of movement of the capital is essential for the functioning of a globalized economy. The concepts of national economy and national markets are gradually becoming obsolete. Products no longer have an origin, capitals no longer have a residence, while resources and markets are virtually everywhere. Such a reality has become possible only to the extent to which the flexibility of the traffic of information enabled one to ignore the physical distance between management, owners and clients. If in the period between the two world wars and even a long while after the Second World War the question of access to resources and to the work-force was the main criterion for the designing of economic policies, today resources may be transported or synthesized locally, the work-force may be, at least in some fields, located away from the retail markets for the end product, while the markets themselves become the main limiting factor. Globalization aims precisely at the unification and liberalization of market access. Such a tendency led to dramatic changes in the specialization of labor. The metropolis gets de-industrialized and re-orients toward services and the manipulation of symbolic products, while the periphery is getting industrialized and becomes the main provider of high technology products.

The organizational characteristic of economic globalization is production and marketing through world networks. Consumption is becoming more uniform on the lines of a hegemonic, North-American or Western economic model. The world is MacDonaldized and Coca-colonized. The global market is a centrifugal market which repulses anything that might limit it: states, nations, families, religions, anything that tries to resist the process of generalized social atomization. We are witnessing a process of the defeat of willpower, of the negation of the political: if the market decides everything, what is politics good for? And what is there to do about this inevitable development?

Looked at from the point of view of economic success, the process of globalization has countless advantages. It mobilizes values and resources in a better way, it ensures a democratization of consumption and favors a global treatment of the crises involved by economic growth. From this perspective, it is better adapted to the challenges that we are facing and it may lead to the injection of rationality in the use of resources and to a better access to knowledge, information, and well-being. For this reason globalization is currently regarded with optimism, although there is also a certain pessimism generated by the political risks of the phenomenon. The violence in Davos, Salt Lake City and Seattle has shown that globalization produces simultaneously adherents and opponents, and that it engenders concern both in the West "exporting its model of development" and in the place of destination.

13.3 The Romanian dilemma: ethnocentrism or 'interculturality'

I have previously stressed the role of the economic mechanisms of globalization. However, to stop at this point would be to look at the phenomenon in a reductionist manner. Actually, there is an economic and political duality of globalization. Globalization is a process that requires a system of political legitimacy. From this perspective, **the**

concepts of international politics are obviously increasingly subsumed to the need of politically legitimizing globalization. It seems that the most exposed area is the cultural one. If in the field of the relations of production and consumption the world accepts with relative ease the pressures of globalization, in the field of culture the reaction is more powerful. We might conjecture that this phenomenon of rejection has its origins in the specificity of North-American culture. Globalization brings and tends to force into the destination areas elements of the American cultural pattern; the Marcusian one-dimensional man breaks the national boundaries and impregnates the whole world with the model of a culturally one-dimension man. This cultural uniformization is what the globalization-engendered crisis that involves the national coordinates of each particular group has exposed early on. In such a context, the Huntingtonian theory becomes relevant and blends with the theory of globalization; Huntington is pointing precisely to the shock that civilizations under the impact of globalization are witnessing. He is offering a theoretical apparatus for a geo-strategy of globalization.

Although Huntington may sketch the crises and the potential threats that come from globalization, he does not offer a solution for them. It is difficult to believe that the forces and the interests that stand behind globalization could accept their failure in front of cultural incompatibilities as a given. They have to offer a project of international politics able to surpass these limits and to justify the forces of globalization.

The political concept that tries to solve this problem was born in the USA before the First World War. Its main supporter was Woodrow Wilson who, caught between the traditional American isolationism and the need to involve the US into the world war, found a principle able to unify the two seemingly opposed imperatives. The principle was moral in nature and it defined America as a missionary power aiming to impart to the whole world the democratic ideals that were at the foundation of the American order. This outlook on the "mission" of the United States proved long-lasting and survived unmodified all changes of context and balance of power that the world has been undergoing ever since. What the main superpower is now proposing to the world is a model of political and economic organization based upon a pluralist democracy and a market economy.

What is typical to the American outlook of the construction of states is actually a by-product that is more or less related to the imperatives of globalization. The historical genesis of the United States is not a given but a model to be followed. The lack of national specificity becomes a positive value opposed to the "nationalisms" of the Old World. The federal character of the state is seen as challenging the traditional experiences of the unitary states. A whole political philosophy is exported together with capital investments or security to the non-Western world.

The mechanisms of the construction of the new order are compatible with the existence of a one-pole system and they are imposed to the new members of the club of democratic states both by political and military means, and by economic ones. NATO, the World Bank and the International Monetary Fund become the main instruments in the reconstruction of future democracies, while other bodies diminish their role either due to their inability to operate effectively, or because they are no longer compatible with the new geopolitical realities. **The UN, just like the entire system of specialized institutions, is going through a worsening crisis, which is ultimately likely to affect its legitimacy. Paradoxically, a body with a universal vocation turns out to be less flexible with respect to the process of globalization than regional structures (NATO and the OSCE).**

Naturally, this model cannot be followed by everybody. It is as a matter of fact energetically contested, and there are areas which the model has not even reached. In certain geopolitical spaces the model is imposed with priority and sometimes even by force. The experience of former Yugoslavia and especially of the Kosovo conflict proves that the option in favor of this model is not essentially free. It is accepted that other areas should be free to practice a different political philosophy. In the case of Russia, but by no means of Russia alone, we have a sort of inverse projection of the isolationist Monroe doctrine. Nevertheless, we are witnessing a gradual reaction against this "exceptionalism" that tends to lose acceptance. One has to stress the fact that the overlapping of the spheres of political interest and of economic operation, respectively, is not perfect. **Economic globalization is considerably advanced in comparison with political globalization and practically**

it is the former that dictates the rhythm and the area of expansion of the latter.

Is there a desirable attitude toward this state of the world at the beginning of the third millennium? What should Romania's evolution be in the context of globalization?

To oppose globalization would be both unrealistic and contrary to Romania's real interests. Globalization is a process that has its obvious advantages and to reject it would be to abandon the development in the direction and rhythm of today's world. To notice the challenges and the perverse effects of globalization is not to move away from it. As a matter of fact, to identify the possible ill effects and to find ways to eliminate them is a matter of utmost concern not only to the enemies of globalization but also to its proponents. It is difficult to prove that globalization has unilaterally positive effects only for some of its agents, and only disadvantages for the others. The process is actually complex, new, and surprising and, in spite of having been adequately predicted by some visionaries, it has found the world unprepared to face it.

Romania has entered the process with certain handicaps. During the last days of communism it was even more isolated than the system that it was a part of. This implies greater costs of the efforts to burn the stages that separate us from the others. During the ten years after the change in political regime the progress has been inconsistent and sometimes followed by backlashes. If in terms of the consolidation of the democratic framework the developments have been articulate, in the economic field the initial handicaps have been amplified. Political hesitations and the serene acceptance during 1997-2000 of a serious economic downfall have rendered Romania unable to take advantage, at this moment, of the benefits of globalization.

European Union integration is a strategic option for Romania. It would enable us to withstand the impact of globalization with lesser risks and greater benefits. By means of its size and its economic power the European Union is a much better vehicle of globalization than an isolated national economic system. Politically speaking, European integration would ensure a positive valorization of the existing democratic framework and would enable us to keep those elements of national identity that proved viable in the case of other EU members states.

The geo-strategic reality of the clash of civilization (or maybe merely that of the clash of international policy options) – even if we do not ultimately accept Huntington's thesis – is present in our very neighborhood. The crisis in former Yugoslavia was relevant in this respect. It cannot be said that the way to solve these tensions and conflicts was the most adequate. Military interventions did not lead to peace but to a continuous subterranean conflict based on violence and intolerance. The risk of contagion of such instability is even larger as we inhabit an area in which historical policies of balance of powers and territorial compensation measures have led to a mixture of populations, cultures and religions.

We are still far from having found a solution for the ancient tensions or the new ones. At least for the time being the only available solution must stress the consolidation of stability, where stability exists, and the integration in collective defensive systems. From this point of view, Romania's option for Euro-Atlantic integration and its efforts for internal balance and stability are fundamental national and international conditions.

The two forms of integration, European and Euro-Atlantic, are adequate answers to the challenges of globalization and are, for this reason, fundamental objectives assumed by Romanian political parties. The option for European and Euro-Atlantic integration is one of the few unifying principles that still operate in Romania after the change in 1989. **This minimal consensus probably springs from the positioning of the will to integration in the unifying space of national interest**. Unfortunately, although the will to integrate is still a cohesive force operating on the Romanian political class, the concrete details of political programs circulated by the various parties and coalitions are often contradictory in terms of the ways and priorities of pre-integration reforms. **A decisive option in favor of integration should not be seen as giving up the principle of protection and promotion of national interest**.

Globalization is increasingly challenging the limits of the legitimacy of the actions of nation-states, both on internal and on international level. Globalization, in fact, tends to limit the state in manifesting its sovereignty. In the process of globalization, the geographical boundaries of the states come up as obstacles in the path of market unification, hindering a free allotment of resources on a much larger scale than that of the national territories.

The problems the world is confronting at the moment have such amplitude that it increasingly tends to go beyond the national-type answering capabilities. Pollution, the shortage of power resources, financial crises of international crime can no longer be settled by isolated national efforts, and states themselves can no longer constitute sole subjects of international relations. Thus is born a trans-national legitimacy, sublimating the traditional 'reasons of state' and imposing a normative system directly at odds with the old sovereignty. Willingly or not, states are witnessing a diminishing of their sovereignty, a so-called devolution of institutions, while trans-national entities acquire encroachment rights, politically and military as well as economically. At the opposite end is the tendency toward subsidiarity, absorbing, at the community level (regional or local), a large part of the quantum of sovereignty that until shortly before had existed at state level. **The national state thus seems subjected to a double pressure, from the supra-state and from the infra-state levels, in order to delegate and restrain its sovereignty.**

Under these circumstances, it is to be assumed that one of the political tensions that globalization will increasingly emphasize is precisely that between the nation-state and the international community in which that state exists.

The issue of political options that comes up in this context, and that is highly pressing for Romania as well, refers to the degree and rhythm in which this diminishing of sovereignty can be accepted. Protecting state sovereignty is not an end in itself, but rather a consequence of the different historical circumstances in which state were created and evolved, as well as of the different level of economic development.

The more strongly and directly does the leveling force of globalization act on the cultural model of a national community, the more intensely does the community tend to react. This becomes the source of tensions both between various national groups, and between the ethnic majority and minority with which it lives in the same state's territory. In truth, this is not a reminiscence of an exclusivist nationalist ideology, but proof that national fundaments are more complex and inalterable than one would think. They bring together specific structures of civilization, with economic and political interests that have not extinguished their viability, and that would probably resist assimilation to the unifying melting pot of globalization.

The experience of the nationalist groups of former Yugoslavia, as well as of the countries from the former Soviet empire, prove that, after relatively long periods of integration into trans-national state communities, the intimate resorts of cultural identity are still strong enough to act according to Huntington's notion of the conflict among civilizations. An experience – apt to cause concern – regarding the effects that the de-nationalizing pressures of integration and sovereignty limitations have in the circumstances of globalization, is represented by the recent accession to power of Austria's nationalist right. When certain values, considered legitimate by a national group, are under threat of aggression, even of a symbolic kind, and even in a state with a high level of economic development and a well-consolidated democratic tradition, it still is possible to excessively reaffirm state sovereignty and exclusivist nationalism.

The Austrian experience alarmed the states of the European Union, but other democracies as well; not only because a European state accepts the accession to power of an extreme-right party, but also because it is an alarm signal as to the risks generated by pushing forwards communitarianism to the detriment of national groups' aspirations to protect cultural and state identity. This signal is all the more upsetting, as it might not be characteristic of an insulated case, but the prelude to an ampler social movement throughout a rather large part of Western Europe. The recrudescence of the nationalist right, contesting communitarian policies that affect the freedom of economic options, the protests to opening the labor market and the migration of capital to other markets, with direct consequences on the degree of employment in home countries, are so many more topics of political debate in the states of the European Union.

More and more theoreticians, but also politicians and representatives of civil society, note that globalization represents at the same time an abstraction (capital, labor, values, information), but also a series of concrete and painful effects (the increasing precariousness of the work place, transforming labor in itself into a preponderantly abstract and isolated activity, a new mode of consumerism, a new way of access and of protection of the access to the traditional rights of the citizen). It is these unwanted side effects of globalization that have lately led to an increase in the numbers of skeptics, and, not lastly, to a shading of the optimists' position.

Romania's integration in the flow of globalization must be prepared through well-designed political programs, that would take into consideration both the severe crisis we are going through and the favorable circumstance created by the European Union's opening toward integrating new members. The issue is merely to find resources inside the country, first of all political, but also material resources to reach a development rate that would make it possible to predict the actual moment of integration. To this stage must still correspond a system of protecting local capital, but also of stimulating foreign investments. The process of liberalizing the market must not turn into the 'anarchization' of the market. The consolidation of democratic mechanisms remains a most important task; and this must not be necessarily understood as a diminishing of the state's authority and implicitly of its sovereignty.

Preparing European integration means more than economic performance; it also means placing national identity at a level that ensures its viability, in the circumstances where the integration will do away with part of its mechanisms of institutional protection. From this point of view, integration must not be mistaken for assimilation. The performance criteria set by the European Union to its candidates target, among others, the capacities of the national economy, but also of other social and cultural structures, to cope with an environment that disintegrates, among others, those national structures that must still be kept in function. To be caught in the leveling mixer of the Union or, at world scale, of globalization, without having competitive economic structures and valid mechanisms of protecting social and cultural identity, represents a major risk both for the integrator and the integrated. A precocious integration, with non-mature economic and social mechanisms, causes internal crises, but also propagates them throughout the entire integrative group.

It is clear that one of the premises of integration presupposes a diminishing of sovereignty, in the sense that decisions of the integrating community acquire force of action inside the national state. This tendency is gradually amplified as integration moves forward, but it does not presuppose the unilateral renunciation to the characteristics of the nation-state from the first moment of integration, not to speak of the period before it. **Neither the unitary character of the state, not its national character can be compatible with integration. What can be challenged here is rather administrative centralism, the inefficiency of the mechanisms of democratic control or the incorrect functioning of the mechanisms of subsidiarity.**

Globalization implies increased risks if a country's level of development is low. From this perspective, external risks cannot be separated from the fragility of the internal economic and political system. The more unstable is the area, the more dangerous it becomes when internal policies fail.

Romania must not and cannot oppose the phenomenon of globalization. What is important is to be ready to react to the challenges of globalization. We must distinguish between the objective process of globalization and the risk that it be confiscated and used to serve obscure interests.

In order to cope with globalization, we must come out of the underdeveloped area; otherwise we shall only collect the negative effects of this process, while the positive aspects will be prohibited to us. Preparing for regional or global integration first presupposes consolidating one's own national and state entity. Integration is not strictly equivalent to losing one's national identity and the dissolution of the nation-state.

Integration presupposes harmonizing national interest to the auxiliary and super-state interest. Federalization and 'regionalization' are possible, but not compulsory solutions. The solidity of democratic structures and internal stability are essential arguments for integration. Economic and cultural competitiveness are essential conditions in order to confront the shock of globalization. The lack of competitiveness and of a sense of identity security transforms the shock of globalization into a shock of civilizations.

Globalization generates new rules and mechanisms of the inter-state relations. International organisms tend to overpass state sovereignty. Without a consolidation of international legislation, such a process could become dangerous, as it might introduce inequalities between the actors of the international political stage, encouraging the politics of force and dictate. Assuming obligations must be simultaneous with assuming responsibilities, but also with acquiring rights and guarantees. Globalization is a dominant, but not singular process. A responsible diplomacy must harmoniously combine the principles of traditional diplomacy to those of integrationist diplomacy.

Although there are strong manifestations of one-dimensionality, the world is still built on the fundament of diversity. In a diverse world there can be no unilateral diplomacy. A certain degree of openness toward all azimuths is in agreement with the globalizing tendency. In the circumstances of globalization, traditional geopolitical distances and criteria no longer represent efficient means of validating the visions of international politics.

Globalization reverses the relation between direct and diffuse threats. The capacity to react to undetermined and increasingly abstract threats becomes essential to one's own security, but also for the security of the world in which we are integrating. Globalization is not the end of the line for human evolution; it is a process that will essentially affect the world. However, neither its advantages, nor its threats can be rendered absolute.

CHAPTER FOURTEEN

THE AGES OF EUROPE

14.1 The challenges of European integration

At the beginning of the new millennium, Europe is facing a great challenge: the extension of the European Union. It is a compulsory process for the future of the continent, and on its success depends the prosperity of Europe's citizens. Today, Europe is the defining area as regards the future of international relations, and, in this sense, the following years will be decisive. The events of Europe will have repercussions far beyond the borders of this continent.

If in the first ninety years of the 20th century, Europe was the center of international politics, this was mainly due to negative reasons: rivalries between European powers, leading up to the first world war; European turmoil contributing to the launching of the second world war; even during the Cold War, the hottest area was on the European continent. When, in 1989, the Cold War reached its unexpected ending, many people within or outside Europe thought that the age of euro-centrism was over. And yet, Europe is still center-stage on the international scene. The fall of the old walls set Eastern Europe free, but forced Western Europe to face the problems of the former communist bloc. Emigration became an explosive social issue, and the economic crisis of the states undergoing a transition from a planned economic system to a market economy system led to the impoverishment of most people in these countries.

The European construction, to which Romania has committed its forces, has among its main goals that of offering a new means of economic regulation. The new age of capitalism brings along, next to an indisputable leap of productivity, new economic and monetary inequalities, especially between rich and poor countries. An extended European Union, in the service of its component peoples, will have to include a set of common democratic values, of more efficient means of market regulation and of promoting sustainable development by fighting environmental problems. But, above all, I see a European Union made strong by its proximity to the citizens, to their aspirations toward social progress and new freedoms.

The process of extending the European Union will change its ways of functioning and - from the moment when it assumes its political dimension - even its very nature. As the domains of intervention of the European Union are further extending, citizens demand, in justice, that its decisional structures be more democratic, more transparent, more efficient, and that they respect the principle of subsidiarity. The states of Western Europe need not only economic prosperity, but also political stability and security. There can be no EU extension toward the countries of Central and Eastern Europe until the European organism shapes its own foreign and defense policy. Today, the EU is more than just a common market. It connects its members by a network more substantial than any economic association: the EU is becoming a security alliance.

For the first time in the last four hundred years, there exists a colossal opportunity of unifying the European continent following a peaceful political project. The extension of the European Union is an imperative of the continent's internal stability, and it answers the desire of the countries included in the former communist bloc, to integrate into the European structures. The EU combines the promise of economic prosperity with the integration into the traditional international organizations; the EU has a special significance also for the internal structures and procedures of its member states, allowing for their national reconstruction. The intensity and profoundness of the connections between member-states equals to guaranteeing a common security system for the entire continent. Finally, the mere perspective of accession considerably makes easier the task of the governments in those countries preparing for EU accession, i.e. the task of convincing their own electorate to accept difficult economic adjustments, necessary for the economic and political reform.

All governments of Central and Eastern Europe have assumed the commitment to the democratic model, with its main components: the rule-of-law, free elections, freedom of speech and market economy. This is the negotiation platform for thc eastward extension of the EU. The EU has extended before, but never to such a degree. In the past, it has enrolled small groups of easily assimilated countries. After the end of the Cold War, the EU declared that in principle it was ready to accept any country that would state its commitment to the values of the rule-of-law. However, the process of integration proper only began after the Kosovo war, when to the small group that had already begun the accession negotiations (Hungary, the Czech Republic, Poland, Estonia, Slovenia and Cyprus) were added the other countries of Central and Eastern Europe, among which Romania.

Nevertheless, there remain numerous questions regarding the rhythm and amplitude of the extension process. Firstly, the institutional reform within the EU, a compulsory pre-condition for any acceptance of new members into the European club, seems to proceed with difficulty because of the conflict of interests between bigger and smaller states, as to the differentiation of the voting shares within the commission, and as to the political embargo on Austria. Even the requirements of the EU are sometimes arbitrary and difficult to fulfill. Let us take as an example the communitarian 'acquis' (the corpus of EU laws and norms that each candidate state must adopt). This legislative corpus (of approximately 80.000 pages) grows faster than the capacity to assimilate it of the legislative systems of these candidate countries. Another delicate issue is the particular time when the first new members should be accepted. There are already discontent voices from the candidate countries, especially from those that have begun the negotiations in the first wave, and that are no longer disposed to keep supporting unpopular economic measures imposed by the EU in the absence of a firm date of acceptance. There is, then, the problem of accepting Turkey in the process of negotiations, a controversial decision made at the Helsinki summit. The insistence of the USA had a great contribution to the acceptance of this country at the negotiation talks; however, the controversies within the EU are liable to obstruct the extension process.

Nevertheless, no matter what obstacles there may be in the way of EU extension, there is no alternative to it for the security and stability of the continent. Neither the Western countries, nor those of the former communist bloc can ensure a prosperous future for themselves in the absence of an ample institutional construction that would bring together both sides of the continent in one political identity.

On May 12, 2000, in a discourse at the Humboldt University of Berlin, the German minister of Foreign Affairs Joschka Fischer put forward the suggestion of 'an institutional re-founding of the European Union', that might lead to a future 'European federation' composed of a small number of states, 'the future gravitational center of Europe'. This Federal Europe would have the benefit, as the German head of foreign affairs saw it, of its own Constitution, a bicameral Parliament and a president elected by universal suffrage. Joschka Fischer's proposal aroused numerous pro and contra reactions in the European political and journalistic environments.

I believe that the topic of federalization must be approached with extreme caution. First of all, it is necessary to delimit the economically prosperous area of Western Europe, where the nationalist issue is less acute, from the countries of Central and Eastern Europe, where the Soviet domination had stifled for fifty years the manifestation of a national identity which most of these states had only acquired as late as the last century. It is now difficult for these states to entirely renounce their national sovereignty prerogatives within the project of a United Europe. If in the field of economic policies, the globalization of commercial exchange and the increasing interdependencies between countries inevitably lead to a loss of the regulating competence of the states in favor of the transnational organisms (such as IMF, the World Bank, the World Trade Organization etc.), in international politics, the authority of the nation-states still subsists. For the countries of Central and Eastern Europe, delegating the European Commission to represent their foreign affairs and defense interests will only happen if their voice is authoritative enough in Brussels.

Still more dangerous, though, is the other pressure exercised on the nation-states – i.e., "regionalization". Local nationalisms and interethnic hate have taken the empty space left by a de-legitimized communist ideology. Encouraging these tendencies, as it happened in former Yugoslavia, had tragic repercussions. In Western Europe, the solution of decentralizing the administrative decision on the ground of subsidiarity is one of the pillars of European construction. In that area, though, ethnic tensions are mitigated, and the institutional frame already in place allows for peaceful settlement of conflicts by negotiation. But Eastern Europe does not fulfill these minimal conditions that would intermediate between various ethnic and nationalist passions at play. There lacks that impartial judge, accepted by all conflicting sides, who would dictate the rules of the game – as the war of Yugoslavia has proved. Any potential conflicting hotbed of this region risks to gain amplitude, redefining the borders and territorial autonomy being the main issues on the agenda of this area's ethnic minorities. By interpreting communitarian legislation on the rights of minorities, those interested can even go as far as claiming self-determination on ethnic criteria. On this mined land, the launching of territorial claims or of extended autonomy claims can entail, as in a domino game, a destabilization of the entire area. The solution adopted by the great powers in the case of Kosovo (extended autonomy, with the possibility of obtaining independence by referendum after a period of three years), still has several contradictions that place under doubt the present provisions of international law. Isolating the Kosovar crisis in international relations, so as not to transform it into a precedent, and its 'imperviousness' in order to prevent a destabilization of the Balkans, are *sine qua non* conditions of normalizing this geopolitical area.

After the Kosovo war, the European Union saw as a priority the establishment of its own defense capacity, without relying on the American leadership. The French minister of Foreign Affairs, Hubert Vedrine, even mentioned Europe 'as an agent of stability of the world'. Without rejecting the usefulness of NATO as the main world provider of security, the long-term interests of the European continent require a European structure of defense and foreign affairs. I shall only refer to two examples that justify the above assertion. The anti-missile defense system designed by the American administration was not negotiated with the European partners within the NATO structures. The European states, like most other powerful states of the world, oppose this much improved American defense system, that would consolidate the hegemony of the United States. Another example refers to the situation of South-Eastern Europe. After the war of Yugoslavia, the EU is not willing to give up to the United States the political and economic supremacy over the countries of that area. The stability pact for South-Eastern Europe is a preponderantly European creation, and is supported financially by the EU alone. To the extent that national vanities are overcome, and that these responsibilities are delegated to communitarian institutions, the EU will soon be one voice on the international stage.

I believe that the European project will only succeed if a new doctrine starts to function within the international community, based on the progressive interests of countries and among countries – a community based on the equal value of each state, on the founding of rights and reciprocal responsibilities. This does not mean that states will no longer pursue their own interests, or that there will be no occasions on which these interests will turn to be contradictory, to a degree that diminishes or amplifies the wish for mutual understanding. Without nourishing illusions, I can but notice that our problems are shared on an increasing scale, and that societies and economies are threatened when there is no understanding concerning the settlement of such problems. The European Union represents the most obvious manifestation of the necessity that nations cooperate among themselves. The common interests and problems have led, in this case, to mutual responsibilities and mutual advantages.

14.2 Romania and the new economy

The economy of the world is moving from a predominantly industrial society toward a new set of rules – the informational society. The dynamics of the new economy are strong, and digital technology makes the accessing, processing, collecting of data and the transmission of information an increasingly easier and cheaper activity. The scale of available information creates huge opportunities for its exploitation into new products and services.

The experience of the United States and the European Union proves that the new technologies can promote economic growth and can provide workplaces. However, the success of this new economy will depend on the ability of consumers to fully profit from the opportunities thus created. In order to do this, they must acquire the skills that enable them to access the desired information and to successfully interact on the Internet.

On the European level, certain measures were taken to promote the informational society: the liberalization of telecommunications, the establishment of a clear legal framework for trade, and the support granted to the Research/Development sector. These policies evolve at the same time with the necessary structural reforms, in order to increase productivity, from the development of digital technologies to a favorable fiscal environment and the respect granted to the rights of intellectual property.

Accessing and using the Internet, by computer or cable, should become common for our country as well. In order to achieve this, Romania must act against its structural weakness and overcome the handicaps that keep it from quickly developing digital technologies:

- the Internet and trade access is generally costly, slow and insecure;
- there lacks a dynamic, enterprising culture, service-oriented;
- the public sector is not active enough in order to allow for the development of new applications and services.

Romania will have to focus preponderantly on actions that address these handicaps: ensuring cheaper access to the Internet;

computerization electronic commerce; a faster Internet for researchers and students; financing IT enterprisers; accelerating informatization in governmental institutions and public administration. Each action targets specific objectives that need to be reached as soon as possible.

At a global level, the development tendency in production and economy is most important for all participants. The problem is how to make sure that, when the situation is stable, the different social groups will have found their places in the new world order and in the new division of labor. Most admirers of the successful 'new economy' model seem to be unaware of the scale and nature of the sacrifices that this model presupposes. They never mention poverty or the increased economic inequality, though these are important aspects, often brought to bear in debates.

Trust-Flexibility-Sustainability. I believe that this triptych of concepts defines genuine democracy, and ultimately defines the expectations of the citizen who refuses to be a 'per capita', a humble taxpayer and the victim of an obtuse administration. Paraphrasing what I thought is defining for Romania's present stage, the passage from Marx to Coca-Cola, I should say we are passing from an age of tyrannical administration to an age of the modern citizen, free to build a career on any meridian, to acquire a bi-, tri- or multilingual family and to place his savings in any corner of the world, a citizen who can connect live to the mayor of New York, London or Paris and obtain an audience through the Internet.

Therefore Romania is facing two major simultaneous changes that demand from us to leave aside everything we took for granted and to move on to a new lifestyle. The good news is that this change, imposed by the new economy, means more freedom of initiative, of movement, of creation. And we have been long expecting these opportunities.

What is there to do for a social-democratic government in these circumstances? My answer is: begin a firm battle for modernization, without missing beats, without hesitations, in order to fully enter the new world. The three concepts I have mentioned at the beginning seem to me the major goals of this battle for the future, a battle which I assume next to my cabinet and party colleagues, next to all our compatriots who have understood that there is no other chance.

The new economy presupposes a major change, not only of rules, but also of mentalities. What seemed solid and efficient when I started out in my career, now seems morally outdated. From here results that the rate of erosion of various categories of problems, beginning with the technical products, lifestyle, objects of material civilization, and ending with the way in which a campaign, a government or a family can be conceived are changing at quick pace, and the society must be ready with new solutions to the citizens' expectations.

We are living in the middle of a crisis of trust that is difficult to combat and difficult to manage. We need an effort, to which the new technologies can greatly contribute, an effort of persuasion by consistency in our obedience to the law and to the rights of each category, of each individual in particular, in order to be able to build a climate of trust and accountability.

We must be able to join in the rhythm of life of a genuine global-village businessman, who has asked a question this very morning and needs the answer today at noon. Thus can we build the trust that I was mentioning, and that we all need. Every single mayor must be able to receive quickly and directly the requests of his local community. Every single communitarian service provider must be able to react in the shortest time to any kind of request. This means integrated management, this means computerized databases of the system that is provided for, of the service equipment and teams, it means real-time databases of service subscription and verifiable invoicing. Moreover, this must mean a competition that would diminish prices and visibly increase quality.

A dynamic economic environment, in which regulations keep up the pace with market transformations, a strong economic environment capable of imposing changes in the philosophy of governance and in the competence model of various professional categories, this is what we believe must be built in Romania. In order to get there we need not pull down the entire economy, but on the contrary, we must give a chance to companies that are still breathing, we must bring back to the operating room the companies with serious tumors, but with yet other healthy components. In this process of straightening and normalization, we need, we must use the new methods of enterprise management, which make it possible to trace down on the computer not only every *leu* spent and every piece contributing to the whole, but also every contract under way.

No doubt, this is useful in an economic context with no financial blocking, with no crisis affecting the entire production flow. We hope to be able to unblock entire industrial systems, as we investigate and support the access of Romanian products to as many markets as possible. Consequently, the need to interact is rising at every level of social life. The need for blitz competence is also rising, a complex competence with immediate reaction abilities, with a capacity to model several possible situations, and a capacity of multi-disciplinary analysis.

The exigencies of electronic commerce mean not only operating speed, but also delivery abilities, flexibility of communication and transport, integration into global systems, and all these systems will only accept us if we are competitive and compatible. The first measures to be taken will be:

- the computerization of local governments
- creating training mechanisms at various levels in the field of informatics, for various user categories
- encouraging the decrease of technical support charges – e.g. of communications in order to enhance Internet access
- taking steps to intensify communication activities by electronic means, and supporting the companies and institutions that will develop interfaces with the citizen

Globalization means a re-evaluation and re-discovery of the spiritual richness and experience of humankind. These assets become the property of us all, giving us an extra chance to be creative and winning. As the prosperity of our compatriots is a priority target, we shall militate not only in favor of short-term efficiency, but also in favor of building premises for long-term success, and these premises are offered by the new economy.

CHAPTER FIFTEEN

ROMANIA'S IMAGE WORLDWIDE: AN UNMARKETABLE PRODUCT?

"Any country weakened by starvation,
plagues, difficult chores
or unstable institutions
draws upon itself the unrelenting lust
of its neighbors."

Jean Levi

The power of mass media today can no longer be questioned. The omnipresence of the means of mass information, the process of information circulation in real time are facts of the contemporary world. Geopolitical changes, at least in the last ten years, are to a great extent due to the influence of mass media.

Foreign politics has also undergone transformations as a consequence of this technological revolution. The opinions of the majority, as they are transposed into the results of public opinion polls, are taken into consideration by political decision-makers in an increasing number of countries. It is not a 'democracy of opinion', but rather an 'opinion regime'. This is a reality, whether we see it as negative or positive. In the richest and strongest countries, public opinion is submitted to an informational bombardment with a strong emotional content. As a result of the 'media effect', there appear chain reactions in the citizens' ranks. Political officials are forced to face enormous pressure every time they prepare to adopt a public decision. A government can do nothing else but submit to the demands of public opinion. It is its daily role.

Every single day, the press provides interesting reports, new information, subtle analyses, sometimes even useful guidelines. But, at the same time, the press often dramatizes and simplifies its analyses, compares the incomparable, practices selective amnesia, privileges the ephemeral and anathemizes excessively. For a country attempting to promote its external image, ensuring the support of mass media is essential. Romania not only failed to create a positive image in Western mass media, but also had to cope with a hostile press campaign. As it would be impossible to approach this topic along the entire period generically called 'transition', I shall only refer to the period of the last four years.

We cannot proceed to a clear evaluation of international press reactions concerning Romania's social and political evolution and its standing in the world, without a few general introductory remarks. We can discern five major characteristics: post-electoral euphoria in 1996, perplexity before the lack of performance of the new government, the effects of NATO's intervention in the area, the shock caused by opinion polls predicting a reverse alternation to power, and the preoccupation with Romania's perspectives. These particularities related to the case of Romania have not been excepted from the general features of structuring information and opinion based on main sources: correspondents of agencies and newspapers accredited in Romania, embassies, internal political forces, specialized structures serving banking and international business circles. However curious it may seem, all are dominated, in different ways, by what the jargon of information media calls 'the audimat'. One transmits and publishes, not necessarily what is seen, but what is requested, or what the correspondents or diplomats think might capture the attention of the recipient. Evidently, priority is given to yellow press reports and analyses, whether this means cyanides, the miners' march and handicapped children, or acute interethnic conflicts and governmental crises; such topics constitute the safest vehicle of penetrating a domain at least as competitive as the merciless competition to monopolize the markets.

Especially significant among the whole of international comments are the syntheses occasioned by the celebration of ten years since the revolution of 1989. In a synthesis presented by *Radio Free Europe* and signed by Jeremy Bransten, entitled 'Ten years after the bloody revolution of 1989, public disillusionment prevails', the author states: 'Ten years after the revolution and three years after the accession to power of pro-Western leaders, partisans of a free market economy, Romania suffers from collective depression'. The conclusion brings us back to the euphoria following the 1996 elections. The results of those elections were then interpreted not only as a democratic normalization, by means of the first instance of peaceful alternation to power, but also as a defeat of 'the communist forces', a genuine 'departure from the past'. That is why the disillusionment is explained not so much by the lack of performance of the administrations coming and going in quick succession, but rather by the fact that the new administration was forced to go for reformist, unpopular measures, that had been avoided by the previous Executive. The author adds that 'it is still unclear whether the present policy of economic reform will lead to better times. The question now is: will the simpler Romanians have the patience to once again take in other promises for a happy future?' The synthesis concludes with the opinions of the Romanian sociologist Vladimir Tismaneanu, who states that the popularity PDSR enjoyed at that time 'is merely the result of a disillusionment with the new government. One may expect a vote that expresses this disillusionment, and if this disillusionment is followed by another, there is a danger of having groups alien to the parliamentary trends using this kind of situation.' This last sentence seeks to be a warning based on the opinions of anonymous observers: 'If such an evolution takes place', say these observers, 'and if Romania's economic decline continues, this country risks being left behind in the race for integration into the main European trend, including into organizations such as the European Union and NATO. The challenge of the following decade will no doubt be making sure that the Balkans ware not once again torn from Europe by a movement of the Iron Curtain a few kilometers to the East'.

In other press articles dealing with this topic, one can notice the inversion of ideological criteria that can be attributed to an insufficient distancing from the past of the authors, or to an insufficient distancing from the black-and-white practice specific to the Cold War. The tendency is not alien, though, to the effect of internal political disputes in Romania, nor is it alien to the consequences of ambitious trends of the same nature coming from abroad. Incipient traces of these can be found in a series of 1998 commentaries, while a certain apprehension as to Romania's evolution started to show its teeth, leading up, during its last days, to a veritable campaign for the salvation *in extremis* of our country. The most representative in this respect is an almost programmatic article by Daniel N. Nelson, published on December 28, 1998, in the *Washington Post*, under the title 'Forgotten Romania needs Western helps, and needs it urgently'. As its conclusion, the author writes: 'These are a few initiatives worth considering: public and unequivocal support for Romania's accession to NATO in the next round; strong diplomatic supportive signals by means of top-level visits to Bucharest; inviting Mr. Isarescu to Washington and, if possible, the establishment of the Romania 2000 Fund, launched by a major stimulating contribution of the United States, by approximately 100 million dollars.' Nelson concludes his suggestion with this final observation: 'The grant given to Romania must not mean military involvement or great sums of money. But it does mean the refusal to wait until intolerant demagogues come to power, or until the country is flooded by a paroxysm of violence. Then surely Nicolae and Elena will laugh in their graves'. In other parts of the article, preparatory to these conclusions, Nelson is more specific. A troubling opinion poll, he writes, shows that 'a majority of the Romanians believe that life under Ceausescu was better, and two thirds believe that the country is led the wrong path'. The author states that president Emil Constantinescu, confronted with the upsurge of revolt against 'crime, corruption and the deterioration of living standards, discharged the Prime Minister,

Radu Vasile, from office. Probably somebody forgot to tell him that, according to the Romanian Constitution, presidents are not allowed to discharge prime ministers'.

This treatment of the situation of Romania, combining the ideological approach with appeals for help, became characteristic especially after the Kosovo war, simultaneous with the evocation of the damages suffered by Romania as a consequence to the support lent to NATO intervention. On July 23, 1999, *International Herald Tribune* published, under the signature of the British analyst Tom Gallagher, an article revealing that Madeleine Albright had declared that Europe had to pay for the reconstruction of the Balkans. Her statement was in obvious contradiction to that of the German Minister of Foreign Affairs, Joschka Fischer, who had declared on July 8, in Bucharest, that 'the Pact must not be understood as a modality of granting material and financial benefits to compensate economic losses; on the contrary, its goal is to promote the possibilities of a long-term development of this region'. Further on, the author evokes what he considers to be the consequences of a disagreement in attitude: 'The Occident must no longer ignore the consequences of letting Romania go astray. Next year there will be elections. Already now, the ex-communists who held power until 1996, seek to stir interethnic turmoil in Transylvania, a province with a large Hungarian minority. Adrian Nastase, the most likely strong man of the country if pro-Western reformists lose the battle, has predicted a hot autumn in this province. He claims that NATO's tearing apart Kosovo from under Belgrade's control creates a precedent that will weaken Romania's capacity to keep Transylvania at bay'. On February 7, 2000, *The Washington Post* discusses once again on the economic consequences of NATO's intervention in Kosovo, dwelling, in a correspondence from Galati, on the anti-NATO feelings that a potential blocking of the Danube might cause. 'In fact', the article goes on, 'here rumors have it that the alliance bombed the bridges not because it tried to paralyze the Yugoslav army, but because it planned to strike South-Eastern Europe and to stimulate the commerce on the Rhine, Europe's other great commercial river, to the advantage of Western Europe. Conspiracy theories spread here as fast as the fog of this winter, wrapping the docks at the mouth of the river... However strange such ideas might seem to Washington and Brussels officials, they have undermined NATO-s positions here and have diverted the attention from Yugoslavia, Belgrade and Serbia in general'.

In yet another synthesis on the ensemble of Central and Eastern Europe's revolution in the ten years elapsed since 1989, entitled 'Euphoria was replaced by disillusionment and prudence', the same analyst of *Radio Free Europe*, Jeremy Bransten, divided the states in question into two major groups: a) the few countries for which this decade meant the freedom to succeed in economic and social reform; b) most countries, for which these years meant the freedom to choose populism, nationalism and economic failure. He includes Romania in the second category. 'The geographic factors, the factors of industrial development and democratic experience are different in The Czech Republic compared to Romania... But, while the characteristics of relative prosperity are more visible in Prague than in Bucharest, the attitudes of the two peoples are not all that different'. Starting from the witticism of a leading Czech sociologist, that 'it is easier to make fish soup out of an aquarium than the other way around', he writes: 'From the point of view of honesty and social responsibility, both Prague and Bucharest, says the sociologist Siclova, we have soup fish rather than aquarium'. Bransten continues: 'In the Czech Republic, the unreformed communist party ranks second in opinion polls, and in Romania, the ex-president Ion Iliescu and his neo-communist associates rank first, way ahead of the present governing coalition'. The confusion reflected in many analyses gets deeper as the realities of the ex-communist countries are less easily fitted into the old recycled Kremlinologists. Siclova is of the following opinion: 'I think it is highly important for us, the ex-communist countries, to discuss our experiences among ourselves; because we are yet presented as freakish animals or aquarium fish. We are analyzed by Western political pundits and politicians, but I do not believe that this is the best approach. There are many things about us that Western people simply do not understand'.

Trying to lend more coherence to his analyses, another *Radio Free Europe* commentator, Michael Shafir, writes, confronted with an avalanche of Romanian and foreign opinion polls, with different evaluations of a fundamental feeling of disappointment: 'How must we interpret these figures? To have them yield the conclusion that a return to communism is imminent or merely probable, this time without Soviet tanks, would have the same value of protecting historical repetition. Instead of rushing to quick generalizations, it would be wiser to examine each poll in its immediate context. After all, all public opinion specialists warn us that opinion polls are a reflection of an immediate situation. The very same Romanian poll that renders a schizophrenic image of Ceausescu situates president Emil Constantinescu as ranking second (18% among the politicians who caused the greatest disasters to Romania). No one can take this for real, no matter what their position is in respect to Constantinescu. In other words, the respondents answered having in mind immediate performance criteria, and they will be ready to shift opinions as the biased impact of daily difficulties make room for other guilty parties'. A saying that this analysis overlooks is that there is never a cramming for failure. Unless the author of the article has another kind of guilty parties in mind.

From what we have seen so far, it ensues that, in spite of the ratification by foreign diplomats and politicians of the thesis embraced by Romania's exponents, namely that our country is a factor of stability in the Balkans, it is in reality considered a potential factor of instability, both because its internal political and economic 'frailty' and because of its vulnerability to the surrounding evolution. From this point of view, Romania's domestic and foreign policies, dominated by circumstantial preoccupations, do not manage to look convincing in the final round of talks of the Romania-European Union Commission, held in the spring of 1999. Europe Weekly writes that 'in spite of a politeness manifest on both sides', the European Union diplomats considers that Romania is the country where replacing ministers has become a substitute for reform. Eventually, this opinion turned into a thesis claiming that at the basis of reform stagnation lies the way politics is practiced in Romania. In a correspondence from Bucharest, published by Le Monde on the eve of president Constantinescu's visit to Paris, the author stated: 'Economic reform is also down because of internal political tensions.

The victory won in late 1996 by the center-right coalition... has not managed to administrate the arranged marriage within the coalition. As a consequence of this portrait (n.b., the correspondence exposes the contradictions manifest in the coalition), Romanians have developed a tendency of turning their backs to politics'.

To this day, Western media, whatever their sources, have not been able to solve their fundamental dilemma: is the special instance of Romania caused by the obstacles that the opposition might have placed against reform, in order for them to regain power due to acute economic disappointment, or is it caused by the weaknesses of the governing coalition? Despite it all, these publications do not forget the basic deficiencies of the policy of the European Union and the Western world as a whole. And I am not referring to analyses inspired from within Romania, attempting to raise help. In an article published by the *Washington Post*, under the joint signature of Steven Rattner, deputy manager of the financial group Lazard Freres, and Michael Froman, distinguished member of the Council of Foreign Relations and of the German institution Marshall Fund, a different point of view is displayed. Under the title "Try to introduce more vigorously a vital economic artery in the Balkans", the two authors state: "The largest country of the region, Romania, which seems to come close to surpassing the impasse in its relations with the International Monetary Fund, can only contract external loans with a 17% interest. A weak governmental coalition can hardly control expenditure or reduce increasing corruption, while inflation is rising to 50% annually. As for the contribution of the United States, we notice a surplus of coordinators, very little money and a lack of connection between these two components. Europe is acting slowly in injecting euros, and even more slowly in articulating a concrete vision for the integration of the Balkans into the rest of Europe. The Occident must focus on long-term solutions'. After presenting a harsh picture of the political and institutional conditions of Romania, the authors add: 'No drastic measure, such as instituting a monetary council, could settle these issues'. The position of the International Monetary Fund, of severe conditionality, though necessary, will not be sufficient, as 'in many cases, the Balkan states do not have the technical and political capacity to answer such a pressure. It is therefore necessary that the Occident make a joint effort in order to ensure the technical support needed, while at the same time maintaining a pressure on the Balkan governments to reform, and even going over their heads where possible. As the structural reform progresses, we must see that the Balkan states open to one another and, more importantly, that they integrate into Western Europe – which will demand from the European Union a responsible economic policy, especially in the commercial domain. Above all, we must not let the region fall into an economic disintegration based on ethnic cleavages. We must try – and try harder than before'. The publication of such analyses raises the question, not only as to how they are received and debated in the Western decision-making cores, but as to how they are debated and exploited by the decision-making cores of the respective countries, including Romania.

Such a manner of reacting became, in the analysis published in *Le Monde Diplomatique* by the French expert Catherine Savary, a source of undermining the credibility of all actions past and present. It shows, for instance, that propagandistic 'politicianism', together with the existence of precarious objective conditions, are placing under doubt the way a fundamental component of the reform, privatization, is truly conducted. The article reads: "The statistics of privatization in Russia, as well as in the Czech Republic, Romania, Poland or other countries, are 'arranged' function of what the foreign creditors, the International Monetary Fund or the European Commission are expecting. These countries are trying to prove that they have committed to the right path. They privatize everything, including companies that did well within the old structure, and sometimes they move to privatize even though there is no real contribution of capital'. The author concludes with a peremptory statement: 'The capitalism now in full process of instauration is missing capital and organic bourgeoisie'. The article touches upon many other issues illustrating the topic of its title, 'Eastward, Transition to the Unknown".

Both *Washington Post* and *Radio Free Europe*, in analyzing this impact, find that the division into previously used categories is no longer sufficient: liberal countries and countries that have not yet broken the bond with the past, pro-Western political groups and neo-communist groups. Michael Shafir, in an article broadcast on February 3, 2000, by *Radio Free Europe*, stated that 'while Romania displayed concern as to the evolutions in Austria', the temptations of a similar evolution go beyond the cleavages established in previous commentaries. He says: 'In Vienna, Schuessel, moved by the conviction that the end justifies the means, is trying to make the Freedom Party look like a respectable, democrat party, which it obviously is not. In Romania there existed a similar situation, when the Social Democracy Party of Romania, led by the ex-president Ion Iliescu, joined forces with the extremists: The Greater Romania Party (PRM), the Romanian Party for National Unity (PUNR) and the Socialist Labor Party (PSM). But now, Radu Vasile seems ready to move on, by building a neo-fascist party. He must be carefully watched for the tendency of lending it what the Germans call 'a respectable look'. That PNTCD has fundamentalists among its members, the views of which are not far from those of the extreme right, is not something unique. But PNTCD as a whole is not an extremist group and, as it is known, it was believed for a while that Vasile belongs to its pragmatic, anti-fundamentalist side. A Romanian proverb, quoted by Iliescu in support of his alliance with PRM, says that "you have to befriend the devil if it helps you cross the bridge." But the devil turned out to have used the friend to cross the bridge himself and then to throw the friend in the waters. This is not something unique to Romanian politics either. Using the examples of Hungary, where Csurka's extremist party was wooed by the party in power, FIDESZ, and of Slovakia, where the alliance between Meciar's party and the Haider admirers is re-launched as the National Slovakian Party, the author concludes: "In the context of this alliance between Schuessel and Haider one has to monitor closely the emergence of a similar trend in East-Central Europe".

Washington Post picks up this type of analysis to show that EU advanced candidates and NATO members are prudent with respect to criticisms of the developments in Austria but harsher in their criticism of the European Union for involving itself in Austria's internal affairs. The article quotes the former Czech conservative prime minister Vaclav

Klaus, a would-be umpire of his country's politics, who states that "Haider is a smaller evil than the European Union's attempt to attack the final decision of one of its members."

A paper of the Johns Hopkins University expert Charles Gati warns future EU members that meeting the political conditions set in Brussels also means "accepting lesser sovereignty". *Radio Free Europe* goes even further to accuse right-wing prime-minister Viktor Orban of having entered a pact with Csurka's extremists and having tolerated the anti-Semite pronouncements of government members. Hungary currently seems to be an oasis of political stability and is therefore not something for the West to worry about. But international pressures, such as the report published in December 1999 by the Anti-Defamation League, could force Orban to change his attitude. One may notice that after a period of initial ideological euphoria and 'triumphalism' in the international and especially Western press, the special case of Romania is now receiving more attention. As the favorite topic of the state of minorities receded from prominence after the signing of the treaty with Hungary, the participation of the UDMR in the government and the end of the Council of Europe supervision, the problems of reform, the chances of Euro-Atlantic integration, and the internal political evolution became paramount questions. Although the question of national minorities is from time to time discussed either with respect to the Hungarians or with respect to the Roma population, the Czech Republic and Slovakia are now in the spotlight.

After Hungary's admission to NATO, *Nepszabadag* published a warning, signed by a Hungarian political scientist, that "no matter what Romanians think, there will not be a second wave of NATO and EU integration for them because the first wave marks the new European frontiers beyond which there will be no foreign investments and no transatlantic security." This December 1997 article was followed by a somewhat more balanced one in the March of 1999. This time it was argued that NATO admission put an end to Hungary's downfall, dominated by the Trianon Treaty, which left the country "without two thirds of its territory and population". The article also states that "the future will not recreate the past." The new geo-strategic position of

Hungary will also ensure "the protection of Hungarian minorities in the neighboring countries, in spite of the fact that in Serbia, Romania and Slovakia some political forces still play the Hungarian card." The newspaper article also declares that "for the first time since the Trianon treaty the aspirations of the Hungarians are supported from abroad." But this also creates obligations to Hungary: "The same way that we have had to give up the redrawing of borders, we now have to give up the territorial autonomy of the Hungarian minorities." This could be, says the article, compensated by the implicit acknowledgement of collective rights and the federalization through 'regionalization' under the umbrella of the European Union. The French journalist Alexandre Adler noted in an article titled "The new world after 1989" that the rapid move of Central and Eastern Europe to the West after the fall of the Berlin Wall could be responsible for the "liquidation without protests of the unity of Yugoslavia and of the Czech Republic". Moreover, he believes that such a process is far from over due to the vulnerable spots in the area, among which he counts the uncertainties "with respect to the political unity of fragile nations such as Croatia and Romania, and the future of Moldova, which had its own small war in 1992-1993." These uncertainties are directly connected to the possibility of a rapprochement between Kiev and Moscow, which would turn Ukraine into "the major stake of the next decade."

In an interview taken by *International Herald Tribune* the Foreign Minister of Bulgaria, Nadeja Mihailova, expressed her opinion that the whole evolution in the Balkans would have been different, had Bulgaria and Romania been NATO members as the Kosovo crisis started. She stated: "Had Bulgaria, Romania and other stable democracies been admitted as members, the Kosovo conflict would not have taken place. The breaking of Milosevic's monopoly on information has been a debated issue. In his propaganda he used the example of Yugoslavia's neighbors, pointing out that, in spite of their relationships with NATO, Bulgaria and Romania were less developed than Yugoslavia. For this reason, the encouragement of their admission is "the key to the future stability of this region." After this March 1999 interview, *Le Monde* published an article titled "Unrest in the Romanian

Transylvania" signed by Professor Joseph Yacoubi of the Catholic University of Lyon who noted, among others, that "everything was going all right until Hungary entered NATO and the Yugoslavian war began." Using UDMR statements as arguments, the author states that "the Hungarians cannot accept a grade of good behavior from the Romanian government and reject its double-faced policy. They believe that the problems of national minorities are not solved and refuse to become an export sample for the Romanian government." The author also shows that the evolution of ex-Yugoslavia re-values the thesis of territorial autonomy of the minorities. Writes Yacoubi: "One can hear voices declaring that if autonomy is not obtained through the Parliament it will be secured by a bottom-up movement." To conclude, he notes: "It remains to be seen whether autonomy should be exercised from within existing societies, as provided in international law, or by questioning the national frontiers... Will the Romanian debate over regionalism, federalism and autonomy serve the deepening of the democratic process in the direction of a multicultural society, or will it become an alibi for an evolution in the sense of separatism and ethnocentrism?"

The improvised character of the solutions and reactions in these press comments shows that a real dialogue and a profound debate on the problems of historical transition in the old communist countries are not actually unfolding. There are however plenty of opportunistic mass media positions that mimic the engagement of the West and the reform in the East. An accurate reflection of Romania's image in the Western mass media is still an object of desire for most of the opinion leaders in our country!

15.1 A Romanian model of inter-ethnic cohabitation

The redefinition of international relations, the breaking-up of nation-states into regions, the internationalization of the market, the end of history or the tendency of English to become a universal language – all these issues have their roots in the phenomenon of globalization. Perceived as a leveling pressure, the processes that create globalization in different fields are interesting due to the identity crises that they engender. These crises are one of the main sources of inter-ethnic conflict and although they manifest themselves periodically they are in a permanent state of latency.

The national state is facing a double challenge. One challenge comes from outside and it is represented by the uniformity-generating globalization. The second challenge is a certain degree of subversion from within and it is related to 'regionalization' as a phenomenon that produces diversity and distinction. Is the national state the guarantor of a measure of tolerance and of solidarity that are able to prevent ethnic conflicts? The answer is in the negative. In fact, one may assert the contrary insofar as the means of solidarity presuppose an antinomian relation with an Other. These means are intimately related to culture and language as they only unify by excluding, more or less explicitly, the ethnic minority citizen. It remains to be seen whether the nation state will survive or succumb in front of the existing pressures it has to face. But it is important to understand that it is not a sufficient source of identity and solidarity precisely because it places these two concepts in opposition in spite of the fact that it operates in an ethnically heterogeneous space.

Regions demand their rights on the background of such identity crises. In many European countries the tendency is to coalesce around a smaller but more powerful identity denominator. Flanders, Walloon, the Basque Country or Catalonia, the Pandan or the Tirol regions, Northern Ireland or Scotland are too numerous examples to admit classification as exceptions. They can no longer be hidden behind a process of European unification that is linear and unavoidable. We cannot fail to notice that we are actually inhabiting two Europes: one undergoing full construction, the other threatened by isolationist, disintegrationist calls. Isolation is perceived as a source of superior integration.

If we define 'regionalization' as a process of coalescence around the smallest local identity denominator it becomes easy to understand the meaning of the concept of spatial solidarity. When this source of identity is solely ethnical and linguistic, it produces isolation and a tendency to separate from the Other. However, there are countless factors besides ethnicity and language that generate identity and solidarity in a given area. They can be related to local economic relations, to a common past, to a common network of transportation and communications, even to local language and dialects. All these factors blend with each other and all identify the inhabitants of a certain area as such. The territory, by means of its many sources of local solidarity, is a factor of cohesion and stability. It generates spatial solidarity defined in terms that do not presuppose the traditional exclusiveness based on ethnic criteria. People may have different cultures, religions and mother tongues but share goods, interests and understand each other in dialect, in the "language of the place". In their worlds, they share the experience of alterity, of cohabiting with different people.

Peacemaker Territories are therefore based on the existence of strong spatial solidarity. They are areas without interethnic conflict, inhabited by people bound by their interest in a set of common values. Their need to be perceived as distinct will not involve ethnocentric arguments and will always be oriented outward, against the involvement of hierarchically superior entities (the government, local administration) in strictly local affairs. In this way Peacemaker Territories depend on the respect for the principle of subsidiarity, too often mentioned in programs and, especially in Eastern Europe, too little applied in the practical administration of provinces.

The most important source of conflict in South-Eastern Europe is the resurrection of retarded national ideals. The un-fulfillment of these ideals conserved a mystical character and kept them alive in spite of their latency during the communist period. The artificial conglomerate of former Yugoslavia could not satisfy the thirst for national identity of the ethnic groups that were part of the federation. Mummified until 1990, these ideals turned into doctrines of violence and engendered inter-ethnic wars and crimes.

Unlike all other Balkan countries, Romania knew no such conflict. Moreover, it does not even have the ethnic problems that most Central European countries are facing, even though the risk of such conflict is lower in Central Europe than in the Balkans. Naturally, this is not to say that extremist parties, xenophobia and vehement nationalism are absent. Nevertheless, there are no ethnic conflicts or, at worst, they are limited to rare individual conflicts. Radical parties are a small minority in Parliament, they are not associated to terrorist organizations, are not explicitly fascist, and do not specifically advocate the elimination of individuals belonging to ethnic minorities.

The general climate of ethnic tolerance is one of Romania's major trump cards. It is the result of a venerable tradition of cohabitation in an ethnically heterogeneous space rather than the object of political projects. Romania's geopolitical position has had a decisive role in this respect. The existence of Romanians unfolded amidst an impressive number of other cultures with which the autochthonous spirit had to communicate and interact. The heritage of this past is the creation of a space of tolerance and interculturality (cross-cultural negotiations), which survived the "gunpowder barrel" and the leveling forces of communism.

Sketching a model of interethnic cohabitation for our country will be possible after an analysis of areas of solidarity in Romania and of their relation to the absence of conflicts. The lesson of peaceful cohabitation and of the respect toward the Other is probably the most valuable contribution that Romania can make to the process of construction of a stable and united Europe. Backing this trump card by all possible means (theoretical works conceptualizing the Romanian model of interethnic cohabitation) might be a way to compensate for the at least short-term performance deficit of its economic and productive system. Below are some possible directions for such as study:

- The contribution to the creation of a theoretical apparatus meant to consolidate the Romanian case in favor of a European construction realized with respect for sub-continental and sub-national identities.

• Offering an answer to the resolution of interethnic crises and conflicts; the dilemma of preventing versus managing crises.

• Building new theoretical foundations for the process of coalescing and developing civil society nuclei at the Eastern-most periphery of Europe; the structures of civil society perceived as a buffer against the potentially conflicting cleavage of Center and Periphery.

• Ensuring the theoretical coherence of a model capable of being exported on the whole continent (and especially in the Balkans) as a mechanism for the construction of a new Europe.

• The invalidation of the legitimacy of the processes of regional atomization, of the dismemberment of nation-states as result of smaller identity denominators.

The bodies established by the Romanian state in order to facilitate our rapprochement with the European Union (especially the Government's Department of European Integration and the Brussels Commission negotiating Romania's EU admission) currently lack the power to elaborate their own programs and projects. Most often the activity of these institutions is limited to the simple reception and translation of documents and proposals coming from European officials. **In order to facilitate Romania's rapprochement with the European Union the communication between the two sides in the process of integration has to work both ways rather than in just one direction**. The same deficiency pertains to civil society associations. Civic activism and the actions aimed at popularizing the corpus of EU norms cannot make up for the conceptualization of the Romanian specificity among the countries seeking European integration. Considering the sacrifices demanded from the Romanian population in order for Romania to accede to the EU structures (and especially the predictable wave of dismissals in industry, public services and administration), the legitimacy of European integration will not be ensured merely by the assimilation of the community 'acquis' or by the application of rigid fiscal and monetary measures. It takes an affirmation of our identity in a European context to make the Romanian project stand out among those of the other candidates and simultaneously ensure internal legitimacy.

CHAPTER SIXTEEN

QUESTIONS AT THE END OF THE CENTURY

"If, in his passivity toward the darkest parts of our history, man enlarged his experience so much as to become a new being, shouldn't he be able to renew himself in order to continue his emancipation and conquer his freedom?"

Georges Duveau

16.1 A Tower of Babel of ideologies

The individuals and the community, the nations and globalization, the re-writing of concepts that were thought to be fundamental for the 20th century – here are some of the questions placed at the convergence between the social sciences and political science, between theoretical politics and practical policies. While major political conceptions are in a state of slow decline, radical and protesting ones are springing from everywhere in the *chiaroscuro* of a *fin de siecle* West. Anarcho-capitalism, a form of Protestantism degenerated into right-wing populism, anti-immigration, ideologized veto groups, etc. are peripheral fluxes derived from the loss of substance of contemporary liberal democracy. The volatility of the voting process and the weak participation of the citizens in the "electoral spectacle" are the realities of a world in which a political middle ground between direct democracy and the optimization of political control at all levels of political decision are sought after.

Many critical voices are accusing the leveling Western system of having altered the individual and its relations with the community. **Only the strong survive** is the product of an "American winner cult" slogan that seems to have nothing in common with the ideals of the Enlightenment and of European humanism. Caught for a long while in the game played by the two powers, America and Russia, Europe now seeks to rediscover its old vocation: that of theorizing. The virtues of the old democratic system of reference are brought to the fore in a "grand retour" attempt to find once again the conceptual coherence of a Europe that is a master of its own tradition.

The 1970's confirmed the false rationality and the inability to perform of Soviet-type regimes and persuaded USSR "fellow travelers" to give up on their red orthodoxy. The concept of revolution and the experience of communism in the world of 'tiermondism' acquired a different significance than that of the "older brother". Many factions started to claim themselves from Guevara and Trotsky rather than from the Kremlin. Simultaneously, official Leninism was challenged by 'eurocommunism' and 'althusserianism' as the "new left" was trying to uncover the errors of "real socialism". The Chinese strategic and doctrinaire variations after the cultural revolution, the default of the eurocommunist temptation which failed to reconcile the Marxist dogma of the "dictatorship of the proletariat" with the pluralism of political visions engendered more uncertainty about the fundamental principles of a closed world.

The explosion of social democracy and the transformation of this political trend into an evolutionary path "from within" (the Bad Godesberg program is the birth certificate of this new way) was another dimension of the European politics of the 20th century. The critique of the dogmatic rigidity and of radical presuppositions, the adoption of pluralism and of an environment of competition of ideas and programs, reformism and the rediscovery of the positivism of moderate thinking, were the attributes that enabled social democracy to have its notable successes in the Northern countries, as well as in the German and Anglo-Saxon world.

The ideological color of a century or an epoch is not and, indeed, cannot be uniform. The buds of programmatic ideas and projects always bloom, and they amend the systems violently or symbolically. The new left, the new right or the "preventive anticommunism", the third way, etc. only indicate that in the political practice discourses never converge. The reconstruction of social Darwinism, sociobiology and ethnology, the evacuation of ideological sites by the new trend of political anthropology, the discovery of the Europeanized ethnic as opposed to nationalist ethnocracy (in the "different but European" catch-phrase), the return to European elitism and traditionalism – all these things mean nothing other than attempts not to stop globalization but to prevent the deformation of the world in which democracy was born.

The economic crisis of 1970-1980 was preceded, according to the historians, by a cultural and political crisis. "The thirty glorious years" of Keynesianism and the welfare state were receiving the blows of conservative neo-liberalism. At the same time, it turned out that convergent centrism or the hypothesis of systemic convergence as a tendency of apparently antagonist ideologies – and, consequently, the appeal to "the end of ideology" – were not viable scenarios.

The crisis of ideologies and the lack of a horizon for "sustainable consumer societies" rekindled the flame of theory. The prolongation of the general insecurity generated by crises in diverse areas of the globe, the intellectual challenge mounted against globalization seen not as enlargement but as the imposition of an excessively-Americanized model, the rediscovery of the dissident-vocation in the cultural sense of the word, the contestation of the old way of doing politics, the emergence of "new age" religions – all indicate that the world of the new millennium suffers from "diseases of faith" and fails to confer a clear, prospective meaning to the old symbols.

16.2 The return to religion

The lines were written at a time when the echoes of a surprising gesture of penitence by the Pope (on March 12, 2000, as the Pope celebrated the Day of Forgiveness in San Pietro, he called on behalf of the Catholic Church for forgiveness for its mistakes) are not entirely gone, a moment when the Christian world prepares to celebrate 2000 years of existence. If by now Malraux's words have circled the globe, while the "ashes or religion" alternative remained just a topic for intellectual disputes, the 21st century is looking us in the face, as if inviting us to make a choice in this famous dilemma.

Alongside other states in Eastern Europe, Romania has been forcibly secularized during the last 50 years. Communist regimes promoted the opposition between the atheism officially supported by the Party and the religious tradition of the people. Religiosity was put to ideological use and the institution of the church was evaluated and promoted to the extent that is served and subordinated to the goal of creating a "new man", scientifically and materialist-dialectically minded, devoid of mystical and religious convictions. In the first years of communism religious life in Romania was rich, with stable and well-represented traditional churches as well as a great number of religions and creeds liberalized between 1944 and 1948. Shortly, however, political-administrative and social measures deformed the normal evolution of religious life.

Toward the end of the ninth decade, as the signs of the system's fall started to become visible, communities of religious men and women gathered around their churches were targeted by political bodies seeking various ways to destroy them. The spark that ignited the events in Timişoara in December 1989 shows that the fears of the regime were not without cause.

In spite of the efforts of the communist regime, the post-1989 world demonstrated that the need for the sacred did not disappear among the population. The religious feeling survived, albeit diminished, degraded and disfigured. Sometimes this feeling gave birth in public life to aberrant manifestations – the adoration of leaders, the 'fetishization' of symbols, the 'hermetization' of structures. The diminishing and the degradation of the religious feeling is, according to the sociologists, a reason for the neglect and the violation of values and for the subordination of spiritual life to immediate, pragmatic, materialist interests.

In the field of religion, the Romanian transition made its debut with an explosion of religious feeling and especially of religious practice. Attending the church – a habit that had up to that point either been repressed, or inauthentic, or clandestine – became a mystical and cult-related manifestation. Religious practice and the overt acknowledgement of one's belonging to a certain cult meant to many the abandonment of the communist ideology and was seen as a "certificate" of moral guarantee and political credibility. One remembers the agitation around the question posed in the 1996 electoral campaign by Emil Constantinescu to Ion Iliescu: "Do you believe in God ... ?"

Things have gradually changed and the pressure of daily life diminished religious enthusiasm as well as the façade-religiosity of those that had been conjuncture refugees under the umbrella of faith. Profound religious feeling is something that belongs to each individual's private sphere. To judge each other by our views with respect to the transcendent, to blame each other for the (non)existence of that "oceanic feeling" (about which Romain Rolland was so ardently writing to Sigmund Freud) sounds frighteningly close to the 1990 "who's not with us is against us" slogan.

One often speaks today about the profound crisis of values, about alienation and purposelessness. People are looking for answers, for something to alleviate their concern. Each of us has the right to believe and to disbelieve. Belonging to one cult or another, theism and atheism, can no longer part the world into good and evil, in angels and demons. Irrespective of denomination or belief, the religion that has to unite people is that of respect for their rights. This should be the horizon of the new millennium.

Before we look for new solutions, before we preach in a radical vein strange religions, failed experiments and curious trends, we need to reassess things that we are supposed to have already obtained: tolerance and respect for the world in its diversity. Unfortunately, when people look around they see only disorder and violence, modern anathemas and economic excommunications. The latest, Weberian catchword refers to the structural inability of Eastern European peoples to integrate in the real rhythm of civilized – that is to say, Catholic and Protestant – Europe. Orthodox peoples are said to be slow, conservative, traditionalist and hostile to change. Catholics are said to be larger in number, richer and more evolved in missionary practices, in philanthropy and intellectual fields. The orthodox hide their complexes and delay their problems ... our brothers to the West often say, as if deliberately forgetting the hiatus that erected the Red Square next to the Church of Saint Vasili Blajenii, the man "mad unto Christ".

The globalist ideology, the "planetary consciousness" has a correspondent in religious life: ecumenism. Just as nationalism seeks to speak in the name of the entire nation, so globalism attempts to speak on behalf of the entire world. Its emergence is seen as a necessary stage in an evolutionary process. Until the Utopian ideal is fulfilled, the world will have to agree not only on the single currency but also on the book from which the word of God shall be imparted.

When Marx said the religion is *opium for the people* he could not even guess what the 'desacralization' of the world would bring about: people who commit suicide, who take drugs, drink alcohol, feel depressed, commit murder, feel alienated. Millions are fervently looking for their own identity or for a miraculous therapy that will reinstate their personality, will offer them a glimpse of identity, a moment of ecstasy, or a superior consciousness.

The great religions seem unable to offer answers for all. The 20th century was the century of the division of belief, of unprecedented proliferation of religious groups. The latter understood the human need for communication, structure and meaning and turned it into a commodity. Hence the paradox: in a free, divided and apparently excessively permissive world many choose a totalitarian, sectarian structure and reject the incomparably more democratic institutions of the great religions. The success of the sects comes from the fact that they offer a meaning for life that is freely chosen rather than acquired by birth or social compromise. Whatever their vision of the world, they are an alternative to the life outside: alienating and chaotic. By imposing order in exchange for the surrendering of freedom they offer a purpose. Whether this purpose actually has anything to do with reality is inconsequential.

How will religions develop in the new Era of information and 'robotization'? Where will orthodoxy reside in the world of chips and circuits conquered by *homo cyberneticus*? Will the latter be able to live alongside the *homo religiosus* as a reminder that both of them belong to the same species of *homo sapiens*? The catholic churches seem to have serenely accepted the access of information technology inside the altar. The reason is simple: adaptation is a natural consequence of their pragmatism, of their wish to survive in a secularized world. The Western parishes keep their balance books, the list of parishioners and the patristic publications on computer. The priest in the confessional keeps his eyes tuned to the laptop screen, his ears tuned to the confessing individual, and his soul tuned to God. The public can access the Bible on a CD-

ROM. The latest Internet idea in this field is the confessor-server. You strike out a few more sins and ask for forgiveness. Another step toward the virtual church! Ecumenism materializing on the chat server.

So far, where religions meet there is still a lot of suffering: Jerusalem, Chechnya, Kosovo, Sarajevo, Algeria, etc. Explosions, fundamentalisms, fanaticisms, extremisms. The ecumenical movements are still weak – yet the institutions still extend their tense, official hand. Each religion wants to be exclusive – the price to pay is democracy and sometimes the lives of the believers.

The orthodoxies in the ex-communist countries are placing too great a crown upon their heads and come to the fore whenever they believe that their national identity is in danger. The orthodox world sees the rest of the Christian world as aggressive and set to conquer, as not only attempting to politically recapture but actually to convert orthodox regions, whether by means of 'Uniatism' or in various other ways... Because it is the incarnation of Truth, the orthodox says, Orthodoxy has been persecuted by the West, by the Ottomans and by the communists as well.

Religious violence is still making victims and generating disasters in spite of the profane explanations of laymen. One might say that religious violence is one of the red threads that the history of the last 2000 years has been weaved with. But, to return to the Day of Forgiveness celebrated by Pope John Paul the Second in San Pietro, so publicized and so politicized – one might say we are facing a new beginning, even though it might be a symbolic one. There were voices even within the Catholic Church that contested the Pope's gesture: how imbued with democratic spirit is even the Church! On the other side of the barricade are those who wish the *mea culpa* had included everything, names and deeds and all. The mud and blood of the "non-evangelical ways" of preaching the Truth of the Bible should have been brought before the Cross especially placed in San Pietro.

Preoccupied by the imposition of their own Truth, believers everywhere seem to forget and impinge upon the basic values of their own creed. Saint Paul thought that Heaven was connected to our world by a bridge as thin as a single hair. So did the Arab mystics. Eliade describes similar representations in all world religions, symbolizing the difficulty of passing through earthly life in order to reach the knowledge of true Life. To make an analogy, we might say we find ourselves, as so many other times in history, on a hair-thin bridge to Heaven. Or to Hell. Religion might be an answer to the world's great problems, though certainly it is not the only one. There are yet too many voices crying for those who have died in its name.

There have been more wars waged in the name of religion than for any other cause. Millions died in these wars. In the name of God – of Buddha, Adonai, Christ, Allah – people have been massacring each other for thousands of years: Christians killing Jews, Jews hating the Muslims, Muslims using their arms against Hindus, but also Christians fighting Christians, Shiites fighting Sunnites, Shiites fighting Hindus. Everybody wants to rid the world of evil, everybody screams Peace, Peace together with their prophets. And in the meantime the churches pray for the same feverishly desired ... Peace.

When will all people hide in another Pandora's box all evils and find again the joy of living together peacefully? If we look around we can only guess that the day is still far away from us. Thinking about the waves of blood that have flowed and the interminable wars that plague parts of the world and threaten others, some believe that all religions should be done away with. Others would like to unite them all into one. But under which sign? None of the great religions offered political recipes, for this would be beyond their purpose. It is clear, though, that religions need an integrating vision that cannot work without an adequate political vision. The restoration of human rights should be the imperative of any social ideal. Otherwise the Dostoievskian parable of Jesus thrown into jail by the Grand Inquisitor and accused for the terrible mistake of having offered man the freedom of belief instead of bread and happiness would become true: people could surrender their freedom in exchange for the realm of the Peace to come.

We all wish a better and safer world but the deeper we look into the past the clearer the future appears and the better we see that for the time being nobody can provide real guarantees that the terrible utopian experiments will never kill our hopes again. The road to tomorrow is still long and the memory of Paradise is getting more and more blurred. And all this while the ideals of religions are lo longer causes but reasons for acts that right some and wrong the others. In other words, ideals are means to ends that we are not aware of. Maybe this is the essence of the Pope's *mea culpa*. A gesture that God only knows whether it is or is not a prophecy ...

CHAPTER SEVENTEEN

FROM KARL MARX TO COCA COLA

If the First World War brought about a consolidation of liberalism and the fulfillment of the fundamental goal of the 19th century – the principle of nationalities –, the beginning and the end of the Second World War seem to have discredited elitism for good, in all its forms, from the political to the ethno-racial one. The new generations raised under the signs of the bipolar world and of different economic worlds tried periodically to build new projects by combining the various pieces of an ideologically and culturally motley puzzle. Toward the end of the period, the world seemed to reach some sort of ideological balance in the ideology of the right, at least after the success of Thatcherite militancy and of the Reaganite new economics. This ideological balance did not lead to integration but simply put the system on the solid bases derived from neo-liberalism and conservatism. "I love my country but I am afraid of its government" became a cliché slogan for US protesters. The meaning of "revolution" – until long a term of the Marxist dictionary –, has been refashioned and applied function of the "beliefs and myths of the group". Freudo-Marxism, the influence of nihilism and anarchism, combined fragments of Maoism and the thought of the Frankfurt School, Guevarism and the music of protesters, the perverted gnosis and spiritualism, etc. created the image of timeframes that do not converge but rather drift away.

Social projects and the autonomy of the social were also claimed in this country after 1989, especially since the direction in which to operate the transition to the new society was missing. The economic crisis into which Romania plunged at the beginning of the 1970's, the taste for contestation of a society that had been politically oppressed until 1989, were not favorable to a system based on consensus.

The violent criticisms of liberal, Anglo-Saxon universalism and individualism came not so much from the social democrats – still in retreat at that time – but from the "new right". From a number of political and cultural questions: the right to difference, the right to alternative lifestyles, feminism, ecology, yuppies movements, individual autonomy, etc. The phenomenon manifested itself in Romania and other countries of the former communist bloc by a mistaken understanding of regionalism and collective autonomy against individual autonomy. Devolution – which in the West refers to institutional and/or economic devolution – was understood by some as devolution of sovereignty and federalization.

Here, close to Europe's soft belly, inter-ethnic relations were always colored in different, contextually dependent nuances. The panic attacks that surrounded the fate of the hundreds of thousand of refugees during the Yugoslavian crises and the devastating bombings should make the adepts of "direct solutions" plead for civilized cohabitation in the spirit of dialogue and mutual acceptance. Nobody outside or inside can accuse post-Decembrist Romanian governments of having been "majority aggressors" espousing a "national criminal politics, meant to exterminate the ethnic or religious minorities, the whole Hungarian minority in Romania..." The conflict between multiculturalism and ethnocentrism remains unfortunately a reality engendered not by the usual cohabitation but by the "directions" taken by political forces that seek to control the social group that they claim to represent.

There is a Latin, a Catholic, a Protestant and an Orthodox Europe but no one can define *a priori* a line of separation between them. Romania is an orthodox country that is also Latin in spite of the fact that the political imagination of some agents places it in the Slavic world. There is nothing abnormal in a Latin orthodoxy, just as there is nothing unnatural in an Arab orthodoxy – the orthodox world has always been a complex one, the development of which is always in need of a deep historical analysis. Secondly, one has to stress – especially for those who see the orthodox church as incapable to progressing in the Western way – that the Western model is neither catholic nor protestant, but that of a consumerist, secularized, capitalist society. Consumerism tends to level and standardize. The Coca-Cola civilization cannot be the wave of the future but merely a temporary hegemony, a mirage provoked by the mercantilism of uniformization and the simplification of values. It is obvious that the different forms of anti-capitalism or anti-liberalism (subsumed to a Karl Marx-type of civilization or to neo-fascist types of corporatism) seem completely obsolete, though all forms of civilization are inherently unstable, just as all political regimes are inherently mortal, corrupted by the corrosiveness of time.

Neither is nationalism a malady or a product of the orthodox spirit – Protestants and Catholics also knew this political-cultural affliction. On the contrary, orthodoxy is carefully cultivating memory and tradition (which some mistakenly describe as "anti-modernism" and "nationalism") and for this reason the dialogue with different civilizations is more fragile, though not devoid of substance. Huntington's famous "clash of civilizations" thesis is, in spite of some interesting observations, extremely simplistic. The literature on which he grounded his study was probably preponderantly ideological and less historical in nature, at least with respect to Eastern Europe.

The totalitarian regimes have exerted a great influence on the feeling of national identity by supporting a form of nationalist communism

(I refrain from using the term "national-communism" because its resemblance to Hitler's national-socialism exists only in the "ideological" intentions of those who have circulated the former concept). But this fact should not automatically trigger a total rejection of the discourse on the nation or the right to affirm it, simply motivated by the fact that the communists did the same thing. This line smacks of Marxist authoritarian thought – it was Marx who thought that the nation was a typically bourgeois concept, which emerged and became prominent in the days of capitalism, but with no reason to exist in the new proletarian order.

The question still facing Romanian society refers to the model or models that it has to follow in order to modernize. The social-democratic model may offer a viable economic and social-political alternative. But in order to be fully functional this model requires that Romanian social democrats should work together and put it into practice as a common project. It is known that societies, both the developed ones and those undergoing development, have to choose between the liberal conception – creating more market flexibility but reducing services and social protection –, and a welfarist conception that is likely to insist on the national interest and on the major options. Today socialism is no longer seen as a messianic and dogmatic ideology (and even less as a communist movement, in spite of the fact some Romanian parties still refer to the "communist danger" in order to hide their own political failures.) Nobody wishes to return to the old ideological rigidity that pushed us away from the realities of today's world. Social democratic ideology must be seen as stressing the importance of a set of universal values, capable of offering hope to people.

The principles of liberalism – individualism, efficiency, competition, competence – explain how economy and society work as a whole or how the production of goods should be secured, but fail to provide for an optimum of social organization, fail to explain how the need for education, health, etc. can be satisfied. Efficiency, competence, competition and individualism have to be supplemented by justice and solidarity. This is the core of the social democratic alternative and it is a pity that the proponents of right-wing or center-right doctrines refuse to acknowledge this fact.

The principles of social democracy cater to social needs: caring for children, young people and the elderly, access to culture, health and education. Some right-wing or center-right political actors believe that securing social assistance and services (which they aim to privatize completely) offers opportunities and benefits to a minority. But citizens demand otherwise: they demand basic utilities, including access to heat and hygiene, health, and education. These needs cannot be satisfied as long as you're capable only of organizing what is profitable in the short term, and only for a limited category of "vassals". Therefore this doctrine has in mind first of all "the offensive" against the deformation of Romania's dramatic realities, against the causes of the corruption of social justice and solidarity, against those politicians for whom politics is reduced to political games and petty schemes.

The social democratic model can only be based on a set of ethical and moral values. It has to spell the end of the excesses and abuses that have marked the last years of this century. Through firm action and on the basis of the values of humaneness and solidarity we have to show that social democracy offers a form of long-term leadership for Romania – by optimizing social control at all decision levels. Speaking of values, we have to say this clearly – our model is a republican one, a model of republican integration in the tradition of European secularism. This means neither exclusion nor atheism. I believe that the social democratic organization of society leads to a larger acceptance of differences, be they cultural or religious. One should not understand from this that 'leftism' involves the absence or the persecution of religions or beliefs.

I am certain that the success of any model supported by a politician, political party or coalition cannot be complete unless this model becomes part of the public debate, of a dialogue with civil society, with the unions, intellectuals, academics, economists, businessmen, etc. The social democratic alternative does not seek to control society by means of laws (ordinances, decrees, etc.), but rather sees itself as a model based on the needs of civil society. **The best work-method for a politician is to approach all problems without false certainties, without looking for differences and hyper-ideologizing them, but rather by trying to find new ways to exchange opinions**

while acknowledging the values that unite us. The differences are sources of enrichment and nobody can claim to have found a unique model or a unique ideology that is universally applicable. The politician as well as the civil society and the parties and the powers that be must "open doors and windows" and listen to each other.

We live through a technological revolution in an age in which the understanding of solidarity and social justice has changed. The disappearance of the great industrial complexes and of the production lines and their replacement with semi-intelligent machines shows that man can turn back to his "primitive" ways "as a shepherd" – "a shepherd of machines" as Felipe Gonzalez put it (Gonzalez; 8). Man is no longer part of a machine, as he was during the first and the second industrial revolutions. What are the consequences for social solidarity of this change? Will its impact be profound? The development of post-modern societies is already witnessing transformations that shatter the solidarity within companies, families and human districts. Today, in the age of late capitalism, companies are no longer places where men and women are part of the production lines, but places where fewer men and fewer women lead or monitor the machine – as "shepherds taking care of flocks of machinery" in the same words of Gonzalez.

Now that we can see the world of the end of the millennium, the question we have to answer is what kind of left-wing policies can a social democratic alternative design and implement. May a leftist government implement macro-economic policies that are not interested in finding some equilibrium with the international environment? The answer is obviously no. Healthy macro-economic policies are a *sine qua non* for the construction of a solid social-economic base, without inflation and without compromising the system's distributive machinery.

Everything will depend on savings and on the ability to save internally. If we accept macro-economic goals aimed at balance and stability, the assessment of the government's actions should be based on the sources of income it has chosen or on the ways in which the income is spent – who pays, how it pays, how much and who are the beneficiaries of the spent money. It is here that the differences between the social-democratic and the neo-liberal doctrines arise.

Today we are witnessing a clash between the liberal democracy and economic liberalism understood as fundamentalist liberalism which excludes the role of the state and is upset by the interference of political authorities. In other words, there are liberals in economics or "liberal economists" that can be a danger both to liberal democracies and to an open society. These neo-liberals are at pains to exclude any kind of political intervention of the state and pretend that the market will always solve the problems at the right time. Europeans have learnt from the "mad cow" crisis that the market cannot always solve any problems. For this reason we cannot simply accept something that seems positive, the surrendering of social cohesion, and the degree of social integration we have obtained. No politician should forget that the social legitimacy of liberal democracies is, more than the vote, a factor of social cohesion.

How can we design or sketch a model that can take us further? Of course, the state can no longer be viewed as an entity above society that interferes all the time, regardless of circumstances. On the one hand, we cannot have a "balloon" state based exclusively on social policies. But neither can we accept a "skeleton" state that humbly bows before every interest that hits it. It is necessary to look to the future beyond the models of the populist state and of the client state. Politics and public interest are not reducible to the interest of the consumer. Businesspersons are always more liberal when they meet other business people than with themselves. They ask for liberal measures from other businesspersons or countries or governments but also ask for "captive markets" and for the freedom to eliminate their competition.

We should keep in mind the role of public authorities, and I am thinking not so much of an entrepreneurial as of a managerial role. In short, we could say that the role of the state would be to provide for physical and human capital. Although this language might seem to belong to a businessperson rather than to a leftist politician, it is still the language adequate to reality. A language that should be understood by the right-wing as well.

We should speak of the business community and should be very specific when discussing the problem of education, of the development model that we wish to design and the sustainability of this model. How shall we manage to train young people in the next ten years who will use their competence and intelligence in Romania rather than abroad? The exodus of young people in the powerful economic systems leaves no hope for consistency. Moreover, young people lack information with respect to integration in social schemes or programs. It is most alarming that they have no access to credit because they are not “trustworthy” to the “old boys”. It will be extremely difficult to improve their condition with fiscal measures because a large number of small- and mid-sized companies operate outside the tax circuit and employ young people under terms that are unfavorable to them and contrary to the work ethics.

I would like to end this in a different mood. After the Cold War we, Easterners, found out that the outlook of the great powers concerning the building of sub-regional bodies (generally for economic and trade purposes) changed. Integrated developments such as MERCOSUR point to “ways forward” and encourage us to support the idea that this is the right way of organization in the new one-dimensional world and it could be an attempt to rehabilitate international relations.

The various economic and political models generated results insofar as economic growth was regarded as important. But it is necessary that the model of growth should extend its benefits upon a larger part of the population. The Keynesian welfare state days are over. Nevertheless, I cannot share the opinion of neo-liberals concerning the limitation of the benefits of social cohesion and solidarity. For this reason it is necessary to find a “way of social cohesion” not only from the perspective of the politicians’ attitudes toward those who voted them or from that of subjective impulses toward solidarity. The coexistence model that we live with, that of liberal democracy itself, is at stake! It will not survive for long if an abyss opens between the rich and the poor members of society, providing the ground for populist and extremist demagoguery.

By Way of a conclusion

The nations' march through history, populated with murder, injustice and experiments that legislated and legitimized "the law of the strongest" to decide in the name of an Absolute Good, is far from over. On one part of the barricade there are the optimistic futurologists, the prophets of a new "golden age" of humanity; on the other – generation upon generation of people sacrificed for causes they do not accept or even understand. Between theory and the real life there is the political decision, the decision of **here and now**, meant to bring at least bits and pieces of the dream of the future into the daily lives of men and women.

Romania is itself a part of the great battle for the future, ready to assume both the mistakes of the past and the sacrifices of the present. The role of the political class at this moment is doubtlessly one of historical significance and overwhelming responsibility. At a crucial point in time, a time which seems to have lost its patience, thc only possible attitude is lucidity, looking boldly at the future while keeping an eye on the existing reality, led by the major imperative of change, in the spirit of unconditional humanism: we build for men and women, they are the goal and not just the means of our ideas, theories, ideologies, here and everywhere...

We still have a long and harsh way to travel. There is no longer a way back, in spite of the warnings uttered by "Cassandras" with their eyes fixed upon the dangers posed by the "Trojan horse" of center-left politics. The ideal of social democracy is to offer everybody the social and economic basics, a decent life and a decent existence, not in the populist spirit of communist egalitarianism but on the solid basis of development. I insisted in this book on the traps of neo-liberalism that can compromise for good the efforts made so far, rendering all past sacrifices useless. History would merely record another failure and the lives of millions would be pushed into the garbage bin of time, while other barbaric experiments will get ready to enter the stage.

The process of globalization which is currently unfolding forces us to reevaluate our own tradition and national identity. I believe that the answer to the dilemma before us will only be found if we manage to achieve a fruitful synthesis of our two options: an unconditional integration in the Western world, also by assimilating in full its values, accompanied by an autarchic retreat inside our own borders, be they symbolic or real. As difficult as finding a middle path may seem, it is still possible. In the first place, I do not believe that Romania, just as any other small state, can afford a retreat from the tendencies that characterize the Western world. The free circulation of capital and of the work force, the real-time circulation of information and free competition are the vital values that Romania needs. At the same time, they will not be operational unless the social body fully assimilates them. In the opposite case, what would the theories and explanations of the failure be good for when the only alternative would be our recruitment in a loop of history that we have just come out of? On the other hand, I do not see integration as a Procrustean amputation of an integrating Romania. A successful process requires a harmonious interdependence between the global and the national.

Romania's battle for the future should not be fought with the weapons of rhetoric. The present placed before us a unique alternative: **to be or not to be in history**! If our answer to Hamlet's dilemma is "absent", the loser status will only offer us a tragic life in a place that I would call, once again, the Vallachian Nothingness.

POSTSCRIPT
TO THE AMERICAN EDITION

This book is just a personal collection of reflections about the future of my country and the world's changing trends. The issues involved here have become part of a worldwide debate. The book contains some original contributions to this debate. Romania is a special case. I tried to analyze the rather fixed and static nature of the Romanian economy and, wider, its society. There are interesting comments and policy proposals in this book, in most of the key areas of political modernization. The reality of the Romanian political and economical climate has changed now since the book's first publishing. The energetic action of the new government has improved the country's prospects for the near future. Of course, there are no spectacular results concerning the rise in living conditions, but the population has now a greater political experience and does not expect miracles to happen. In spite of a year of tough political decisions, the Romanians still trust their democratically elected government and I'm very grateful for this.

From the beginning of the Romanian transformation in the early 1990's, the leaders of our democratic revolution voiced their unshakeable commitment to the fundamental values and principles of the free and prosperous nations of Western Europe and the United States. From the first, successive democratically elected governments have confirmed the aspiration of all Romanians to join the institutions that form the foundation of the Euro-Atlantic community - NATO and the European

Union. We have always understood that, if Europe was ever to become truly whole and completely free, the new democracies of Central and South East Europe would have to join the two complementary and mutually reinforcing pillars of the Trans-Atlantic community.

Since 1990, we have moved ahead on a long and often difficult road toward Romania's re-integration into the European family to which we rightfully belong and to which we have substantially contributed throughout our history - Constantin Brancusi, Eugen Ionescu, George Enescu and Mircea Eliade are just a few resonant names in this regard. Considering the starting point of our transition - Romania's situation in 1989, I marvel at what Romania has been able to achieve in little more than a decade. The "distance we have traveled" from the most autarchic and repressive political and economic system of Central Europe to present day Romania is a monument to the power of democratic ideas and the economic dynamism of free markets.

The failure of the policies conducted by the opposition that led Romania over 1996-2000 undermined the citizens' confidence in this country's future and compromised, at the level of public opinion, the reform, which has become to many Romanians synonymous with poverty and unemployment. Within this difficult economic and social context, **a considerable percentage of the electorate chose a government of a social-democratic type. The new image and the new policy-making approaches of the Social Democratic Party were the main arguments which determined the population to switch it's political options. Crafting a new political party, perfectly adapted to the new democracy demands, were my main goals** at the time in which I wrote this book and they are still now. **I always believed that the Social Democratic Party has some noble, but also difficult national tasks to achieve: rebuilding the economy, protecting the democracy and making the administration system functional.** In this context, despite all risks, I have chosen to take **the responsibility of making a minority monocolor government, that is supposed to accomplish the reform works in all fields.**

The principle of the balance between the major requirements of the market economy and those of social protection and solidarity is one of the basic elements of this governance program. **A fundamental principle of action of the Adrian Nastase Government** is the observance of the separation of powers within the state and granting to Parliament its natural role as legislative body.

By the way the governance Program was elaborated and by the measures that are going to be implemented, **the Executive wishes to enhance the stability and coherence of the legislative framework, and offer transparency and credibility to its decisions**.

In view of the evaluation of the economic, social and political situation, and consistent with the provisions of the electoral offer, **the Nastase Government has established the following priorities for the ensuing governing period**:

· relaunching economic growth;

· fighting poverty and unemployment;

· restoring the authority of the state and of its institutions;

· diminishing bureaucracy, fighting corruption and criminality;

· furthering and accelerating the process of integration in the European Union and NATO.

Instead of an abstract approach and of focusing the governing effort upon the area of macro-monetary balances, **it needs a pragmatic outlook, open toward real economy and the needs felt, in the most direct way, by the country's citizens**, and, to this purpose, it sets as successful indicators of its economic policies the real and enduring growth of the Gross Domestic Product and the sensible and generalized improvement of the living standards of Romania's citizens.

The enduring economic growth is being achieved by updating industry, agriculture, infrastructure and services. Education, training, research and culture are major vectors of our development strategy.

Restoring confidence in the act of justice and in the mechanisms of enforcing law and public order shall be urgent goals for the future Executive, to the end of ensuring the protection of the citizens' rights and security.

National interest, the imperatives of the moment, the risk of the fragile equilibrium of democracy breaking due to social tensions and pressures **call for political responsibility and cohesion on the part of the democratic political forces**, regardless of their doctrines, so that the new government be installed immediately and start the immediate implementation of the established governance program.

In order to secure a solid social and political basis to support governmental initiatives and programs, we shall consistently **adopt a working way based on political, social and economic dialogue, and on consultation with the political partners and public opinion**.

Certainly, there is more to be done. Perhaps we made some mistakes, perhaps we had some hesitations. **But one thing I am sure of is that we are now irrevocably on the road toward the integration of our country into the political, market and security institutions of the West**. Romania is not only a committed European democracy with a strong case for invitation to join NATO at the next Summit in 2002, but we are also engaged in accession negotiations with the European Union, with the goal of achieving full membership by 2007. It is no longer a question of whether Romania will come to join these institutions, but rather of how soon. Standing here today, I cannot give you a precise date when Romania will be a member of both NATO and EU. But I am certain that, on that date, our resolve and hard work will bring a strong and reliable ally to NATO and "value added" to the community of Trans-Atlantic democracies.

BIBLIOGRAPHY

M. Albert - **Capitalism contra capitalism**, ed. Humanitas, București, 1994

L. Anthony & R. Nekkaz, **Millenarium. Quel avenir pour l'humanite ?**, Robert Laffont, Paris, 2000

H. W. Arndt, **Economic Developement: the History of an Idea**, Chicago University Press,1987

J. M. Barbalet - **Cetățenia**, ed. Du Style, București, 1998

J. Baudouin - **Introducere în sociologia politică**, ed. Amarcord, Timișoara, 1999

H. Bergson - **Les deux sources de la morale et de la religion**, Albert Skira, an neprecizat, Geneve

I. Berlin - **Four Essays on Liberty,** Oxford University Press, 1969

S. Bernard - **Sociologie politique interne**, Presse Universitaire de Belgique, Bruxelles, 1982-1983

J. Blondel - **Political Parties: A Genuin Case for Discontent**, Wildwood House, Londra, 1978

N. Bobbio - **Dreapta și Stânga,** ed. Humanitas, București, 1999

M. Botez – **Lumea a doua**, ed. Du Style, București, 1997

R. Boudon - **Tratatul de sociologie**, ed. Humanitas, București, 1997

T. Brateș, **Privatizarea.Durerile facerii 1990-1997,** ed. Economică, București, 1997

Ph. Braud - **Grădina deliciilor democrației,** ed. Globus, București, 1996

L. Brown – **Starea lumii 2000**, ed. Științifică și Tehnică, București, 2000

Silviu Brucan, **Generația irosită,** București, 1992

Silviu Brucan - **Stâlpii noii puteri în România**, ed. Nemira, București, 1998

Silviu Brucan – **Treptele tranziției spre capitalism,** ed. Nemira, București, 1999

Z. Brzezinski, **Europa Centrală și de Est în ciclonul tranziției,** București, 1995

Ian Budge, Hans Keman - **Parties and Democracy. Coalition formation and government functioning in Twenty States,** Oxford University Press, 1990

Alfred Bulai - **Mecanismele electorale ale societății românești,** ed. Paideia, București, 1999

Anton Carpinschi, **Doctrine politice contemporane. Tipologii, Dinamică, Perspective**, Iași, 1992

A. Carpinschi - **Deschidere și sens în gândirea politică**, ed. Institutul European, Iași, 1995

M. Castells, **The Rise of the Network Society**,Oxford, Blackwell, 1996

P. Câmpeanu, A. Combes, M. Berindei, **România înainte și după 20 mai,** ed. Humanitas, București, 1991

J. Clarke, A. Cochrane, E. McLaughlin, **Mission Accomplished or Unfinished Business? The Impact of Managerialization** în vol. **Managing Social Policy**, London, Sage, 1994

G. Corm - **Noua dezordine economică mondială. La izvoarele insucceselor dezvoltării**, ed. Dacia, Cluj-Napoca, 1996

R. Dahl, **Who Governs?**, Yale University Press, 1961

Ralph Dahrendorf, **Reflecții asupra revoluției din Europa,** ed. Humanitas, București,1993

R. Dahrendorf - **Conflictul social modern**, ed. Humanitas, București 1996

M. Dauderstadt, A. Gerrits, G. Markus, **Troubled Transition. Social-Democracy in East Central Europe**, ed. Friedrich Ebert Stiftung, Bonn, 1999

D. Deletant – **Biblioteca Sighet**, ed.Fundația Academia Civică, București, 1997

A. Dimitriu - **Note de drum. Lupta pentru supraviețuire a**

social-democrației române. 1944-1980, Fundația „Constantin Titel Petrescu", București, 1994

M. Dogan - **Noile științe sociale**, ed. Alternative, București, 1998

A. Downs - **An Economic Theory of Democracy,** Harper & Brothers, New York, 1957

Ioan Drăgan (coord.), **Construcția simbolică a câmpului electoral**, ed. Institutul European, Iași, 1998

O. Duhamel, **Les Democraties**, Presse Universitaire de France, Paris, 1993

M. Duverger - **Les partis politiques**, ed. Armand Colin, Paris, 1973

L. D. Epstein - **Political Parties in Western Democracies**, Frederich A. Praeger Publishers, New York, 1967

S. Fineman, **Emotion in Organization**, London, Sage, 1993

M. Focault, **Power/Knowledge, Selected Interviews and Other Wr itings 1972-1977,** Harvester Press, 1980

Viviane Forrester - **Une etrange dictature**, Fayard, Paris, 2000

J. Freund - **Political essays**, Beveridge, New York, 1987

R. Frydman, A. Rapaczynski - **Privatizarea în Europa Răsăriteană: este statul în declin?**, ed. Oscar Print, București

Graham Fuller, **The Next Ideology**, Foreign Policy, nr.98, 1995

J. K. Galbraith - **Societatea perfectă**, ed. Eurosong & Book, București,1997

E. Gellner - **Condițiile libertății. Societatea civilă și rivalii ei**, ed. Polirom, Iași, 1998

Anthony Giddens - **The Third Way**, Polity Press, Cambridge, 1998

Felipe Gonzalez, **What is "Global Progress" Commission?**, Maritime House, Londra, 1996

J. Gray - **Dincolo de liberalism și conservatorism**, ed.All, București, 1998

J. Habermas - **Sfera publică și transformarea ei structurală**, ed. Univers, București, 1998

V. Havel - **Power of the Powerless**, Armonk, New York, 1990

A. Hirschman - **Abandon, contestare și loialitate**, ed. Nemira, București, 1999

E. Hobsbawn, **Secolul Extremelor**, ed. Expert, București, 1998

S. P. Huntington - **Ordinea politică a societăților în schimbare**, ed. Polirom, Iași, 1999

M. Ignatief, **Needs of Strangers**, Penguin, New York, 1994

I. Iliescu, **Revoluție și reformă**, ed. Enciclopedică, București, 1994

C. Iordache – **Clasa nevrednică**, ed. IRINI, București, 1997

R. Inglehart - **The Silent Revolution: Changing Values and Political Styles among Western Publics**, Princeton University Press, 1977

P. de Laubier - **Introduction a la sociologie politique**, PUF, Paris, 1983

L. Joffrin, Ph. Tesson , **Ou est passe l'autorite**, NiL Editions, Paris, 2000

V. Kamber, **Poison politics,** New York, Free Press, 1999

K. Kumar, **Civil society again: a reply to Cristopher Bryant's social self-organizations, civility and sciology**, *British Journal of Sociology*, vol.45, No.1, march, 1992

J. LaPalombara, M. Weiner - **Political Parties and Political Development**, Princeton University Press, 1972

Kay Lawson (coord.) - **When Parties Fail. Emerging Alternative Organizations** , Princeton University Press, 1988

P. Lenain -**„FMI-ul"**, ed. C.N.I. Coresi, București, 2000

Rene Lenoir, **Quand L'Etat disjoncte**, Paris, Grasset, 1995

D. Lipton , Jeffrey Sachs, **Creating a Market Economy in Eastern Europe: the Case of Poland**, Brookings Papers on Economic Activity, No1:1990

J. Locke – **Al doilea tratat despre cârmuire. Scrisoare despre toleranță**, ed. Nemira, București, 1999.

Joseph de Maistre, **Istorie și Providență,** ed. Anastasia, București, 1997

D. Marin, **Criza reformei. Eu sunt român?**, ed. Economică, București, 1999

S. Martin Lipset - **Political Man. The Social Bases of Politics**, The John Hopkins University Press, Baltimore, 1981

T. May, M. Landells , **Administrative Rationality and Delivery of Sicial Services: An Organisation in Flux**, International Conference on Children, Family Life and Society, Plymouth, 1994

V. Măgureanu - **Studii de sociologie politică**, ed. Albatros, București, 1997

Y. Meny - **Politique comparee**, Montchrestien, Paris, 1989

P. Minford , **The Role of the Services: A view from the New Right**, în M. Loney (coord.), **The State or the Market: Politics and Welfare in contemporary Britain**, London, Sage, 1991

A. Năstase - **Drepturile omului. Religie a sfârșitului de secol**, IRDO, București 1992

A. Năstase - **Ideea politică a schimbării. Discursuri politice**, București, 1996

D. Nelson (ed.) – **Romania after Tiranny,** Oxford University Press, 1992

K. Ohmae - **The End of the Nation State - The Rise of Regional Economies**, New York, Free Press, 1995

Mancur Olson - **Creșterea și declinul națiunilor**, ed. Humanitas, București, 1999

J. Ortega y Gasset - **Revolta maselor**, ed. Humanitas, Bucuresti, 1994

G. Orwell - **Selected Essays**, Penguin, London,1957

G. Orwell - **1984**, ed. Cartier, Chișinău, 1999

V. Pareto - **Traite de sociologie generale**, ed. Droz, Geneva, 1974

Vl. Pasti, M. Miroiu si C. Codiță, **România - starea de fapt**, ed. Nemira, București,1997

D. Pavel, **Cine, ce și de ce? Interviuri despre politică și alte tabuuri,** Ed. Polirom, Iași, 1998

Cr. Preda – **Modernitatea politică și românismul**, ed. Nemira, București, 1998

Cr. Preda – **Occidentul nostru**, ed. Nemira, București, 1999

R. Prodi, **Alloccution au Conseil de l'Europe: valeur ajoutee et valeurs communes,** Strasbourg, 25 janvier 2000

A. Przeworski - **Democrația și economia de piață**, ed. All, București, 1996

M. Ralea – **Ideea de revoluție,** ed. Albatros, București, 1997

I. Ramonet – **Geopolitica haosului,** ed. Doina, București, 1999

I. Rațiu - **În fine, acasă**, ed. Univers, București, 1999

J. Rawls - **Political Liberalism,** Harvard University Press, 1971

C. Rădulescu-Motru - **Psihologia poporului român**, ed. Paideia, București, 1998

R. Reich - **Munca națiunilor**, ed. Paideia, București, 1996

D. Sandu - **Sociologia tranziției. Valori și tipuri sociale în România**, ed. Staff, București, 1996

G. Sartori - **Parties and Party Systems: A Framework for Analysis,** Cambridge University Press, 1976

G. Sartori - **Teoria democrației reinterpretată,** ed. Polirom, Iași, 1999

T. W. Schultz, **The Economic Value of Education**, New York, 1963

R.-G. Schwartzenberg – **Statul spectacol**, ed. Scripta, București, 1995

Ph. Seguin - **C'est quoi la politique ?**, Albin Michel, Paris, 1999

D.-L. Seiler - **Les partis politiques**, Armand Colin, Paris, 1993

A. Severin, **Lacrimile dimineții**, ed. Azi, București, 1995

J. Sevillia - **Le terrorisme intellectuel. De 1945 a nos jours,** Perrin, Paris, 2000

E. Shills, **The Virtue of Civil Society**, ***Journal of Gouvernement***, Winter Press, 1991

S. Strange - **State și piețe**, ed. Institutul European, Iasi, 1997

A. de Tocqueville - **Democracy in America**, New York, Vintage Books, 1954

F. Thom - **Limba de lemn**, ed. Humanitas, București, 1994

G. Țepelea – **Însemnări de taină,** ed. Fundația Culturală Română, București, 1997

R. Vasile – **Se închide cercul,** ed. Nemira, București, 1999

N. Văcăroiu - **România , jocuri de interese** , Carte interviu de Gheorghe Smeoreanu, ed. Intact, București, 1998

M. Walzer - **Spheres of Justice. A Defence of Pluralism and Equality**, Basic Books, New York, 1983

*** - **The Encyclopedia of Philosophy**, Paul Edwards, New York,1971

*** - **The Lugano Report, On preserving capitalism in the Twenty-first Century, with an Appendix and Afterword by Susan George**, Pluto Press, London & Sterling Virginia, 1999